UNIX® TEST TOOLS AND BENCHMARKS

*Methods and Tools
to Design, Develop, and Execute
Functional, Structural, Reliability,
and Regression Tests*

Rodney C. Wilson

Prentice Hall PTR, Upper Saddle River, New Jersey 07458

LIBRARY OF CONGRESS CATALOGING-IN-PUBLICATION DATA

Wilson, Rodney C.
    Unix test tools and benchmarks: methods and tools to design,
develop, and execute functional, structural, reliability, and
regression tests/ Rodney C. Wilson.
      p. cm.
    Includes bibliographical references and index.
    ISBN 0-13-125634-3
    1. Computer software -- Testing. 2. UNIX (Computer file)
I. Title.
QA76.76.T48W65a m1965
005.1'4 -- dc20   95-10555
                                                         CIP

Acquisitions editor: Mike Meehan
Editorial assistant: Dori Steinhauff
Cover design: Aren Graphics
Cover design director: Jerry Votta
Copyeditor: Camie Goffi
Art production manager: Gail Cocker-Bogusz
Manufacturing Manager: Alexis R. Heydt
This book was composed with FrameMaker on a UNIX platform.

© 1995 Prentice Hall
Prentice-Hall, Inc.
A Simon & Schuster Company
Upper Saddle River, New Jersey 07458

The publisher offers discounts on this book when orderedin bulk quantities. For more information, contact: Corporate Sales DepartmentPrentice Hall PTR One Lake StreetUpeer Saddle River, N.J. 07458 Phone: 800-382-3419Fax: 201-236-7141 E-mail (Internet): corpsales@prenhall.com.

Printed in the United States of America

10 9 8 7 6 5 4 3 2 1

ISBN   0-13-125634-3

Prentice-Hall International (UK) Limited, *London*
Prentice-Hall of Australia Pty. Limited, *Sydney*
Prentice-Hall Canada Inc., *Toronto*
Prentice-Hall Hispanoamericana, S.A., *Mexico*
Prentice-Hall of India Private Limited, *New Delhi*
Prentice-Hall of Japan, Inc., *Tokyo*
Simon & Schuster Asia Pte. Ltd., *Singapore*
Editora Prentice-Hall do Brasil, Ltda., *Rio de Janeiro*

TO

DEBRA

AND

MY PARENTS

Contents

Testing Methods and Definitions

CHAPTER **7**   **Load and Stress Testing** **81**

CHAPTER **8**   **Quality Assurance** **95**

Test Technology

CHAPTER 14   **Test Tools** **183**

CHAPTER 15   **Test Harnesses** 237

CHAPTER 16   **Final Remarks** 254

 # Preface

Purpose and Organization

This book is the result of many years of software and hardware development, test and QA experience in a variety of systems and applications software development and integration environments. Chapters 1 through 8 deal exclusively with testing methods and strategies in the UNIX environment. Chapters 9 through 16 discuss tools and technologies for testing and benchmarking software in the UNIX environment. Definitions and terms are provided throughout to describe various test strategies, methodologies and technologies that are known to provide the greatest ROI. Development and use of a common vocabulary is a critical step toward the successful definition of a common software development process that can be used across the entire organization. This book is recommended as a handbook to be used in the definition of test plans, procedures and processes. This includes many of the processes associated with the design, development and execution of software tests.

Tools and Techniques for Verification and Validation

The reader is exposed to many techniques, tools, and actual test programs for software verification. The purpose of verification is to measure and improve many of the human aspects associated with the development of software products. Verification also involves analysis of the software development process to confirm that the product is being built correctly. Without a well documented development process, software verification is a very difficult, if not impossible. Validation testing techniques and technologies are equally important to verification and are used to ensure the right product is built according to customer requirements. In other words, the purpose of verification and validation testing is to prevent surprises by ensuring that the right product is being built right.

Content

Four key strategies form the foundation and methodology for the design, development and execution of software tests. These methods include: functional, structural, reliability and regression testing. Performance test tools are equally important to software verification and validation testing and are also explored in detail. Functional testing, which is often called black box testing, is one successful method of software verification and validation. It is often based upon user documentation that is usually generated from product requirements. Structural analysis and structural testing include many techniques to evaluate the product implementation (i.e., source code or documentation). Several static and dynamic structural testing and analysis methods are discussed in Chapter 3. Chapter 14 includes many tools related to structural analysis and structural testing. Reliability testing based on testability methods provides a preventive rather than reactive approach to software failures. Tools and methods related to reliability testing are discussed in Chapter 14. Regression testing is an equally important subject. Regression tests are used to ensure that product source code changes do not introduce either new or old failures. Unfortunately, many organizations believe that this is where the bulk of testing resources must be deployed. Unfortunately, the regression test system often becomes the only focus at the sacrifice of functional, structural and reliability testing. Many best practices associated with unit, integration system and acceptance testing are discussed for both short-term or long-term software development process improvement.

Audience

Software verification and validation testing and benchmarking is one of the most important areas of study for system and application software engineers. This is due to the high cost of testing, benchmarking and maintenance of new and existing software products. Quality assurance and development engineers, managers and professionals must understand how to perform functional test design, development and execution in order to improve customer satisfaction (quality) and reduce development costs (defect repair). This text has been written for use by both students as well as seasoned software engineering professionals. This includes individuals involved in the battle of bringing high-quality products and services to market on-time or ahead of the scheduled competition. The need for better methods and tools to design, develop and execute functional and system test cases remains a major challenge for most companies. Few courses, and even fewer books, cover this and other challenges by using practical examples based on modern-day technology. This text will provide many examples using the UNIX operating system; however, many tools for other operating systems are provided as well.

QA and Benchmarks

It is important to include in any text on software testing, information regarding the interpersonal and cultural aspects associated with software QA. Chapter 8 includes a discussion of both benefits as well as challenges associated with QA. This includes information that would have been extremely helpful to the author many years ago. Chapter 8 provides many tips and traps to avoid for anyone desiring to change or start a career in software testing or QA. Software test and performance analysis are two critical areas of study. Benchmarking the software development process is included as well; however, performance tools (benchmarks) for measuring software from a quality analysis standpoint is critical. Chapter 13 is devoted to the subject of benchmarks as tests for the UNIX environment.

Automated Test Tools

State-of-the-practice tools for automated regression testing of GUI and non-GUI applications is one of most popular topics of-the-day. Chapter 1 includes many tips and traps associated with automated testing. For example, one common trap associated with automated testing occurs when functional and structural testing are disconnected from the automated regression test system. The end result, with this common method, is a set of ad-hoc tests that may fail to verify or validate the product.

Another trap occurs when test design and development is not properly planned. The best that can be expected is often automated chaos (or something even faster) as a result of using test tools. Regression tests that have no functional value or provide little source code coverage must always be considered for their ROI. Software testing is a strategic activity; tools can only be used to improve the methods and practices which are already employed.

UNIX Test Tools and Benchmarks

Providing world-class products requires world-class techniques and technologies for software verification and validation. These techniques and tools must be used across the entire development life-cycle. Locating and hiring individuals who possess these and other skills will continue to be a tremendous challenge for the majority of modern-day software engineering managers. I intend the text to be a valuable tool in the process of producing the highest-quality software products possible. Adaptation of all methods and tools presented would be impossible. Therefore, careful selection of specific methods and tools from each area (functional, structural, reliability and regression) is suggested. Locating a product or function for quality improvement can be a major challenge for any organization. Therefore, suggestions that are useful in providing a focused approach to quality improvement are provided throughout.

I make no warranty of any kind with regard to the material and shall not be liable for defects contained herein or for incidental or consequential damages in connection with the use of this material, either expressed or implied.

Finally, I would like to thank the following individuals for their help in either reviewing or providing the motivation and encouragement to complete this text: Alka Shah-Jarvis, Rao Loka, Ed Miller, Greg Pope, Ed Kit, Ray Kehoe, Linda Prowse, James Bach, Larry Wear, Jeff Payne, Venkat Manickvasgam, Frank Ackerman, Andrew Ferlitsch, John Palacio and several of the faculty and students of the UCSC Extension. I would especially like to thank Peter Ron Prinzivalli for his comments and support in this project, as well as many of the members of the SSQA group. Finally, I would like to thank my editor Mike Meehan for his continued support and encouragement. Also, many of the vendors mentioned throughout this text.

CHAPTER 1

Functional, Structural, Reliability, and Regression Testing Overview

A successful software development and Quality Assurance (QA) strategy will minimize rework and manufacturing costs, reduce field defects and deploy competitive, quality products to customers on time. This can be best accomplished by using standard methods and tools for software development and testing and customizing these practices to the culture and capabilities of the organization. Schedules and quality must not conflict, as is often the case. Many companies still either do not set quality goals, or base their quality goals on the amount of time available (often left over) in the schedule. [CROS79] states: "Quality is free. It's not a gift, but it is free. What costs money are the unquality things — all the actions that involve not doing jobs right the first time."

Poor development processes that do not incorporate formal strategies for test development and execution are the largest contributors to product rework (waste) and customer dissatisfaction (poor quality). This means that test planning, design and development must occur prior to or in parallel with product development.

This chapter deals with the basics of software testing and is the foundation for the remainder of the chapters contained in this text. Even though this is a book on test tools and benchmarks for the UNIX environment, it is important to discuss the methods and strategies associated with testing first.

Many terms and definitions associated with testing are provided in these first several chapters (Part I). It is important that a standard set of terms be used to define any process, procedure or method. Once a standard set of terms and methods are realized, use of various test tools and benchmarks will become much more easy (productive).

Testing is normally considered a Quality Control function since the task is product, not process related. QA, on the other hand, is considered primarily a process related activity. For the sake of simplicity, this book will use QA to encompass both product and process related testing and analysis activities. If the reader is only interested in UNIX test tools and benchmarks, skip to Chapter 9 where the discussion of test products and tools begins.

1.1   Motivation for Writing this Book

In this chapter we will discuss proven strategies and techniques for the development and maintenance of successful software processes. The following four test methods are used together to form a consistent methodology (process) for software verification and validation across the development life-cycle:

1 Functional
2 Structural
3 Reliability
4 Regression

Over ten years ago, as one of many unsuspecting members of a growing software quality management nightmare, I was baptized through fire by the need for better approaches, methods and tools for software development and testing. There was a great need for testing methods and tools to assist in the release and delivery of quality products to customers on time (according to schedule estimates). In my case, this began during my employment with a UNIX system hardware and software company. During this time, many of my fellow engineers and I struggled for answers to common yet critical software and system quality problems. Many of my colleagues left the testing and quality functions and went on to other areas, but I simply could not leave this nightmare unresolved. Those of us who remained even formed a group (started by Pete Prinzivalli) that grew to include many different companies, both large and small in size. We would share both success stories, as well as battle scars, in our continual search for answers to complex software quality and reliability problems. Many of our common problems had to do with organizational politics (see the chapter on quality assurance for details). I believe that these meetings almost became like therapy for many of us who attended each month. If you are involved in the development or test of software, it is strongly suggested that you find a local group like the Santa Clara Valley Software Quality Association (SSQA), (a task group of the American Society for Quality Control).

In those days, there were few books on software quality and testing. In addition, most references were very theoretical and difficult to associate with current, real company problems. Many of the references available had very advanced and brilliant concepts and ideas for testing; however, most techniques were too sophisticated and complex to implement in the midst of common everyday problems (e.g., kernel, networking and application panics, core dumps and hangs). The ANSI/IEEE standards were also available (most of them in draft form). However, most of the material was so comprehensive and overwhelming that attempting to adopt many of the principles defined in the various standards was analogous to giving a rocket ship to an infant or child.* However, we quickly learned to provide R&D engineers with a simple release requirements checklist based many of the IEEE standards (see Appendix E). The checklist, or outline, described the expected criteria for QA acceptance prior to system testing. This technique proved to be an excellent way of improving communications between development, support, test and QA engineers.

Unfortunately, not a great amount of change has occurred regarding test development, execution and analysis techniques in the last ten years; however, there are more test tools and companies than ever before.† Even though the tools and techniques for software testing have improved greatly over the years, the complexity of the problems that the software is expected to solve also has increased; thus, the situation is not really much better than before [LEW92].

1.2 Functional, Structural, Reliability and Regression Testing

Increased customer satisfaction and rework reduction are the goals of testing. Efficient and effective test strategies and methods can improve productivity (long-term) by providing more time for engineers to focus on product development rather than maintenance and support.

- *Functional testing* ignores the source code of a program and focuses solely on the outputs or outcomes generated in response to test inputs. In other words, functional testing involves comparing product behavior to documented functional requirements.
- *Structural testing* takes into account the source code and all other Configuration Management (CM) items of the product or application under test. This type of testing requires the source code or a detailed design

---

*Most companies were comprised of adolescent QA and engineering departments.

† Compared to the advances in microprocessor technology.

specification to analyze the implementation details as a result of performing functional testing.

- *Reliability testing* is performed to determine if the required functions have performed without failure under stated conditions (requirements) for a specific period of time.
- *Regression testing* verifies that product modifications have not caused unintended effects and that the product still complies with its specified requirements.

Functional testing using product requirements documentation must be considered a prerequisite to structural, reliability and regression testing. After all, it really doesn't matter how much of the internal product has been tested (structural testing); if the product does not meet the customer's requirements, you and the company both will be unsuccessful (i.e., a great product without a customer).

One of many common problems that is resolved using functional testing is when the software developer questions why a product must be placed on hold when a feature that "no customer would ever use" does not work. When the functional requirements are defined and become the acceptance criteria for release, these discussions are defeated (assuming the functional requirements document exists and is testable, complete and accurate).

1.3   Reasons for Testing

There are many reasons for testing and the following are just some of the many potential motivations:

- Testing for success
- Testing for failure
- Testing for quality
- Testing for customer satisfaction
- Testing for reliability

All of these approaches to testing are valid and there are many more. What is interesting is that often when you ask most software developers about testing, they know very little about the subject, for many reasons. One common reason is that testing is perceived as boring and non-creative. Another major reason is that only 10-15% of all developers are ever trained in testing techniques [GRA93].

The testing maturity process usually starts with testing for success and is then followed by testing for failure. However, the ideal approach to testing must always be that it is a natural part of the entire development process from start to finish (part of the corporate culture). Cultural change is one of many goals and motivations behind the development of this text. Culture change is the key to software quality improvement. Software test tools and benchmarks will only be successful when they are used to support a documented, organized and efficient development process.

1.4   Challenges to Testing

Test design and development can be more challenging than product development in many cases. This is because the tests must be of a higher quality and reliability standard than the software under test. Tests that do not compile or execute combined with poor-quality products still yield poor-quality products.

I once spoke to an engineering manager about how his group was going to test a new product that was currently under development. He said, "They were not interested in finding bugs during coding using tests, instead they were more interested in conformance to the standard coding style. Anyone that cannot meet the standard is simply fired." This is clearly an interesting, if not disciplined (fear-driven) approach, to software development. However, if functional tests are not designed and developed as the product source code is written (hopefully before), how do you know when you have successfully completed the product? Moreover, how do you determine that the product has been built according to the customer's requirements?

1.5   The Purpose of Testing

Testing allows the development and quality engineer to measure the success or failure of a product to its internal and external requirements. This means that you must write many "dirty" tests to try and break the product for each "clean" test that shows the program works properly (according to the functional specifications). The ratio of dirty to clean tests is six to one (or more) for mature organizations, however, the opposite is true for immature organizations. Unfortunately, the majority of companies are immature (i.e., SEI Level 1) and do not write "dirty" tests. Having more companies write more tests (dirty or clean) is another motivation behind the development of this book.

1.6   Quality and Testing

Quality is often described as a measure of the customer's view as to how well a product meets the customer's requirements. Releasing products to customers without comprehensive testing based customer requirements can best be described as gambling with your company's integrity. Regardless of how well you may be able to write a feature, function or product, errors are bound to occur and engineers must not be made to feel guilty for coding mistakes. Instead, developers must be able to learn and improve as a result of a coding, design or requirements failure. Reviews are strongly recommended as a test method to increase knowledge, as well as motivate engineers to write solid specifications, designs and code from the very beginning. Two major sources of errors are often:

1 Requirements are often lacking entirely, or if they are present, they are usually ambiguous, self-contradictory or incomplete. As a result, the programs that are considered finished may perform exactly as intended by the development staff; however, when the program is used by the customer or end user, it may not satisfy the original requirements.

2 On the other hand, even when unambiguous, consistent and complete requirements exist in the specification, the number of test inputs is usually too large for comprehension (test development and execution).

1.7   Verification and Validation

An independent test process that proceeds in parallel with development attacks both of the sources of error named above. With regard to the first source of error, an independently developed test design specification provides an unambiguous and consistent set of requirements for software *verification* and *validation*. The test specification is written in the user's language, so agreement on the desired behavior can be reached prior to having executable code. With regard to the second source of error, the execution of independently-developed tests provides a form of redundancy in the development process which enables errors to be uncovered and corrected within the confines of the development process. The terms verification and validation are defined as follows:

• **Validation** is the process of evaluating a product during or at the end of the development process to determine whether it satisfies functional requirements. One way to accomplish this is to use the validation test suites covered in later chapters. In other words, are we building the proper product?

- **Verification** is the process of evaluating a system or program to determine whether the products of a given development phase satisfy the conditions imposed at the start of that phase. In other words, are we building the product properly?
- **Verification and Validation** is the process of determining whether the requirements for a product are complete/correct, each development phase achieves the requirements of the previous phase, and the product matches customer requirements. One way to accomplish this is through the use of requirements, design and code reviews. (Tools to help perform reviews will be discussed throughout.)

Verification includes all of the activities (checkpoints and milestones) conducted during the software development life-cycle process to prevent and detect defects. In other words, the verification process answers the question: is the product being *developed* correctly? The question is how do you monitor this without a well documented development process? Once the product is built, validation or conformance with the functional requirements is analyzed to detect and contain program coding faults and execution failures prior to product release.

Functional testing is just one method of performing both verification and validation; however, verification can also include activities such as code inspections, walkthroughs, peer and structured reviews of source code. Another successful verification method includes static analysis of product source code using a checker program, such as the UNIX utility **lint**.

1.8   Errors, Faults and Failures

So what is the evolution or root cause of most software bugs? The following three terms describe the evolution from error to failure:

- An **error** is a human action (mistake) that produces an incorrect result. For example, an incorrect action on the part of a developer. The greatest return on investment can be gained by improving communications between project team members and therefore resolving errors before they become faults in the source code. This is why structured reviews have been so successful toward preventing defects. However, technologies such as **mosaic** and **netscape** can also be helpful in improving communications between the project team members. See the chapter on test tools for more details about **mosaic** and other related technologies.
- A **fault** is an incorrect logic step, or data definition in a program. A fault is commonly referred to as a defect or bug. Many faults often hide in

source code and are only noticed when the fault is executed and thus produces a failure.

- **A failure** is the inability of a system or program to perform its required functions within specified functional requirements. Failures often result in problem reports that are entered into a problem report database for defect repair.

The evolution of an error to a failure can account for the majority of either schedule delays or poor-quality products. It is believed that most companies spend approximately 50% of their total time in defect repair. Think about the potential impact in revenue if less time were spent in defect repair and more time was available for new product development. Providing a testing methodology supported by suites of tools to improve productivity is the desire and motivation behind the development of this text!

1.9   A Testing Hierarchy and Test Assertions

So, what are the key components associated with testing? The following terms are commonly used to describe testing:

- A **test** is any activity in which a program is executed under specified conditions, the results are observed or recorded, and an evaluation is made (test success or failure). There are many potential types of tests. This text will focus on the most practical types of tests.
- A **test case** consists of a set of test inputs, execution conditions, and expected results developed for a particular objective. For example, to exercise a particular program path (structural testing) or to verify compliance with a specific requirement (functional testing).
- A **unit test** is a separately testable element of a program. Ideally, a unit test uses the smallest set of program inputs and outputs possible. The term unit test can be very confusing, especially since the scope of a unit can change from one program to another (sometimes called an invocable component).

From these definitions, a hierarchy of tests can be developed, as shown in Illustration 1.1.

This illustration does not imply that a test must be comprised of more than one test case and that a test case must be comprised of more than one unit test. Unit tests are often further decomposed into subtests. The combination of multiple tests is sometimes referred to as a test suite or test library. A test library may consist of many individual test suites.

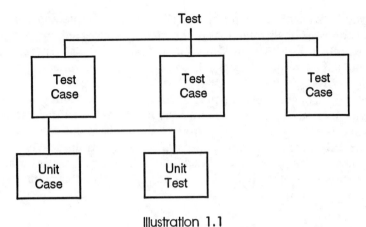

Illustration 1.1

Another related term is *test assertion*. This is a logical expression specifying a program state that must exist during testing. Alternatively, a test assertion includes a set of conditions which must be satisfied at a particular point during execution. A test assertion is used to validate a specific behavior of one function and is contained in a test program or script. For example, does the UNIX **read** routine return (assert) **EBADF** when a bad file descriptor is passed as the first argument? The value of a -1 in this case is returned by the calling function by **read**.

To design a **read** test assertion, the engineer simply needs to make sure that the first argument passed to the function does not represent a valid open file descriptor from the UNIX **open** function. This is a functional test (test assertion) based on the UNIX **man** page (on-line information from the manual), which describes the functional behavior of the software under test. Illustration 1.2 is a simple example of the functional test assertion program for the **read** function:

```
#include <stdio.h>
#include <errno.h>
main()
{
char *buf;
extern int errno;
if ( (read(-1,buf,1) != -1) || (errno == EBADF) )
 printf("read assert error for EBADF \n");
/* Test other ways read can fail */
```

Illustration 1.2
read test assertion

If you look carefully, you will notice that this simple and small test provides one of the very basic elements of a test case—expected outcomes. The test assertion expects that the **read** function will fail and anticipates this as the "expected" output as indicated by checking both the return code, as well as the global variable **errno**.

Many developers prefer tests that do not display output unless there is an error. They also often object to tests that display non-error information unless a verbose option is selected. The advantage to the verbose option approach is that there is more data to analyze. The disadvantage is that unless a verbose option is available, there is less information available for debugging, maintenance, analysis, etc. In either case, always provide an option for verbose output with any test.

1.10 Common Testing Problems

Many recommendations will be provided to resolve many of the classic quality problems associated with testing. The following list will help the reader to better understand the difficulties associated with the development of a successful verification and validation strategy. These items are just a few of many potential problems that can prevent companies from providing better products:

- Unclear quality definition, goals and objectives
- Quality personnel lack the required time to resolve issues
- Schedule delays by uncovering problems late in the life-cycle
- Testing is often slow, inconsistent, reiterative and boring
- The test cases continue to change (one of my favorites)
- Employees are required to be patient and dedicated
- Poor employee morale

1.11 Automation, Planning and Stages of Testing

Many of the problems listed above can be reduced, if not completely eliminated, through the planned development and execution of automated test technology. However, automated technology must be based on a standard methodology. The methodology must incorporate the strategies of functional, structural, reliability, and regression test development and execution. Having an automated regression test suite comprised of poor-quality functional tests does not improve productivity or quality! A plan is required, otherwise automation of chaos will simply provide faster chaos. It is also important that the architecture of the test library be such that if one test fails it will not result many other tests failing (i.e., single-point not multiple-points of failure).

Engineers must be motivated by achieving customer requirements as a quality objective prior to the start of any new project. Otherwise, new projects will lack the focus and attention required to successfully develop, test and release quality products. Automated test technology can provide consistent, accurate and efficient test development, execution and results for analysis. Test results must be reported as a by-product of having a clear definition of product quality requirements, goals and objectives. Automation provides more time for all engineers to focus on the investigation of test suite and product failures, rather than executing laborious manual tests. Another benefit is the reduction of test execution throughput time and monotony.

Scheduling can also be improved once quality data have been collected using methods such as the COnstructive COst MOdel (COCOMO) [BOE81]. Organization of the data, however, is also critical to the success of a well-balanced product and test development and execution strategy. Automation remains the primary focus for most QA organizations today. However, using formal methods for verification and validation must always be considered prerequisites to automation. Understanding the organization of testing as it relates to the product development process is paramount to success.

Five key steps are involved in the software verification and validation test process. Each step must be performed in parallel or ahead of the product development process to be successful (provide the maximum ROI):

1 Planning
2 Development
3 Technology with Development
4 Execution
5 Analysis

Starting with a solid test plan for test development is just as important as starting product development with a complete and testable requirements specification. Automation does not remove the need for test planning, it makes it even more important!

1.12 Test Plans (Step 1)

Test plans form the backbone of verification and validation testing when it is performed across the entire product development life-cycle. Test tools can only be as successful as the test plan that is developed prior to and during their use. Test matrices must also be developed from the test plan to more clearly and specifically state the operations and conditions to be tested. Test matrix operations (product functions) and conditions (test inputs and expected outputs) are used to perform *cause-and-effect-graphing*. Cause-and-effect-graphing is a technique used to map inputs (causes) to specific outputs (effects) and it considers test combinations of functional test events. Adding a test matrix to a test plan moves the process forward from test planning to test design. Therefore, a test matrix is often considered the test design specification.

An outline and checklist example test plan is contained in Appendix E. Creation of a test plan is the critical first step required in the design, development and execution processes for both functional, integration and system level test cases. The following best practices can be adopted for test plans and test design (matrices):

- Create a best practices team to create templates, examples and methods. Create a handbook and workshop as a result of the team's effort to promote the material for corporate-wide exposure.
- Test plans are usually best when produced by both the engineering and software QA functions. Engineering often has the technical details; however, QA can help determine missing customer requirements (when they act as the customer's advocate).
- It is critical that test plan focus is on content, not just format. A checklist using the [IEE94] standard is useful as a model or outline (Appendix E).
- It is important to move the most robust test plan sections to the front, as energy often tends to decrease during the development of a test plan. (Another reason why methods are presented in this text prior to tools!)
- The emphasis of the test plan must lead toward automated test development and execution.
- Test plans are always best when they are tightly coupled to functional specifications and requirements documents. The cross-referencing of requirements defined specifications to functional tests in the automated regression test system is critical. More will be said about requirements traceability in the next chapter.
- The test plan is only complete when the product feature set is stable. A well-defined set of milestones must include test plan sign-off instead of waiting until the code and functionality is complete.
- The completion of test plans is a critical milestone in the development life-cycle and is vital to the successful transition from prototype to production-level product maturity.
- Some companies do not allow code to be integrated into the central CM system, unless an adequate test plan is available. This can go a long way toward improving internal customer/supplier relationships.

1.13 Unit Testing (Step 2)

The software development group has typically been responsible for the creation or development of unit tests. Unfortunately, a unit test is often considered to be a test case connected to a problem report from a customer. Instead, a test case from the customer is usually the result of not having a unit test in the first place. Unit testing is part of an overall process that includes many activities and is best described as:

> **Software unit testing** includes test planing, acquisition or development of tests and measurement of the test results against functional requirements.

Often, there is not enough time to develop tests and still make project schedule deadlines and milestones. This decade will continue to be a time when automated test development will continue to increase in interest and momentum along with automated capture/playback technology. Automated regression tests help provide extra time by automating the test development process, capturing events (tests) for playback and comparison with baseline golden result files. Unit testing must be performed before interface, system and acceptance testing is performed using assertion-based tests derived from the test plan and test design documents. Another way to state this is that API tests must be conducted before functions are tested together as a complete product or system.

Unit test development and execution often become part of the critical path since they are often developed last and yet required first. This is a difficult problem since design and implementation details are often required to complete unit test development and execution prior to integration, system and acceptance testing. Using a standard template (provided by the test environment or harness) will expedite the development of unit, interface and system tests. A standard test environment that provides a consistent set of support functions (i.e., print results, compare results, etc.) will make the test development and execution process more efficient and effective. This will also reduce the cost of test development through improved re-usable tests from the central test environment.

When possible, unit tests must be developed along with product design prototypes. These tests must be preserved for reuse during production-based unit testing. Some best practices for unit testing and test development include the following:

- Problem report test cases are used as input to unit test development. The saying, "where there is smoke, there is fire," is especially true to testing. Always start by verifying and validating components to check for smoke before ever attempting to plug everything together (big-bang vs. step-level integration).

- Maintenance of unit tests must be considered a critical part of the product maintenance schedule. Another way of accomplishing this is to have engineering pick up the tab for product support. This practice will increase defect containment test development and execution in a hurry. The major reason that most unit tests are not available during and after integration is because they are not included in the product/project schedule from the start!
- Development of unit and function tests are scheduled to occur in parallel, if not before, product development. I love to hear stories about how developers write the tests before the code and continue to get new development assignments, while their colleagues must remain behind fixing bugs.
- Central test harness technology must be used for sharing tests from customers, engineering, QA and others. Test code re-use is just as important as product code re-use. Why not consider bringing unit tests to market as installation, configuration and software power-on tests?
- Flexible tests, using parameters that can be passed as arguments rather than hard coding values in the program, often result in a minimal amount of rework when product functions change. (Same coding guidelines used as are provided for product code.)
- Unit tests are combined with dynamic and static metrics analysis. If the value added by the unit test cannot be assessed, you are operating in the dark. Use structural analysis and testing techniques to understand the branch or statement coverage provided during testing. (See Chapter 3.)
- Support personnel often provide excellent help in the creation of unit and function tests. Test development requirements can often be based on the same requirements defined for new product demos. Any code, regardless if it is part of the product or a test, must always be highly leveraged or used to the fullest potential possible.
- Unit and function tests that are provided on a *contribution* tape for customers can provide a tremendous return on investment.[*] If tests are never released to either internal or external customers, the motivation for quality will often be missing since people thrive on recognition!

1.14 Interfaces and Integration Testing (Step 3)

Interfaces must be tested as part of unit testing, followed by integration testing. This is the next major step in the product test life-cycle and it is mandatory, after test plans, unit test design and development are complete. Software must be able to function on a base hardware and operating system platform, as is the case with unit test execution. Notice that we are restricting use to a base plat-

---

[*]Contribution tapes may be provided at a minimal charge; however, they must be supported.

form instead of every supported platform during integration testing. This is a major distinction between integration and system testing that is often overlooked by many engineers and test developers. Unfortunately, most individuals often confuse and combine integration with system testing and believe that they are comprised of the same set of activities. Integration testing must be considered an extension to unit testing, where the focus is on testing external functional interfaces between consumers and providers. (The greatest challenge for software development!)

When possible, simulation libraries must be used to test interfaces to and from an external function (e.g., status, exception, and error condition handlers). Functional interfaces must be defined in the requirements specification; however, often times they are missing because the requirements specifications are incomplete and inaccurate. This then results in functional incompatibilities between and within products. It is best if engineering suppliers can obtain and successfully execute acceptance tests for consumer functions prior to releasing source code to central integration. Some of many possible best practices for testing interfaces and integration testing include:

- Unit tests that include interface tests for libraries, commands and GUI functions that save many hours of debugging during the system test phase.
- Consumers create acceptance tests for providers. In other words, when one supplier provides a library for a consumer, the consumer must provide an acceptance test, along with a specification to the provider, for the verification of compliance to the library specification. For example, the standard C function libraries must be well-tested before applications developers are expected to use the libraries. An agreed-upon library test suite must be developed (i.e., POSIX, XPG4, SVID, etc.). Application vendors that provide system tests to their system suppliers for testing operating system changes are very smart! (Duplication of effort is unnecessary re-work!)
- Interface tests must be *tightly coupled* to the product interfaces they test. This often requires test-points or special test code to improve interface testability. For example, if product A uses B and B uses C, interfaces are tested from A to B to C. This is especially critical when product A may release its code prior to C by a factor of weeks or months (often very likely).
- Structural test tools that provide call entry and exit coverage are critical to testing interfaces (integration testing).
- Integration testing must be conducted during everyday development. Don't wait until the very last moment! This means that integration and interface testing is scheduled as part of the development process.

1.15 System and Acceptance Testing (Step 4)

System testing combines unit and interface tests with operating system and hardware platforms and is a prerequisite to acceptance testing. This is because acceptance testing is normally performed by an independent third party or possibly even the customer. Technical expertise in the development of *test matrices* that map operations and conditions against system configurations and features is critical to system test, as it is with unit test development.

Automation of this task is as critical with system testing as it is with unit testing. This is mainly because of the increased complexity often associated with system testing of both hardware and software configurations. I have seen several variables that must be associated with successful system testing:

- CPU version
- Operating system version (kernel/libs)
- Application software version
- Compiler version (includes all software generation tools)
- Network software version
- Firmware version (peripherals)
- Device driver version
- Minimum or maximum memory
- Minimum or maximum disk space
- Zero or maximum network cards
- Zero (headless) or maximum displays
- and many others . . .

Some of many best practices for system testing include the following:

- Tests are automated and documented for a minimum amount of user intervention. See the material provided in the chapter on test tools, as well as the chapter on test harnesses for more details.
- System tests must be integrated with other system tests in the same manner as the products they are used to test. As is the case with integration testing, if product A uses B and B uses C, system interfaces are tested from A to B to C. This is especially critical when product A may release prior to C by a factor of weeks or even months as is often the case!
- Intelligent filters must be created or provided by the test harness for efficient baseline comparisons (actual vs. expected or golden results files). When there is data overload from results files, it will be easy to overlook something important during results analysis. Therefore, filters or scripts that both look for differences, as well as matching strings, must be provided as part of the test execution environment!
- A rigorous set of release milestones must be used to prevent code churn and out-of-date specs during system testing.[*] For example, code freeze

means code freeze! When requirements continue to change, it often means that the product requirements specification was incomplete or inadequate. This is probably one of the biggest contributors to test development and execution waste during the unit, integration or system test phases! (This can kill the successful introduction of a capture/playback tool for automated test development and execution.)

- System testing must be conducted during everyday development. Don't wait until the very last moment for system test design, development and execution! This means that system testing (as is the case with unit and integration testing) must be included in the project schedule and be considered a critical part of the development process, not an after thought.
- Good documentation and training must be made available for system test maintenance and execution to be performed properly. Test development and execution are no different from product development—both require documentation for maintenance and support.

End user testing is also critical for successful defect containment. End users often make mistakes without adequate training and often find problems that unit, integration and system testing phases do not uncover. System testing may also be performed during beta testing[*] or customer acceptance testing.[†] Unfortunately, acceptance testing is often known as *disposable testing* since test cases are rarely *saved* for future use by developers or test engineers. Through the use of Computer-Aided Software Testing (CAST) tools, end user graphical and command operations can be recorded. Therefore, critical problems can be replayed at a later time and reused as part of a complete automated regression testing system.

Automating manual test cases that produce erroneous results will serve no purpose, except for reducing productivity. It is critical that test plan creation is performed in parallel with system requirements and design. Test design, development and automation using CAST and other technology must also be performed throughout the software development life-cycle—not at the last minute.

Usability and fitness-for-use are problems that can be eliminated using iterative functional specification and design cycles, with customer feedback and input using early *prototypes*. If you start with a prototype, then it can include much of the GUI and command syntax you need will need at a later date during bottom-up integration testing. Structural test tools that provide simulation libraries for integration testing using prototypes are probably one of the biggest and important secrets today. The cost of requirements *churn* or the constant modifica-

---

[*] Code churn can be best described as a trashing-like cycle whereby functionality changes so frequently that code development can't keep up with product changes.

[*] An independent party under a contract or verbal commitment to a software provider.

[†] Like beta testing, however, customer's purchase of product or maintenance may be contingent upon the success of this activity.

tion to product features can cost most companies a significant portion of revenue by increasing development and test costs. Therefore, it is critical to understand the needs of the customer and constantly refine and update all documents used for product planning, implementation and validation.

1.16 Conclusions

- Use the functional, structural, reliability and regression test framework to reduce confusion often provided by the myriad of available test techniques, tools and metrics. See Illustration 1.3.
- Always start with function tests that can be mapped to functional requirements.
- Next, measure the coverage of the functional tests with structural testing.

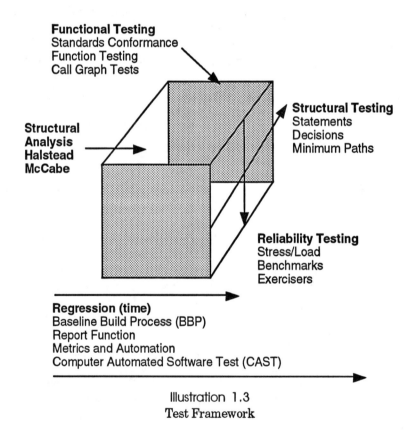

Illustration 1.3
Test Framework

- If the functional coverage is sufficient (mapping and coverage), regression and reliability testing will be much more successful.
- Use customer acceptance criteria, based on complete, accurate and testable functional requirements, so errors are resolved before they become faults and then potentially, customer failures. (Appendix F contains a sample beta test checklist.)
- Complement functional testing with structural testing and analysis. This provides a clear or transparent wall to the box so that what has been tested during functional testing can be viewed.
- Time is always a critical factor in relation to product maturity and quality (customer satisfaction). Therefore, reliability and regression testing must also be considered as equally critical dimensions in a well-developed test methodology.
- Poor planning that doesn't allow for requirements, design and code reviews, never will be fully compensated for by testing.
- Testing must include all activities related to verification and validation (i.e., testing across the entire development life-cycle).
- Planning and structuring the product development life-cycle process is critical to achieving product quality goals. The later in the process that a problem is discovered, the greater the cost.
- Many defect identification techniques are available for use during the requirements and design phases. The following items can be used to help target an area of focus for functional, structural, reliability and regression testing:

  - Customer dissatisfaction
  - Defect density results (problems vs. Lines of Code)
  - Code or functions that support many interfaces (other functions)
  - Static structural analysis (McCabe, Halstead, and Token counts)
  - Functional test coverage (tests vs. functional requirements)
  - Structural test coverage (tests vs. code execution, memory, etc.)
  - Combinations of any of the above

- The V-model is another method that has been proposed for testing across the life-cycle. This model is shown in Illustration 1.4. If you look closely, you will notice that as you move down the V to the code, more details will be required.
- Unit tests are usually always in the critical-path because they are required early in the verification process (i.e., prior to integration and system testing).
- Lack of proper planning for unit test development, execution and maintenance is probably one of the greatest contributors to late or poor-quality products.
- Define the size and contents of the box, then use out-of-the-box thinking!

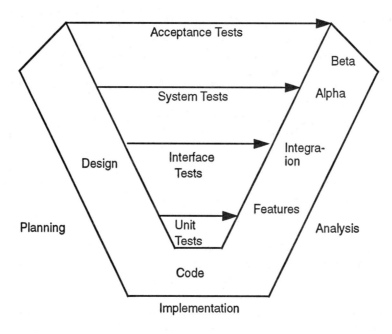

Illustration 1.4

## CHAPTER 2

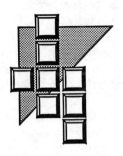 # Functional Testing

Coupling or tracing functional test programs to functional requirements provides a clear vision, not to mention documentation, for test design, development and execution. Ideally, the functional test must be included as either visible or hidden text in the functional requirements and design documents.

Organization and clarity are just two of many by-products of using a standard strategy and methodology for defect detection and containment (verification and validation testing). Furthermore, organization enables management to more efficiently and effectively deploy costly engineering development and QA resources to one or more testing areas (i.e., functional, structural, reliability or regression) based on the need. For example, structural testing can be used to better profile the complexity and integrity of a function once functional testing has uncovered a function or product feature with several failures or defects. Finally, after changes are made, and functional tests are successful or no defects are detected, regression testing must be performed.[*]

---

[*]This is where most QA organizations spend the majority of their time, unfortunately. I say unfortunately because unless functional testing is successful (performed first) no amount of regression testing will be effective.

2.1   Introduction to Functional Testing

It is important to measure the amount of functional tests relative to functional requirements before regression or reliability testing is fully executed. After all, if the functional tests that comprise the regression test suite are insufficient, the regression test suite will be insufficient as well. After functional testing is complete and all functions have been integrated into a system, regression testing must be performed. More about regression testing and CM will be provided in the chapter on regression testing.

Functional testing can also be called *behavioral testing* because it is based on using test assertions that check for specific behaviors (inputs vs. outcomes). The focus of functional testing is to find failures. Another commonly used term is *black box testing* since the source code itself is not evaluated or witnessed during testing, only the written requirements are tested. Standards help improve blackbox or functional verification and validation testing by providing consistent implementation guidelines.

Some of the several different types and areas of testing include (see the ISO-9126 standard):

- Documentation examples
- Performance
- Installation
- Security
- Interoperability (networking)
- Usability
- Reliability
- Scale-ability (notebook to super computers)
- Portability
- Compatibility
- Functionality
- Maintainability
- Availability
- Reliability

2.2   Functional Test Coverage

Functional test coverage is concerned with acquiring test traceability data for all documented external functional requirements. The focus is usually based on customer features incorporated into user reference documentation. However, it is often the case that product documentation will suffer with test design and development when resources and schedule constraints are tight (the result of poor planning). For example, several engineers were interviewed using a set of questions derived from the Software Engineering Institute (SEI) (included in Chapter 16). One specific question had to do with updating design and functional specifications during testing. As one engineer stated, "We don't update the specs; however, now that I think about it, if we did, then technical publications would probably stop bothering me for current information for the manuals."

Functional verification and validation testing will only be as successful as the specification that is used as the basis for evaluation. This also implies that the requirements specification is written such that it can be tested (complete, accurate, unambiguous, etc.).

Testing from the requirements specification is usually the most popular form of verification and validation testing. In the UNIX environment, one of many possible ways to start functional testing is to begin with a major underlying component—the compiler. A later chapter will discuss test suites that can be used for testing the C compiler. Because the majority of UNIX is written in the C language, this is one of the most common places to start functional testing. However, the same principle applies to other operating systems and environments.

Once the compiler has passed functional testing, the standard UNIX and X Window System libraries (e.g., **libc, libX11**, etc.) are tested. Test assertions that cover all documented functionality must be executed prior to system integration. However, this is really a chicken-and-the-egg problem because the compilers depend on system libraries (e.g., **libc**). Conversely, building a library depends on the compiler, assembler, linker, etc. Therefore, you will want to use an iterative or forward-and-backward process for functional testing because of these and other potential dependencies between functions.

Identifying dependencies as part of the planning process is critical to successful integration and system testing. Identifying dependencies is an important responsibility of the test management system or test harness software (e.g., TestExpert from Qualtrak). Test dependencies can also be identified using the UNIX **make** program. However, this method lacks the facilities of a complete database management system.

2.3   The Structured Review Process (Functional Testing)

Testing against a requirements specification or user's manual is obviously much different than examining the comments contained in the source code. However, source code comments provided by the programmer are another very useful method for performing functional testing. This method is especially helpful during the maintenance phase of product development or when third-party source code must be integrated with existing products. Functional verification using source code comments is often performed during source code structured reviews or quality inspections. Reviews usually help provide consensus and team building, whereas inspections are used as a quality improvement (defect containment) method [GIL93]. Verification testing using the source code comments may, however, be considered during structural testing (covered in the next section). Structural review can be considered as black and white box testing techniques.

2.4   Call Graphs and Top-Down Functional Testing

One useful way to implement functional verification and validation testing during the maintenance phase is to use a call graph or call tree to determine what functions to exercise. A major difficulty for this approach in the UNIX environment or others is that the number of options or functions involved in a command or system process is often enormous. Attempting to exercise or call each function in a command, library or system service has also sometimes been called *touch testing* by many companies. The purpose of touch testing using a call graph or call tree is to verify that functions exist in the product and return a sane[*] result. Many tools that will be discussed later provide these and other facilities for functional test coverage, as well as call tree or call graph coverage. Starting functional test coverage by evaluating the results of calling all functions is a good sanity test.

Top-down functional verification and validation testing focuses on interfaces. This method can start by using functions that are commonly found in the customer problem report database or derived from call graphs. Top-down testing starts at the top, or initial function in a program. After this, any other routine can be tested incrementally or using a step-by-step method [MYE79]. However, the general goal for top-down testing is to carefully isolate all dependencies and therefore reduce as many failures as possible prior to system testing. Stub files can also be used, when complete code is not available.

2.5   Functional Testing for Defect Containment

Increasing functional test coverage for products that have high field defect failure rates is one of the best methods for improved *defect containment*. Defect containment is considered a metric whereby problems are discovered later in the product life-cycle (testing)—still before customer shipment. One approach is to compare the total number of new defects discovered for each line of existing or new

---

[*]For example, the system does not crash, hang or the program does not dump memory or create a core file.

source code. Using historical data from previous baseline product source code builds can help engineers and managers provide better estimates for when testing will be complete. This in turn influences when the product is deemed "complete" and product release can occur. (Several metrics reports are provided by many test management systems for this purpose.)

Defect prevention is different from defect detection in that defect prevention is more concerned with methods and technology, such as development environment tools used during product development. For example, a compiler will require conformance with coding standards to eliminate many potential coding faults.

2.6   Standards Conformance and Functional Testing

Several different types of standards are available to the quality engineer for conformance testing. Some of the various types of standards are *de facto*, *de jure*, national and international. *de facto* standards are standards adopted by the customer or user community as a result of hopefully superior technology. *de jure* standards, on the other hand, may be the result of heavy arm-twisting by one or more companies. Several standards-based groups have designed and developed assertion-based test suites that provide functional test coverage for the UNIX operating system. Some examples of standard conformance tests are:

- POSIX Conformance Test Suite (PCTS), based on the Portable Operating System Interface (POSIX) P1003.1
- System V Verification Suite (SVVS), based on the System V Interface Definition (SVID)
- Verification Suite for XPG (VSX), based on the X/Open Portability Guide (XPG)

As interoperability[*] and compatibility requirements have emerged, so has the need for more comprehensive semantic- and syntax-based test assertions, where an assertion is developed based on the published behavior of a specific function. Interoperability and compatibility characteristics that provide communication and execution between heterogenous computer systems and software often drive the evolution of standards documentation. Many other standards are available for compliance or functional verification and validation testing including but not limited to:

- Computer automated design Framework Initiative (CFI)
- National Institute of Standards Technology (NIST)
- American National Standards Institute for C language (ANSI-C)
- Federal Information Processing Standard (FIPS)

---

[*]This often means the ability for programs to operate in a heterogenous network environment.

2.7   Dirty and Clean Functional Tests

Standards-based tests can be categorized as either positive or negative. Positive tests show that a function works properly under normal conditions and are sometimes called clean tests. An example of a positive test is typing in your log in name and password at the UNIX **login** prompt. The user always expects that the **login** and **passwd** programs will be able to properly read and accept keyboard input that matches the contents of the **/etc/passwd**[*] file.

Negative tests look for failures when incorrect inputs and conditions are provided. Negative tests are sometimes called dirty tests because sometimes they don't play fair or according to the requirements specification. Mature software developers write both positive and negative tests before the product source code is ever written. The ratio of negative tests to positive tests is often much greater for most software development projects and can be even greater depending on product or system complexity. Negative functional tests can require significantly more disk space during product development, as test development is integrated with product development. This must be accounted for as part of the verification and validation test planning process.

There are many ways to perform negative testing. The following functional testing techniques are commonly used for stress testing to optimize and improve the test selection process:

- **Equivalence partitions** or **partitioning** is the process of classifying data by type (e.g., integer, character, floating point, etc.) to reduce the total number of test inputs. Providing data or equivalence classes (the results of partitioning) explicitly, from either the right or wrong class, is also a common approach to stress testing.
- **Boundary values** are data that correspond to a minimum or maximum input, internal or output. These values can be specified for a system or program. Boundary value analysis is the study, process or technique used to determine test inputs for functional and stress tests. Boundary values are one of oldest (still useful) approaches to testing, however, they can create a significant number of tests that may not be exhaustive.

The reader must take note that both types of testing have now been automated (e.g., SoftTest, StP/T, etc.) and don't consider combinations of tests. Many other types of negative testing are available as well; the following are just a few of many possibilities:

---

[*]With UNIX System V Release 4, the **/etc/shadow** file contains the actual encrypted password string.

- **Error guessing** is often conducted using random numbers and is testing from experience or through the use of empirical data. Experience is often one of the best skills associated with successful testing.
- **Syntax testing** is a common form of testing where a command or function is often used (tested) without providing the required or necessary options or arguments. Most validation test suites perform this type of testing, by definition.
- **Cause-and-effect graphing** is a functional testing method that uses combinations of inputs that are compared with specifications for matching error conditions (effects).

2.8   Functional Testing (Domains vs. States)

A complete functional test means that the program must be tested using all possible inputs and environments (including combinations). This is impossible since the execution of all possible combinations for a reasonable program with multiple decision statements would possibly take years of computation time to complete. One study showed a very small GUI program had 10" path combinations. However, using domain testing, some of the infinite amount of inputs and outputs can be plotted to identify corner case, vertex, or extreme inputs that touch the boundaries of all possible test cases. For example, with a simple desk calculator (e.g., the UNIX **dc** program), you can randomize all inputs and operations to be performed on two numbers and graph the inputs and results. Next, a systematic or known approach can be used to identify new inputs based on whether the input and operation exposes a new boundary to testing. One systematic technique known as *guided synthesis* will be discussed in the chapter on test tools. Test operation conditions are external circumstances placed on the software under test, rather than test input data or vectors. A complete verification and validation test plan based on a product's functional requirements will determine testing inputs, conditions, operations and outcomes. Again, tight coupling between the specification and test plan is a critical prerequisite to test coverage measurement. Design documentation can provide a better understanding so one can clearly determine error conditions and boundaries for functional testing.

Assertion-based test methods can be used to help develop state machines for testing. This following term is used to define a state for testing:

- **State** is a condition or mode that a program may be in; for example, the pre-compiled state of a program is normally comprised of source code files, include files and other CM items.

States for testing must be based on requirements and design specifications. Begin testing with positive tests first and then migrate to negative tests during the functional testing phase of product development. Another method for handling the problem of test combinations is to develop cause-and-effect graphs from a state table or test matrix. By mapping input and output combinations based on the functional specification, a more clear focus for testing is provided. No tools are known to the author to provide this capability.

2.9   Domain Testing and GUI Environments

Domain testing restricts the range of failures to domains or data set classifications. A failure may mean that the boundaries of a domain are incorrect due to errors in conditional expressions or other control flow statements that specify what numbers belong within the domain. Looking at domains from either the code structure or functional requirements are both valid techniques. However, one always needs to question why an input domain was not specified in the functional requirements when it is contained in the source code and when test domains are based on the source code statements.

Domain testing in Graphical User Interface (GUI) environments is especially useful. An example of domain testing with a graphics application would be a case that would resize a window so small that text could not be seen (less than a single text line). Next, the test case would attempt to read or write text to the window. Other specific tests included in the chapter on stress tests explore these and other areas of testing using boundaries and domains. (See the section on **xcrash**.)

The most common source used to select inputs or a test domain is the product requirements document. Functional requirements and design documents are also extremely useful in helping the test engineer derive input domains for test design and development.[*] It is critical that customers review product, function and design (in some cases) documents during and prior to product design, implementation and test as part of an iterative product development life-cycle.

Another approach to domain testing is to evaluate the test suite by combining structural test coverage tools to compare statement, decision, minimum path and condition/decision test coverage (in that order) with inputs as provided by functional tests. It is also often useful to plot input data with results or messages. As a result, *coverage partitioning* information can be obtained, since this process allows the test engineer to evaluate functional test overlap from one test case to the next. Ideally, one will want regression tests that provide the greatest breadth of functional test coverage possible for the area of change, with as little redundancy (duplicated source statements or decisions) between tests as possible. Most structural testing tools provide these capabilities.

---

[*]It often makes good sense to have the documentation and test groups work closely together if they are not part of the same group reporting to the same manager or director.

2.10 Automated Test Generation

The automatic generation of test vectors (inputs) is a strategy that can be combined with structural testing to complement the current approach to functional testing. Test grammars are one method of automatic test generation by providing the ability to specify a description of potential product inputs and, when combined with various test strategies, provide a powerful tool for automatic test generation.

It is important however, that a test strategy be combined with a grammar to restrict the set of test inputs. Test Generator Generator System (TGGS) is technology from RG Consulting. Data Generation Language (DGL) is another system from Peter Maurer of the University of South Florida which also generates tests using a test grammar.

Another approach utilized by IDE is to use the T Tool to automatically generate tests based on a requirements specification developed using the IEEE 1175 standard or object models. Next, XRunner from Mercury Interactive can be used to execute, record and playback tests that have been generated automatically. QAPartner from Segue Software also provides automatic capture and playback for regression testing.

Another approach to automated test generation is to use structural testing with automatic record and playback facilities. These two facilities provide another method of automated testing. This capability has been provided by VERITAS Software's VistaREPLAY product. The purpose of VistaREPLAY is to verify that as functional testing proceeds, structural test coverage is increasing.

2.11 Orthogonal Arrays for Functional Test Selection

Because the efficient selection of functional tests is critical to maintaining schedule and quality goals, one more area of advanced research the reader might consider to reduce the cost of testing by better test selection is the use of *Orthogonal Arrays* [PHA89]. This approach, also called Robust Testing, suggests a method whereby test cases are selected based on the breadth and scope of coverage that will be provided during functional testing. This enables a balanced or "equal" coverage of all factor levels and pair-wise combinations. By pair-wise we mean that combinations for test cases **a** and **b** would hold true for **b** and **c**. Test cases would be spread uniformly throughout the test domain and the set of input boundaries after a test matrix (plan) would be created. The test matrix would be used to identify the test factors (requirements) and levels (test conditions) for each factor. An example of a test factor would be the power switch on a coffee pot. Normally two levels are associated with this factor (on and off). Once all factors and levels have been identified, a suitable orthogonal array is selected to optimize testing. In general, this method strives to increase the success of functional testing from just the corners and edges to *critical points* within the test data set. This is a very new area of test case selection still to be evaluated by many test developers. However, it has and deserves a growing interest, especially since the number of tests for selection is often very large with most UNIX applications and system software functions. No automated tools are known to provide this capability (at the time of this writing).

2.12 Call Graphs and Touch Tests

These functional tests, as the name implies with the term *touch*, check only the existence and basic operational sanity of a command or function. For example, rather than validating complete functionality of the ls command to list files by checking each option, ls would be executed without any arguments or options and the return code would be evaluated as provided by the UNIX shell. If the status returned was a value other than 0, an error would be suspected. It is also important to consider other outcomes, (e.g., the command didn't complete execution due to a system hang or core dump).

Touch tests can be created by executing function call entry/exit point testing. These tests check what function calls have been both entered and exited. Therefore, call graphs and touch tests are often considered in the last stage of unit and functional test development and are often performed during integration or regression testing. Call graph touch tests are usually positive, not negative in nature. Therefore, their primary purpose is to weed out gross failures and prove the existence of basic functionality. An example of a touch test (or wiggle test) is to execute a command and verify only the return code and ignore the output (this is to be discouraged). For example, to check the UNIX **echo** command, the following two commands from the UNIX **csh**:

%1> **echo hello world**
%2> **echo $status**[*]

Another benefit of tne call graph touch testing strategy is that it can be easily automated and can offer minimal function test coverage when time and budget restrictions exist. Call graph touch tests are always predefined by requirements or user documentation; however, they are often confused with:

- *ad hoc* testing, which is where anything goes for the specific cause of finding a failure. This includes everything from powering off the machine to using a pen to destroy a floppy disk.
- **Random** testing, which is usually accomplished using a random number generator provided by the operating system or application under test. The generator selects some set of tests to execute. With the UNIX operating system, this can be accomplished using the **rand** or **srand** library functions.

---

[*]The UNIX shell interpreter will return 0 if successful, or non-zero if erroneous.

Unfortunately, *ad hoc* testing often produces results that are difficult to analyze and that may or may not always be reproducible. This is a very difficult task to attempt, especially if the program under test is reasonably large. However, if the software under test is mission critical or software safety is important, use of any and all available test methods and tools must be used.* This includes random or *ad hoc* inputs with no boundaries.

2.13 Monkey, Random and Touch Testing

Some people may confuse random testing with monkey testing, because any monkey can come in and beat on the keyboard. Seriously however, I have found several important failures more than once by simply running my hand across the keyboard a couple of times to crash an application or system process. Having a user accidentally place a book on the keyboard and end up with a dead system does not engender a happy and confident customer.

Many serious problems have been discovered during random and *ad hoc* testing. Three engineers developed a set of junk data that they then passed to several UNIX commands and discovered that they would often core dump (write a memory image to a disk file rather than complete successfully). In some cases, many of the commands would crash under certain circumstances [MIL90]. This *ad hoc* form of testing was created as a result of modem communication difficulties they experienced during electrical storms on the east coast of the U.S. These problems often occurred while dialing into a computer system from home. Ten data files were created with various control, escape and other special characters. This type of testing however, requires a special driver to set a variable timer and then force an exit for tests that do not complete successfully or crash, but just hang around forever. This is also an important function for any test harness or driver program that is responsible for the setup and execution of tests. For successful stress testing, a consistent set of test data must be used for all programs for successful stress testing.

Touch tests can also be useful when combined with CM system software. In these cases, after a module or function has been built and installed, a touch (wiggle) test can be used to ensure that the executable program is in the correct location and can at least be executed successfully. Many C compilers will often compile (create an executable program), however, the program may not be executable after several errors are displayed. Once adequate functional tests are available using standards conformance and functional and touch test approaches, structural testing can be applied to either modules that change during development or have a high level of customer dissatisfaction. Only a small minority of all companies are believed to perform any type of structural testing.

---

*UNIX is used in many applications where human lives are at risk (nuclear power plants, medicine, etc.).

2.14 Conclusions

- Start to implement functional testing by using requirements traceability (functional requirements vs. functional tests). Structured reviews are an excellent method of performing functional testing and provide top–down communication across the company.
- Standards conformance testing is one of the best approaches to starting the functional test process.
- A real software standard will include a validation or verification test suite along with the specification.
- Standards testing using static analysis tools (i.e., source code checkers like **lint**) is extremely important prior to function, integration and system testing. (Use the strict ANSI-C compiler, or, better yet, try to compile C programs with the C++ compiler!)
- Start functional testing with clean tests. Then, make sure that there are many dirty tests for each individual clean test.
- Identify boundaries and equivalence classes as part of the functional test design process. Use these methods for requirements, design and code reviews as well.
- Use your imagination during functional testing (i.e., error guessing, syntax testing and domain testing).
- Automatic test case generation can be based on a test grammar or test generation system (i.e., DGL or TGGS). Both methods are useful in generating many tests. The problem then becomes test-set reduction and optimization.
- Automatic test generation tools that require formal specifications (i.e., IEEE 1175) force developers to write more complete functional specifications. After the specification is written, you get tests for boundary values, equivalence classes and cause-and-effect graphs.
- Use automatic capture/playback technology to preserve expert use testing of a product or system. Be careful however, automatic test capture and playback still requires a significant investment (e.g., you still must have a test strategy before you begin test recording).
- Structural test coverage must increase when you execute new functional tests; otherwise you must question the purpose (value added) by the test.
- Orthogonal arrays provide one method of reducing the total number of test cases that will be used for f testing.
- Call graphs and touch tests are useful for function and system testing when you do not have much time and need to find the highest risk areas.

CHAPTER 3

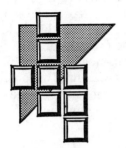

Structural Testing and Structural Analysis

Structural testing is also called white box or glass box testing. It is performed by the engineer responsible for the development, integration or maintenance of a software component or module, subsystem or product. Therefore, access to product source code is required. Structural testing is best performed during the unit test phase of the software development life-cycle. Unfortunately, it is usually performed much later. Structural testing can include UNIX utilities, such as **tcov** (from SunSoft), or memory management analysis products, such as Purify from Pure Software, Inc. The quality control group is usually oriented more toward defect containment after design and code development. However, QA organizations must be involved in code reviews, inspections, walk-throughs and other defect prevention methods that include structural testing and analysis to make significant process and culture changes. The purpose of structural testing and analysis is to find faults in the source code.

3.1   Introduction to Structural Testing and Analysis

You should always attempt to design and develop a sufficient number of tests to assure that every path through the program is exercised at least once.

However, a complete path testing requirement is usually unrealistic or impossible, because some control flow constructs (loops, goto's, etc.) may never complete. Therefore, structural testing is often more productive when tests and product features are carefully selected according to complexity and size as part of a complete defect prevention and containment strategy. For example, with the UNIX kernel, an engineer will want to start with simple daemons like **fsflush**[*] or **init**[†] before instrumenting more difficult functions such as memory management and process scheduling. Function, product dependencies and prerequisites must be considered before initializing the testing. This can be performed using call coverage structural analysis methods. Most structural testing tools provide function call coverage at a minimum.

3.2   Structural Analysis

Structural analysis validates the structural integrity of a specific source code module, component, function or the entire system. It can be accomplished using:

- **Static analysis** is when a program is evaluated based on its form, structure, content, or documentation.

This can be one of the most expensive methods of testing in terms of both time, money, equipment, schedule and other resources. MCrev from QASE is just one of many tools that provides support for automated source code review. Several other metrics and tools are available for evaluating software structural integrity, which is much like evaluating the integrity of a building or any other multi-level or faceted object. Some techniques available for structural analysis include (from least formal to most):

- Peer reviews, mentors and the buddy system
- Code walkthroughs
- Structured reviews
- Code style checking (standards compliance)
- Formal inspections

Two of the many potential benefits of structural analysis are critical to our discussion:

---

[*] This is a system process or "daemon" that runs periodically to perform file system flushes (reallocation) of cache memory pages.

[†] This system process controls initialization and is invoked as the last step in the boot procedure.

- **Minimal unit test case determination** which is a measure used to determine the number of independent paths through a module. A minimal number of test cases can be determined from this measurement. This also is often referred to as C1, *decision* or *branch* test coverage. Statement or C0 coverage only considers statement blocks (e.g., all statements between braces in the C language). C0 is weaker than C1 because it does not consider all predicates (decisions) within a statement.
- **Defect density** is often used to measure the product after design and code inspections of new development or serious modifications. It is useful to compare the number of unique defects to the total component or system size (measured by commented or non-commented lines of code).

3.3   Static Analysis

Static analysis provides *reverse engineering* information, where complexity and other structural information can be used to re-engineer software to reduce complexity. Static analysis is more effective when it is used frequently throughout product development, or as a parallel process to function and module prototyping. It is also a useful technique when examining product designs and source code that are error-prone. The problem of continuing to support a product's algorithm that costs more time and energy to maintain than is required after redesign can be facilitated using structural analysis and other software re-engineering techniques. The end result will be software that is more simple to maintain, enhance and support. This will save potentially thousands of dollars in rework and unnecessary maintenance costs. Quality and reliability, as well as improvements in interface and integration testing, will be provided through static analysis.

Engineers that say "I ran the complexity metric tools and yes the code is complicated, but there is no other way to re-write the code," are failing to understand the entire point of static structural analysis. One of many potential purposes of static structural analysis and testing is to flag or clearly identify complex functions during design, unit code, test, system integration and system test. Some people may feel that complexity metrics which identify the number of decisions present in a module are useless; however, these modules or functions must always be considered of higher risk. They must also be considered the target for new test development, which will result in increased function testing coverage.

3.4   Metrics and Testing

A prerequisite to most structural testing requires a process to prepare the product under test for test analysis. This process often is referred to as:

- **Instrumentation** is when instructions are installed or inserted into hardware or software to monitor the operation of a system or program.

Profiling is one method of instrumentation that can be performed using the UNIX **prof** command. Profiling is used to measure performance; however, it can also be used for structural test coverage analysis.

The two approaches to instrumentation are described and categorized as either *intrusive* or un-intrusive. If the source code is augmented or expanded by inserting probes, wrappers or additional statements around source code statements and functions (e.g., call tree coverage), the instrumentation is intrusive. Un-intrusive instrumentation means that a monitor[*] evaluates the instruction execution at link- or run-time without changing the original source and re-compiling.

Most structural testing products provide augmented or instrumented source as input to the standard compiler. The compiler, in turn, provides the modified source to the preprocessor, assembler and finally, link editor to create an annotated or instrumented executable binary. In time-critical or real-time environments, instrumentation for dynamic structural testing may not be possible; however, static structural analysis is always possible. The standard process for structural testing is as follows:

1 Instrument the appropriate[†] source code for the software under test
2 Evaluate test coverage after test execution and analysis
3 Continue to add tests to the test suite or library until the test coverage is sufficient, or to the agreed-upon amount of coverage
4 Once the test suite reaches the agreed-upon goal or metric, remove all instrumentation from the software under test
5 Re-execute the test suite with the un-instrumented source and compare test results

This process is important because the customer usually does not receive the instrumented version of the product; therefore, that is what must be considered for final test. It is important to mention in this chapter that a rifle shot (not shot gun) approach, or targeted focus, is critical to the success of any structural testing process.

---

[*]This is often accomplished by disassembling the object code into assembly language instructions, and then monitoring test coverage.

[†]Appropriate in this statement can refer to just source code that has changed, or to all source for new products.

3.5   A Rifle Shot Approach

Instrumenting or profiling approximately 12 million lines of source code (the total approximate size of the UNIX System V.4 operating system, other source code and documentation) and then analyzing results will take a long time.[*] Therefore, it is important to identify key modules for instrumentation and analysis. Instrumentation of commands, libraries and then the kernel (system services) is one possible order of test progression for system vendors. However, the severity of problems discovered will usually be in the reverse order. For example, a kernel or sophisticated daemon process problem that halts the system is obviously more serious than a command line option failure with a simple workaround. (However, commands such as *cat* when provided a directory have been known to crash Solaris.) Application vendors must start with core library functions or services first, using assertion-based functional test cases to validate conformance to a published API. This testing can be followed by either commands, followed by graphical interfaces. Finally, complex product-to-product interfaces must be instrumented and tested; however, the selection criteria must be very specific for successful structural testing.

Using static structural analysis to determine the degree of complexity of a function or module is one of the best methods for instrumentation and dynamic structural testing. For example, more than 10 segments or source code statement branches using McCabe's Cyclomatic Complexity static metric is one method of determining module complexity. See minimal unit test case determination from the IEEE Standard for Reliable Software for further details.

Function call graph, call tree and requirements coverage (mapping code to product specifications) are other metrics that can be used for static structural analysis. Static structural decision analysis usually implies counting the number of potential decision points in a function, including complex or compound predicates. A predicate is defined as any segment of code where a change in control flow (decision or branch) may occur. The C language supports multiple predicates or compound statements. For example, the following line of C source code contains three predicates,[†] or decision points:

if ((A == B) && (B == C) || (C==D))

Path coverage, on the other hand, can include each independent path from a function's entry to its exit point (one method of selected paths). One method of structural test coverage between decision and path is called switch coverage. Switch 0 is considered the same as decision or branch coverage. This is when each

---

[*] I know from experience that just instrumenting and analyzing part of UNIX can take several years.

[†] Expecting software engineers to separate each predicate using a UNIX command like indent, for example, is not realistic as proposed by some test coverage vendors.

statement from the beginning of the function is executed at least once; and path combinations are not considered. Switch 1 considers all path combinations one level below each first-level decision point from the start of the function. Switch 2 continues past Switch 1 to the second level of each decision point, so that all path combinations are complete to the second branch from switch 0. See Illustration 3.1 for details.

Interface coverage considers the ability to reference external functional calls or library interfaces. Call entry and exit coverage or S1 coverage identifies what external *instrumented* function calls have been successfully entered and exited. This is most useful during integration testing.

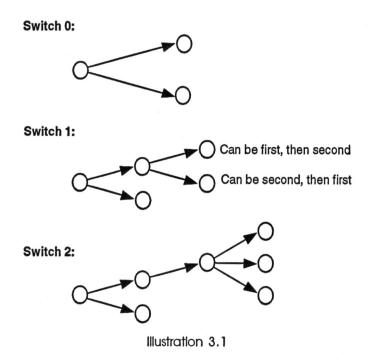

Illustration 3.1

Instrumentation of user-level software can be much easier than operating system services like the UNIX kernel. For example, obtaining dynamic test metrics from the UNIX device drivers requires a special monitor[*] to be built inside of the UNIX kernel to collect and present data. This is often *not* required for non-kernel-related software, since the monitor can simply be linked with the source code to produce an executable that can use the standard input and output services of **printf**. VERITAS Software provides a Kernel Interface Monitor (KIM) that can be included in the kernel as a monitor for instrumentation and dynamic structural

[*]The UNIX kernel does not use the standard **printf** library function.

test coverage analysis. Quality Assured Software Engineering (QASE) also provides a product for kernel instrumentation called MCkrn. This is useful for testing device drivers and other additions to the standard UNIX kernel. Dynamic structural testing and analysis metrics are critical to the verification and validation of either user or system level-software. Some tools provide results without the need for recompilation.

3.6   Dynamic and Static Structural Analysis

Dynamic analysis focuses on the collection of various source code test metrics information during test execution. This metrics can include statement, branch, condition, condition/decision, modified condition decision and multiple condition/decision coverage. Other techniques include coverage partitioning, selective instrumentation and error seeding.

Static analysis, on the other hand, can be provided without program execution and only requires a *map* of the source code structure. Two common static analysis metrics include the Cyclomatic Complexity and the Software Science. Token counts are also very useful for static analysis, and include individual components of a program (e.g., operators, operands, white space and others). Static metrics data can be obtained without ever having to successfully execute a program, because only the structure is analyzed. The use of static metrics analysis techniques is strongly recommended during the design stage to inspect and analyze the complexity of a function or module prior to coding. Static metrics can help software engineering management better determine whether a junior or senior engineer must be used for a specific function or project, based upon anticipated complexity. Schedule estimates for coding and test will be much more accurate when static metrics data are utilized.

It is critical that all metrics chosen for structural testing are always agreed upon by all parties involved, especially the developer responsible for function testing. [GRA92] discusses private vs. public metrics data collection and presentation. He suggests that engineers must be provided first with the opportunity to check their own work and discover defects prior to peer reviews, inspections or central integration. Once the work product (e.g., code, design or requirements specification) has been provided to others, it migrates from a private status to being public. In other words, it passes from being the individual's responsibility to being the project team's deliverable. More recommendations regarding metrics and measurements are provided in the chapter on metrics.

3.7   Memory Management Tools

Another major breakthrough in software testing and engineering automation has been the advancement and development of memory management debugging tools. These tools formerly provided only dynamic system memory analysis based on functional test execution. However, static analysis tools are available today to identify a memory fault without having to execute a single line of source code. However, using static analysis doesn't guarantee that each and every fault will be detected, since the compiler may make optimizations that may not be detected during static analysis.

A major problem with dynamic memory management analysis is that it requires a comprehensive set of functional tests. Many memory analysis and test products can also be used with either source or object code and can direct the tester or developer to areas of code that have not properly allocated or released memory. These types of failures are also known as memory allocation and access violations and they can cause a program to crash or consume more memory than is actually required. This can result in significant reliability or performance failures. Integration of memory analysis and other source code or object code analysis tools (such as the UNIX command **lint**, for example) must be used prior to and during regression testing. Memory analyzers must be used during the implementation and test phases of the product development process (e.g., from unit test to system acceptance test).

3.8   Be Careful With The Data!

The use of test tools for code profiling can be used for both performance, as well as test analysis. [DOW93] states: "You must be careful to gather data for all kinds of uses, otherwise you may not have a complete picture of how the program operates. Someone invites you to take your very first ride in an automobile. You get in the passenger's seat with a sketch pad and a pen, and record everything that happens. Your observations include some of the following:

- The radio is always on.
- The windshield wipers are never used.
- The car only moves in a forward direction.

"The danger is that given this limited view of the way a car is operated you might want to disconnect the radio's on/off knob, remove the windshield wipers, and eliminate the reverse gear. This would come as a real surprise to the next person who tries to back the car out on a rainy day!" It is important during code analysis to distinguish between dead code that is unreachable and code that is simply not easily accessed. Customer satisfaction surveys, user group meetings, defect density and many other measures must be used to make decisions regarding product test design, development and execution. The problem reporting system is one of the most commonly used systems to collect data as input to test development and execution. The test management system must be integrated with structural-testing, problem-reporting tools.

3.9   Conclusions

- To serve as a successful verification and validation strategy, structural testing and analysis must be conducted during the implementation (design and code) phases of product development. (The sooner the better!)
- Structural testing is dynamic analysis of the source code under execution during functional testing.
- Structural analysis is static examination of the source code or implementation. Static analysis does not require the use of functional tests, only a reference implementation.
- Be very selective about the functions you will instrument for static analysis or structural testing.

The following cumulative maturity levels are proposed for structural verification and validation testing:

1 Static complexity analysis (e.g., call graphs and control structures)
2 Memory access violations and leak detection (unit testing)
3 Dynamic structural test coverage analysis (unit to system level)
4 Portability and performance static analysis
5 Portability and performance dynamic analysis

- Level 1 organizations use basic metrics to measure the complexity associated with an existing source code module to determine the relative level of testing and support difficulty associated with a program. Call graphs for program interfaces are used during system-level testing and planning. Also, control graphs, such as McCabe or Halstead, are used for unit level testing.
- Level 2 groups perform some type of memory leak and violation analysis for source code using functional tests. This includes the use of memory analysis tools, like those provided by Pure Software, Inc. It is believed that many organizations simply skip Level 1 activities; unfortunately

this results in a much more reactive and less proactive approach to scheduling and planning. (Poor risk assessment.)

- Next, Level 3 organizations perform some type of dynamic structural test coverage during unit, integration, system and acceptance testing. Unit testing evaluates the number of branches or statements in the source code that have been exercised (tested). During integration, system and acceptance testing, the number of function calls executed as a result of testing is evaluated.
- Level 4 groups evaluate the portability and performance of a source code module during unit testing using UNIX utilities such as **lint**. This technique could be integrated with the static complexity analysis performed in Level 1.
- Level 5 organizations incorporate static portability and performance analysis with dynamic data metrics. This often requires the vendor to have an excellent grasp of customer usage and requirements.
- It is important to note that each proposed level is considered cumulative in that the previous level's processes and technology must be continued to the next level.

## CHAPTER 4

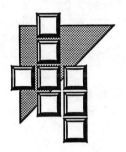

Reliability Testing

Reliability testing focuses on intended software usage. This means that an operational profile is determined or created to describe the average usage of the system or program over its expected lifetime. Reliability tests are created relative to a usage model. For example, if function X is expected to account for only .01% of a system's usage, then a minimum of .01% of the overall testing must test function X. Therefore, reliability testing strives to achieve a Mean Time Between Failure (MTBF) and Continuous Hours of Operation (CHO) rating for either individual programs or a complete system. Unfortunately, many of the models that have been used for software reliability have been based on data derived from computer hardware reliability studies. However, hardware reliability models typically are associated with a manufacturing process that does not correspond properly to the software design process (i.e., manufacturing vs. design errors). The purpose of reliability testing is to organize testing according to the way the software under test will be used. Reliability testing measures reliability in terms of failure density over time (in most cases).

4.1   Introduction to Reliability Testing

Software reliability failures are the results of executing faults in the source code. Therefore, software reliability can be more accurately projected by identifying all source code faults, where each fault has the potential to become a failure. This leads to the following four proposed maturity levels for reliability verification and validation:

1 Testability (dynamic analysis using the fault failure model)
2 Automatic mutation generation for fault analysis
3 Software safety analysis (hardware and software simulation)
4 Testability using static analysis (source code coding guidelines)

4.2   Testability and Reliability

Testability is the dynamic analysis of source code to determine how difficult to test a function or module will be. In many cases, you may determine that testing is not the best solution and that the function must be redesigned or eliminated altogether because of low testability (it cannot be tested). This is often performed without any regard to the functional specification (a white box testing technique).

Automatic mutation generation is the next level of maturity that studies what sections of the source code are better or less able to protect themselves from faults. Safety analysis continues the reliability maturity process by including the analysis of source code reactions to hardware- and software-generated faults. Finally, static testability analysis provides a set of coding guidelines, technology and strategy for preventing faults during code design and development. Testability, automatic mutation, and software safety analysis are all provided by PISCES.

Static testability analysis really should be a Level 1 activity; however, since there is so little information available, it has been moved to the highest level of complexity and maturity. One example of static analysis checking would be to flag any function that accepts, for example, two real numbers between the values 1 and 100, and yet only provides a 0 or 1 as output (a boolean). This function would be difficult to test since there are almost an infinite number of potential inputs and yet only two outputs. This is also known as *internal state collapse,* since the number of potential test inputs for the function far exceeds the number of outputs [VOA92]. Source code testability will be increased whenever a specific input can be mapped or associated with a specific output (traceability). Therefore, one could combine low testability functions with other high testability functions that provide many outputs instead of just two. The best case would be to have the function provide only two inputs (e.g., true or false) and exactly two outputs (positive or negative).

Always consider the testability of a design or source code function during a review. Also consider the testability of a function or system before attempting to measure reliability.

4.3   Testability of Object-Oriented Software

Testability analysis is a fundamental problem for testing object-oriented programs and systems. This is because the benefit of object-oriented design and modeling is to provide data abstraction and class reuse (i.e., function and operator overloading). This benefit, however, often lowers the testability of a function as described above. For example, using a structured design approach improperly (e.g., reusing a variable) can result in a program failure. Most testing tools support the C++ programming language; however, this does not necessarily mean that object-oriented design methods have been used during testing or development.

4.4   Run Reliability

Another metric associated with reliability is run reliability. This measurement is the probability that X randomly selected runs (over a specified period of time) will produce correct results. This is just one of many reliability metrics that can be used as a baseline for reliability testing.

In general, a standard result must first be determined prior to the execution of any reliability test. Also, incremental increases in successful Mean Time Between Crash (MTBC) or Mean Time Between Error (MTBE) must be considered as metrics for continuous quality improvement. Most test management tools provide the ability to monitor key metrics such as run reliability.

4.5   Reliability and CM

Another significant reliability metric is the amount of elapsed time necessary to change or correct a software defect. The UNIX operating system provides either the UNIX System V-based Source Code Control System (SCCS) or the BSD UNIX Revision Control System (RCS) for source code management. It is strongly recommended that functional tests be automatically identified by a source code CM system based on changes, as well as frequency of changes.

One of the common problems that can occur with CM is deadlock. This is when a popular file gets locked by overuse. The end result is those who miss the chance to obtain (check out) the file must then wait an indefinite amount of time to make their changes.*

To improve traceability between tests and product features, integration between the test system and CM system must be provided. This also requires that at least one test accompanying or existing test be modified for each change to the source code under test. This will ensure that the configuration baseline will continue to operate without any regressions or new failures. TestExpert from Qualtrak is one product that provides an integrated facility for tests, problem reports, metrics, and CM.

In general, higher activity modules and functions must undergo more stringent reliability tests, as well as static analysis and dynamic structural testing measures.

4.6   Stress and Load Testing For Reliability

Stress testing is conducted to analyze a program or system at or beyond the limits of its specified functional requirements. In the UNIX environment, this can be when various or all system resources are exhausted for a short duration of time (minutes or seconds). Load or volume testing is successful when limits are exceeded for a long duration of time (usually hours rather than minutes). Stress and load tests overlap with function tests; however, time is a critical variable often associated only with stress and load testing. Therefore, stress and load tests have been included under *reliability* testing.

Several techniques can be used for both load and stress testing (i.e., boundary values, equivalence classes, cause-and-effect mapping, etc.). Both stress and load tests exist when the following categories are exercised to the point of exhaustion:

- System exercisers (peripherals, memory, CPU, etc.)
- Multi-user benchmarks
- Resource limit tests (files, locks, processes, etc.)

Examples of hardware/system devices that can be considered for either system or resource exercisers during stress and load testing include:

- Memory
- Disk/tape/floppy
- CPU and floating point processors
- Serial input/output
- Networking (Local Area Network, Wide Area Network)
- Video
- Floating point co-processor

---

[*]Peter Miller <*pmiller@bmr.gov.au*> provides a possible solution, aegis-2.1, posted as Volume 27, Issues 36-54 of *comp.sources.unix*.

4.7   Exercisers

Exercisers are concerned mainly with stress testing subsystem components or physical devices. Exercisers provide excellent stress or load tests because they consume critical system resources. These reliability tests can also be used for performance comparisons or system-level diagnostics. A sample floppy disk exerciser is provided in Appendix A. (This program can be modified to act as an exerciser for other devices as well.)

4.8   Tips for Stress and Load Tests

Once stress tests are successfully completed for individual resources or devices, the frequency and quantity of tests can be increased for load testing. It is not necessary to limit stress testing to device exercisers. Multi-user resource exercisers can also act as stress tests by simulating a *full or maximum work-load* for several users. Once individual or component-level stress tests are created, either new load tests or existing stress tests can be used in a recursive loop, either in sequential or random order. Test harness tools and capture/playback tools are extremely useful for combining stress tests into load tests.

Using existing stress tests gives assurance that unit test failures will not occur, whereas new load tests potentially (in certain circumstances) will introduce at least one new functional failure (e.g., a missing feature). One example of when a functional failure is introduced by a new stress test is when physical or virtual memory or file system disk space is insufficient for the test.

New load tests designed specifically for pushing the envelope on system limits over a long period of time may uncover unique failures not discovered during functional or structural testing. Using multiple stress tests in parallel with functional testing will provide worst case scenarios for load testing, but they will increase the complexity of debugging problems.

Good stress and load tests will uncover system memory core dumps (access to memory that is out of bounds) and system crashes by passing boundary values and wrong data types. Memory management debuggers will find memory access violations and leaks; however, they are dependent upon the code coverage provided by the function or unit test. With these tools, no valid reasons for memory access violations in delivered software products exist.

4.9   Test Harnesses and Load/Stress Testing

A test harness is a term that is often confusing to people. This term is commonly used to describe a:

- **Test driver,** which is used to invoke a program under test, provide test inputs, control and monitor execution, and report test results. A test harness can be used to build load tests from stress tests.

It is equally important to consider the complexity of the hardware resources during stress and load testing. Multiprocessor architectures must be carefully considered during the development and execution of stress and load tests, because of the characteristics of added complexity.

4.10 Multiprocessor and Multi-tasking Considerations for Reliability Testing

Another important aspect of stress and load testing is the proper distribution of tests in a multiprocessor and/or parallel processing threads environment. Multiprocessor environments mean that more than one Central Processing Unit (CPU) is available for process use or multiprocessing. Parallel processing, on the other hand, can mean that hardware is provided for moderately or massively parallel processing.

Initiating multiple copies of stress and load tests does not necessarily guarantee a symmetrical load distribution on hardware processors, network nodes or other system resources, unless those services are expressly provided by the operating system. This can either occur automatically or manually using library system services. A good balance or job mix is vital to the success of stress and load testing. User simulation with stress and load testing is not adequately represented by one small program with a few arguments executed repetitively (in a loop) to represent each individual user.[*] Multi-user testing that is successful simulates a unique **login** session for each system user. One approach to simulating user activity is to use automated regression testing tools such as LoadRunner and XRunner from Mercury Interactive and QAPartner from Segue Software.

Another approach to simulating multi-tasking and multi-user stress and load testing is to characterize the user as a scientific engineer, office worker or manager. The next step in the process is to then build a set of programs to exercise the system for each unique type of user. For example, the scientific engineer will probably use a compiler, debugger, editor and other development tools. The office worker or manager, on the other hand, will use word processing and spreadsheet applications. During compilation, fast sequential access to files is important to the engineer; however, random access performance will be more important to the manager's or office worker's applications. This leads specifically to multi-user job mix considerations that must be made during reliability testing.

---

[*]In UNIX terms, this means that for each child process that is created using the **fork** system call by the parent process, we are providing multi-tasking services.

4.11 How Much Time Does Load Testing Require?

The decision of how long to test is one of the most difficult aspects of load and stress testing. The development and quality engineer must always consider how long load or volume tests will take to complete before the return on investment is no longer equal to the amount of time consumed. This estimate, for a return on investment, must also include the average cost of labor, machines, technology and schedule. If the cost of a severity 0 problem is $10,000 to fix and release after product shipment, this value must always be considered during development, verification and validation testing. This cost would normally only be based on accounting costs and would not include potential loss of business and sales revenue. If we don't know the cost to repair a customer failure, we are operating in the dark. Without this information, how can we determine the return on investment for any new or existing test development, execution process or technology?

An appropriate rule of thumb for load tests is between 48 and 72 hours. After four days, most failures usually occur through exhaustion of resources such as:

- Inodes[*]
- Files
- Locks
- Processes and other resources

Significant functional or performance defects are rarely discovered after three or four days. Failures at this point are often a *false negative*, which is when the cause of failure is not directly attributed to the test under execution.

4.12 Benchmarking Reliability

Benchmarks can provide not only excellent reliability metrics information that is useful to QA personnel, but they also provide competitive analysis information that can be used by marketing and sales employees to measure anticipated customer satisfaction.

Unlike standards conformance tests, there are no *de facto, de jure,* national or international standards for stress and load testing. However, some organizations, for example, the Transaction Processing Performance Council (TPC), have developed benchmarks for comparing system performance. The TPC number is well known as a standard performance metric, especially for database management operations [GRA91].

---

[*]Stands for index node. This is a unique integer value for each file allocated in the UNIX file system.

Benchmarks are standards against which other measurements may be referred. Successful benchmarks provide good stress or load tests and exhibit many other benefits, including:

- System limits testing
- Acceptance test simulation
- Baseline performance comparisons
- Competitive analysis

Benchmarks have been included under this section with stress and load tests because they can be considered integral components of successful regression, reliability and functional testing. The term *benchmarking* has also grown to include activities such as best-in-breed and best-in-class reviews. These activities exist when customers, as well as suppliers, develop and test processes that are evaluated for best practices.

The other more common use of benchmarks has to do with performance analysis. There are several different categories of performance benchmarks; however, two classes often dominate all others. *Marketing benchmarks* are commonly used for customer comparisons of performance prior to purchase. *Technical benchmarks* are often used by system architects and designers for characterization of performance prior to manufacturing. Marketing benchmarks, like the AIM Suite II and III, are usually more appropriate for reliability testing than technical benchmarks and provide a macro- rather than micro-level focus.

4.13 Mean Time Between Failure (MTBF) and Software Reliability

Setting an appropriate software reliability MTBF is one of several critical metrics for continuous quality improvement. However, a realistic metric must also be considered. Too long or lofty a MTBF goal may be near to impossible to validate through testing. For example, after three days, the system under test may run out of inodes or some other critical system resource. Conversely, too short a MTBF will inadequately test the following:

- **Robustness** is the degree to which a program can function correctly in the presence of invalid inputs (dirty tests) or stressful conditions.
- **Integrity** is the degree to which a program prevents unauthorized access or modification of program text or data.

Another typical MTBF evaluation process would be to install a newly manufactured system and execute reliability tests until system death (crash, hang, etc.). This is also known as a *life test* and it is an equally important method of reliability testing. The reader is encouraged to note the run reliability and Mean Time To Failure (MTTF) metrics from [IEE94], along with a total of 39 metrics for the production of reliable software. Reliability testing in the system software integration environment can be tightly coupled with regression testing as described in the next section. There are several degrees of granularity possible for run reliability. As one example, for a coarse level of granularity, the engineer can use the UNIX command **uptime** to determine the length of time a system has been in operation. The output of the UNIX **uptime** command looks as follows:

uptime
3:20pm up 4 days, 57 mins, 1 user, load average: 0.45, 0.11, 0.04

A higher resolution or granularity measures the length of time until any command or functional failure occurs. Live recorded customer sessions using automatic record and playback tools must be considered critical components for any thorough reliability test. Tools such as FlightRecorder from Mercury Interactive can now record only X events. This means that playback can occur on other systems without the need for program data or text. FlightRecorder is similar to the black box that is located in the flight deck of an airplane. Both are useful for analysis of reliability failures. However, if the crash was a result of a data-dependent function, it may be difficult to completely diagnose the failure.

Unfortunately, MTBF for software often does not work as well as it does for hardware, because the MTBF will be limited to both the time and input values used for testing. Software can have an infinite number of inputs. Therefore, the MTBF results for reliability testing will only be as accurate as the quantity and quality of inputs that are used for testing. One approach to reliability testing is to prove *failure-free* results from random inputs (see [VOA93]).

4.14 Conclusions

- Reliability testing must be incorporated as part of functional verification and validation testing.
- Reliability is often a direct result of product testability. High testability means you can test the product and detect most program faults (i.e., high reliability).
- Leverage or combine reliability testing with other testing activities (i.e., function, system, regression and structural testing).
- Exercisers test basic functions and are useful for reliability analysis, especially when executed within a loop over long period of time.

- Benchmarks are tools for measuring product reliability, as well as functional performance.
- Few tools are known to exist to solve the problems associated with reliability testing. See the section on PiSCES in the test tools chapter for further details on tools for testability and reliability.
- The following reliability methods (in order of maturity) are provided as a basis for reliability verification and validation testing and most are supported by existing technology:

   1 Testability (dynamic analysis using the fault failure model)
   2 Automatic mutation generation for fault analysis
   3 Software safety analysis (hardware and software simulation)
   4 Testability using static analysis (source code coding guidelines)

- TestExpert from Qualtrak is one tool that combines testing with CM and problem management to improve product reliability. Several reliability metrics are provided with TestExpert and other automated test harnesses.

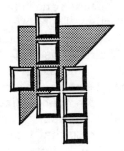 # Regression Testing

*R*egression testing, as was mentioned in the beginning, essentially consists of validating or retesting and comparing baseline results with previously known or expected outcomes to ensure that modifications have not caused unintended effects or failures. This chapter has been explicitly placed after the previous chapters to encourage the use of the tools and methods already discussed. Most QA functions devote the majority of their effort to regression testing at the sacrifice of functional, structural, and reliability testing. This must not occur

5.1 Introduction to Regression Testing

The goals of regression testing are not only to validate the resolution of a previous problem, but to ensure that all previous problems will remain fixed with the latest product baseline. This requires a closely-coupled interface between the test library (regression test suite) and the CM system. The following cumulative maturity levels are proposed for regression testing:

1 Functional V&V integration with CM
2 Structural V&V integration with CM
3 Reliability V&V integration with CM
4 Internal company problem report database integration with CM
5 Customer problem report database integration with CM

5.2   Regression Testing Approaches

The first level of maturity integrates functional verification and validation based tests with product source code within the CM system. Therefore, when source code changes are made and checked into the CM system, the corresponding functional tests are compiled and executed by the test harness as part of the regression test process. This provides a significant incentive for developers to produce functional unit tests, that are integrated with the CM system. As a result, when source code changes are made, the build process will *automatically* include construction and execution of the appropriate tests. It is also important to include a keyword-type of searching mechanism in the CM system so that functional changes to the test can be quickly cross-referenced back to all appropriate product features. The objective is to increase test reuse as much as possible through leveraging existing tests with similar product features. TestExpert from Qualtrak is one product that provides these and other integrated facilities.

The second level of maturity adds to this methodology the ability to analyze and manage functional test execution based on structural test results from Level 1 activities. Level 3 adds the capability of analyzing reliability metrics and associated impacts as a result of source code changes and regression test execution. As product changes are made through the CM system, reliability as well as functional tests will be compiled and executed.

Level 4 maturity adds internal problem report database information to the regression test and CM systems and finally, Level 5 maturity adds customer supplied problems and feedback through the entire system. Both Level 4 and 5 processes provide direction for the regression and CM systems, instead of *ad-hoc* product construction and regression test execution. It is critical that a tight feedback look is provided between CM, regression and problem management systems. All of the above regression test levels require the use of a standard test environment. Along with each level, two keys to successful regression testing are critical:

1 The ability to provide quick (touch-level), full, and regression test
   result analysis
2 The development and execution of a well-organized baseline build
   process

5.3   Regression Testing and QA

Most QA and test engineers are often asked to spend the majority of their time in regression test development and execution. This is usually because there is nothing more embarrassing than resolving a customer problem with a patch release and then re-introducing the same old problem with the next follow-on product release. Some people may call this obtaining experience; however, most customers will consider this *madness* (to put it nicely). One of the greatest challenges to successful regression testing is the ability to properly and efficiently compare regression test results when major or minor functionality changes have been made to the product source tree. One common result of unsuccessful regression testing is that *golden data,* or known baseline results data, will no longer be appropriate for evaluation, comparison and analysis. (Golden data can become rusty very quickly.) This is often a result of poorly-defined product requirements, which results in code-churn.

5.4   Video-taping and Regression Testing

Video-taping customer product usage and the resulting problems can provide excellent input to regression test systems, as well as many other benefits (i.e., better requirements documentation). Video-tape information is indisputable and can help in the determination of the root cause for failures. Video-tapes can also help assist engineering and QA in the development of new and improved design specifications, verification and validation test plans and regression tests. Mercury Interactive's FlightRecorder (currently not a released product) acts as a software video tape recorder and does not require the application under test or program data for replay. This is because only graphics primitives are stored, instead of actual application commands. Performance Awareness has a similar product for recording graphical events that also does not require the application under test during playback. Both products help automate the process of adding tests to an existing regression test system by providing pseudo capture and playback facilities, much like that of a Video Tape Recorder (VTR). Analysis of customer problems using video capture-type facilities can help to not only improve system regression test suites, but also to improve usability design (task analysis) and testing.

Automated regression testing using software tests is an important vehicle that provides the necessary time for new and existing test development and maintenance; however, it requires both planning and management's support.

5.5   Regression Test Reports

After functional, structural and regression testing, baseline test results need to be compared with standard results. A report generator program is critical to intelligently interpret test suite results via a results database. This is probably one of the most important tools, especially considering the volume of data generated by most comprehensive regression test systems. Analysis time is often directly proportional to the amount of data generated. Therefore, it is important that report generation tools provide searching and sorting capabilities to elimi-nate noise-level data. Products that provide smart comparison checking are dis-cussed in the chapter on test tools.

One example of smart or intelligent checking during regression testing is to first check for problems that have the highest problem severity according to the problem management database. It is also important to separate problem *severity* from *priority*. Customer problem priorities often must influence company problem severities during regression testing. Some of the many other possible critical datum collected during reliability testing often include:

- Responsible engineer
- Change request history
- Number of days a problem has been open
- Critical accounts
- Product category

Integrating the regression test system and the reporting function with the construction of software products and tests is a critical component in the software development and test automation process. Several tools for problem tracking are discussed in the chapter on test tools. A baseline build process will be discussed as a final critical element in a successful regression test methodology.

5.6   The Baseline Build Process (BBP) and Regression Testing

One of the more critical processes that usually needs to be established early in the software life-cycle is a BBP. There are two significant aspects to the BBP:

- Configuration items
- Control of configuration items

Configuration items must include source code files and directories located in the **/usr/include** hierarchy, libraries, compiler and other development tools, as well as revision control logs. However, this list must also include test plans, test suites and test programs. The proper timing for code freeze and integration is par-amount to project success. As an example, if the C compiler and standard libraries have not completed some level of functional testing, attempting to build other complicated subsystems (kernel, X server, etc.) will probably be futile. The BBP must be tightly coupled with all components, test cases and suites contained in the functional, structural, reliability and regression test system. This implies that the

CM system include tests as important CM items. Including tests with the product source provides reduced test throughput time and duplication, because applicable test cases are executed based on changes made to a baseline that is then installed on the System Under Test (SUT).

The Testsuite Environment Toolkit (TET) and TestExpert are both discussed in the chapter on test harnesses. These tools provide a scenario file that can be used for this specific purpose (i.e., mapping product changes to test case selection and execution).

5.7 A Fully Automated System

An integrated CM and regression test system will automatically build the product to test, install it, boot the system and software, build the test suite, execute the product using the tests and then send electronic **mail** to the project team with a pass or fail test status. If there is a failure, it must be analyzed, otherwise the baseline build process must be considered unsuccessful. This integrated build, install and regression test system has actually been developed by a company (which I worked for) that provided a moderately parallel super-computer with the MACH operating system from Carnegie Mellon University (CMU). MACH was created for multiprocessor computer systems for symmetrical processing of programs using multiple threads of control. This means that the instructions are divided among different microprocessors or CPUs by the MACH operating system.

5.8 Computer-Aided Software Test (Regression Testing)

Computer-Aided Software Test (CAST) now called Automated Software Quality (ASQ) technology has greatly improved the automated regression test process. I wonder why the name CAST was changed to ASQ by most of the tool vendors? Could it be that the promises of CAST technology were oversold? (Another commonly used name for CAST is "shelfware" because most automated capture/playback test tools often sit on the shelf, instead of the developer's desk.) It is the intent of this book to provide many methods to help solve this and other problems associated with the use of test tools and benchmarks.

Verification is one of the key areas for automated test improvement. The following list is provided to help the reader to understand just a few of the many challenges associated with automated regression testing using capture/playback technology:

- User interface changes cause golden or compare files to be obsolete.
- Building tests from scratch can be difficult (capture/playback tools help, however, the tester must still often edit test language scripts).

- Interprocess communication between remote systems can be difficult, e.g., synchronization between objects and systems.
- Comparing graphics using bitmap files is not always the best approach to verification.
- Intrusive capture/playback tools require testing what you often do not deliver to the customer. Ouch!
- If you don't have a development process for testing, you may just automate chaos faster using ASQ technology (regression testing must be based on a successful functional, structural and reliability methodology).
- Test documentation is usually lacking. ASQ tools help in some cases, but still often do not solve the problems of training and ease-of-use.
- Tests still need to be portable, e.g., absolute vs. relative path names.
- Test scripts are often incompatible between ASQ tools.
- During test playback, the display is no longer usable (virtual server and many ASQ tools already solve this problem).
- Display resolutions and fonts can be different between platforms, making replay scripts useful, except for one type of system (same comment as above).
- Selection of user inputs and combinations of inputs is a major challenge i.e., path and transaction analysis. (This is probably one of the greatest problems with automated testing.)
- Comparison by value instead of by a range (e.g., bitmap file) requires a significant amount of programming effort with most test script languages.
- Environment setup and configuration is often a manual and error-prone process (and a major difference between automated capture/playback and test harness technology). Most test management systems provide a test administration function for this purpose.
- Test planning and design is still a fairly manual process that is critical to success with any automated test tool.
- The use of object-oriented test languages, integrated with the application development environment, seems to be the current approach most vendors are pursuing to solve these and other problems.

5.9   Systematic Testing (Context Free Capture/Playback)

Another approach to regression testing is systematic testing. This is a general term that is often used to describe testing that applies to any test method based on a strategy. This systematic approach is opposed to testing where the engineer may execute some finite number of tests in any order and environment, without any preconceived notion of expected results. It is useful to use manual testing approaches, such as test matrices, prior to the automation of a regression or functional test suite using a test harness or automated *capture/replay* or *playback* tool. Using a context-free or object-oriented record and playback, the application under test can change and the test scripts can continue to function because of a logical to physical mapping that occurs at the lower layer (usually the window manager). More about context-sensitive capture/playback is covered in the section on XRunner from Mercury Interactive in the chapter on test tools.

One of the primary goals of systematic testing is to have an automatic data generator design and develop all the tests identified by the requirements specification and then execute each test using the automated capture/playback tool. This is available with IDE's T Tool, ADL from Sun Labs, TGGS and several other sources.

One of several other possible approaches to systematic testing is to have the software developer include comments regarding possible boundary and equivalence class values inside the source code under test. Alternatively, the developer and tester can jointly provide this information in **README** files for each source directory. Later, a filter program can be used to pick up and review the contents of each **README** file in the source code hierarchy to obtain directions for the generation of automatic test input vectors.

Finally, another systematic testing approach is to incorporate test code into the requirements specification for functional test coverage analysis. This also improves the test documentation by incorporating test information with the product requirements document. This information can include information required to not only design, develop and execute tests, but also data required to support the test environment.

Some of the many common approaches to generating regression tests using an automated capture/playback tool include the following:

- Ensure that the tests are successfully used during manual testing.
- Regression tests must be coded in small modules to improve maintenance and support (same as structured programming).
- Record scripts must be easy to maintain and understand (if logic is added to the record script, make sure to use mnemonic variable names that help others to understand your thoughts and intentions).
- Test scripts must try to account for future changes in the product
- Values that are presented by the application that are variable (e.g., date and time stamps) must not be considered for comparison unless special provisions are made to mask them.

It is important to realize that during automatic playback of the record file, one will no longer be using the physical input devices that were used during recording. Therefore, the engineer may desire to have different physical device driver level tests for the mouse, keyboard and other input devices. See the chapter on stress tests for details regarding exercisers.

State machine testing is another very valuable method of testing that evaluates a finite combination of circumstances or attributes that belong, for the time being, to the program under test. Extended finite state machines use a history mechanism to reduce the number of events to just those operations that are within the program's scope. For example, attempting to delete a line in an editor prior to opening a file is an invalid state. Defining the states (extended or finite) using a test matrix improves the test development process and reduces test development rework. Build an inventory of existing tests and then see if use-models can be validated by linking existing tests together in a test flow. Test management tools are designed to provide these functions, or should be!

5.10 Defect Tracking Systems, CM, and Regression Testing

Unfortunately, in most companies, changing problem reporting systems can be very difficult for several reasons. In the case of legacy problem report data, the data must often be migrated to the new defect tracking tool. Furthermore, training employees to use a new system is often difficult, especially when engineers have already fixed in their minds that a new system is not necessary. Managing change is often one of the most difficult challenges for the software QA professional; however, often the right changes can make the difference between a company that folds and one that is extremely successful.

Understanding the root cause of field defects is often critical in developing a future action plan for recovery. Therefore, the root cause of a defect must always be identified and documented in the defect tracking system. The following types of failures can often be quickly analyzed by the developer and entered into the system:

- Requirements failure (missing requirement in the specification)
- Design failure (algorithm or design defect)
- Unit code and test failure (missing unit test for coding error)
- Integration failure (two or more functions or products not working)
- System failure (platform, operating system version, etc.)
- Other (see details in problem report description)

A solid, complete and well-integrated CM, regression test and problem reporting system is critical to the proper analysis of critical information that can be used to improve future products through process changes. Unfortunately, changing or upgrading the problem management system in most companies is a major feat for several reasons, including: legacy data, learning a new user interface, introducing a new process with potentially more required fields and many other obstacles. However, you cannot and must not simply give up always trying to improve development processes!

In order to influence change (probably the most difficult task associated with QA) and management, you must look for individuals that are hurting and really want help. Identify just one step in the development process that you agree will provide the biggest return on investment. Once the change has been implemented, make sure to advertise this change as a best-practice or best-in-breed method. You will also want to make sure and use brown-bag lunch time presentations, quality awards and newsletter articles to disseminate the success associated with the change. We don't need more tools or process models; we need more team-oriented heroes.

5.11 Conclusions

- Regression testing is driven through the use of functional tests. (It is an important activity to ensure that product changes have not destabilized product functionality, reliability, and quality.
- Functional testing methods and tools must be integrated with the central CM system so that product changes are properly tested using the right set of functional tests.
- Structural testing methods and tools must be integrated with the CM and regression testing systems so that test coverage is measured after functional testing is complete.
- Reliability tests and metrics must be collected and integrated with the CM and regression test systems so that functional changes can be verified after structural and functional testing analysis.
- Internal company problem report database information must be integrated with the CM and regression testing systems so that internal test failures and product changes can be better identified as input to the regression test system.
- Customer problem report database information must be integrated with the CM and regression test systems so that product changes and customer problems can be quickly identified and tested using the regression test system.

- Many capture/playback tools that are discussed in the test tools chapter can be used for regression testing. Some of the many tools discussed include XRunner, QA Partner, preVue-X, VISTAreplay and CAPBAK/X.
- Test harness and management systems are also important to regression testing. See the chapter on test harnesses for products that can be used for regression test management and administration.

 # Metrics

*T*he purpose of metrics is to provide measurable benchmarks for evaluating or *testing* against anticipated goals and objectives. A **test** is defined as: "1. A means of examining or evaluating something. 2. Something devised and administered to determine one's skill, knowledge, intelligence, etc. 3. A criterion in measuring or examining: standard" [WEB84]. Without the use of both pre-release and post-release metrics it is often difficult to discern progress during the software development life-cycle.

For example, without a checkbook general ledger, how can a bank's customer determine if a check will bounce or clear the bank successfully. Another example of why metrics are important is when a police officer gives a speeding ticket to a motorist. Nobody wants to receive a speeding ticket, however, we also know that speed limits are for the safety of ourselves and others. If you receive a speeding ticket, you are allowed to view (verify) the results on the radar (in fact, many officers will require it). What if instead the police officer simply said "I think you were going too fast" and did not have a radar or any other means of *measuring* your speed. How would you feel about the officer's appraisal, especially if you were told that you were going 100 m.p.h. too fast? The carpenter's axiom holds true for software development, and for testing as well—"measure twice, cut once." In this chapter, the following metrics will be discussed:

- Bug categories
- Defect density and containment
- Test coverage
- Bad fixes (regressions)
- Change history
- Size, cost and effort of product
- Documentation problems
- Usability
- Mean Time Between Failure (MTBF)
- Call entry and exit coverage with interfaces
- Project completion time

6.1   Introduction to Metrics

Metrics practices and procedures can provide specific incentives to improve employee morale (as is rarely the case). However, QA organizations often may not add this particular value, or at least the internal and external perceived value is often unknown because metrics are not used. Often, the emphasis for the QA group is counting and finding bugs. This, in turn, results in a much more reactive and less proactive approach with little added value. [BRO75] instead suggests the surgical team approach to software development where the chief programmer is the surgeon who: "Personally defines the functional and performance specifications, designs the program, codes it, tests it, and writes its documentation." The copilot: "Is the surgeon's alter ego and able to do any part of the job, but is less experienced. His main function is to share in the design as a thinker, discussant, and evaluator." QA engineers must be able to act as the co-pilot for our company surgeons in many cases when there is no one else available to perform a code walk-through or inspection. Unfortunately, there is usually only one co-pilot for five to ten surgeons on the average (lower ratios for mission-critical applications). Therefore, our co-pilots need to be able to help provide instruments for our surgeons because many times they will not be able to sit side by side during a major product integration or operation. However, for any instruments or metrics to be successful they must of course be used and well understood as a result of training. The QA function must be able to provide training for the company's surgeons in the latest techniques of functional, structural, reliability and regression verification and validation testing. This is another motivation for writing this book. Would you rather go to a surgeon or hacker for an operation?

6.2   When Defects are Discovered

In general, the greatest number of defects or anomalies can be detected during the requirements phase of the product life-cycle. [BEN93] reports that 56% of all defects are attributed to requirements. My root-cause analysis of one critical customer-site showed that approximately 33% of all failures were due to missing or erroneous requirements. Bender states that fewer defects are introduced during detailed design (27%), and even less (7%) during implementation or unit code. This points to the idea that during integration and system test, only a small number of problems can be resolved prior to customer acceptance testing and First Customer Shipment (FCS) or General Availability (GA).* Unfortunately, the reverse is usually true for most companies. (They spend all their time testing at the end instead of the beginning.)

Milestones and metrics are critical to the visibility of potential hazards during product development. Not having any pre-release metrics and milestones can be compared to an automobile only having one large mirror instead of clear glass for a front window. Therefore, all that can be seen is only what is behind the driver instead of obstacles in front of the automobile. In addition to a clear glass front window, one small rear-view mirror in the center of the windshield must be provided to see what is behind (i.e., post-release metrics, such as defect density). Illustration 6.1 shows how failures and issues must decrease throughout the product development life-cycle when metrics are applied.

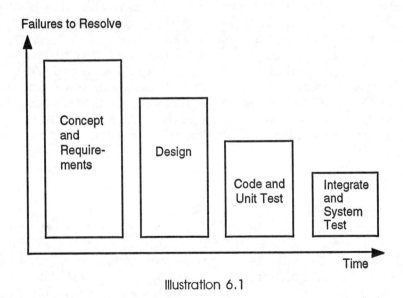

Illustration 6.1

---

*See Illustration 6.1 for details of the ideal relationship between failures and the software life-cycle.

6.3   Caveats to Metrics

Metrics must never be used as a weapon or scalpel against others—especially the surgeon! Often times when this is the case, people will either rebel, cheat, fix the numbers or simply leave the company, or operating room if you like. Many developers fear metrics because they often feel that they will be misunderstood by management [GRA88]. Metrics data can be a big stick to beat people with!

Metrics must be agreed upon by all parties involved and must have an executive staff sponsor to succeed. This means that both individual and company-wide annual reviews must be made using quality objectives as goals. Also, providing incentives to individuals for *fire fighting* with on-the-spot bonuses after shipment, regardless of quality goals and objectives, will always come back to haunt everyone involved. (QA must be involved in a bonus program along with other project team members.)

Quality training is also critical to success as well as process and cultural change. Quality training must include the employees affected, plus all levels of management. Specific quality objectives and goals must be established during training classes and agreed upon prior to each annual individual performance review. Key quality issues must be outlined and developed during training classes and then incorporated into quarterly objectives for annual review. Annual reviews must be replaced with quarterly performance reviews. This is primarily because the dynamics of a project are often too volatile to be left to an annual review process. Senior and executive staff members must drive quality improvement at all levels within the company. (Individual contributors must use personal initiative to drive change in their organizations as well.)

Process change through the use of metrics requires an evolution that often starts with an individual that is in great pain (e.g., someone tired of fixing bugs that is anxious to work on a new project). Do not attempt to collect metrics for every possible development phase (i.e., code, design, maintenance, integration, system test, etc.). Instead, attempt to identify the area of greatest risk. Focus on that area by experimenting with incremental and small changes.

6.4   Bug Categories

Measuring the types of problems encountered and where in the software life-cycle process the problems were introduced can provide better preventive measures. How many problems were discovered in a particular product area (measure of customer satisfaction) or development phase (phase containment metric) can also help focus the unit, integration and system testing efforts.

A **taxonomy** is a scheme to partition knowledge and define the relationships between various components. It is often used for classifying and understanding a vast body of knowledge (raw data is converted to information). Defects are difficult to categorize, because they usually have several symptoms and potential remedies.

Often a root cause analysis is required to determine where, when, what and how failures occurred. One approach is to target a specific customer or company that exhibits a low tolerance for problems and high expectations for product features and capabilities. Problems can first be decomposed into the following FURPS categories as defined by Hewlett-Packard and described by [GRA87] and [PRE92]:

- Functionality
- Usability
- Reliability
- Performance
- Supportability

Further analysis could categorize problems based on unit, function, subsystem, interface, system, multi-user and other types of failures. The following categories can also be used which are unique from the IEEE Standard 1044-1993 [IEE94]:

- Requirements (what function is performed)
- Design (how the function is performed)
- Code (structure related)
- Integration (CM related)
- System (platform related)
- Interoperability (product to product related)
- Usability (training, documentation, etc.)
- Licensing and packaging (delivery as well!)
- Other

Bug categories are important because they provide an important pulse-point for release management and product/process improvement. Ask if the problem is related to what the product does (requirements), how it does it (design), or if the product works (code).

6.5 Defect Density and Defect Containment

How well problems can be contained or isolated during the software life-cycle is a metric that can assist management, engineering and QA in many ways. Metrics improve planning and estimation, and specifically help to determine the length of time required for development and test prior to product release. Several models are available for planning estimation using either the COnstructive COst MOdel (COCOMO) [BOE81] or Putnam Estimation Model [PUT78]. Either lines of code or function points can be used to determine resource requirements, including both time and people (see the section titled "Size, Cost and Effort of Product" in this chapter for details). Resource estimation is based on baseline reliability measurements and new and existing source code to be provided. A common metric that is used is the number of bugs found in every thousand lines of either commented Lines Of Code (LOC) or Non-Commented Lines Of Code (NCLOC). The problem with measuring defect density using LOC is that it does not take into account several factors including:

- Complexity
- Maintainability
- Level of interoperability
- Language
- White space and structure (code or data)
- Comments

The reader must be careful with LOC or NCLOC estimates. Another critical measurement criteria is test coverage. This metric has only begun to increase in popularity as most companies still test using black box techniques (functional testing). Most test and bug management systems provide key metrics that can be used for defect density analysis.

6.6   Test Coverage

Test coverage definitely holds the promise for success in the future for the majority of QA functions today. This is still a fairly new area of exploration for most organizations. Also, the majority of all engineers continue to fear that test coverage measurements, as well as other metrics, will be used to create more harm than good.

Software QA personnel must be trained to provide many important services.* One new and important function is the ability to train others in both technical as well as strategic aspects of source code instrumentation.This means that QA personnel must be able to read source code in whatever language is used for product development. It can also be extremely useful to have training in manual testing techniques prior to using test coverage and automated test tools.

---

*For example, problem report administration, beta site administration, customer requirements collection, etc.

Table 6.1

Mapping Functions To Test Cases		
Function or Operation	Module Name	Test Cases
Read Filed	read.c	read1, read2
Write File	write.c	write1, write2
Print File	print.c	print1, print2
Edit File	ed.c	ed1, ed2, ed3
Copy File	copy.c	copy1, copy2

The development of a test matrix to compare dependencies between product functions and unit and system tests provides an excellent methodology from which to build automated tests. Another useful manual technique is the generation of a test case matrix that identifies test conditions or product modules for each functional operation defined in the specification. This also can be helpful prior to the creation of a test module. See Tables 6.1 and 6.2. The MCman product from QASE provides the basic ability to update UNIX on-line **man** pages with special **nroff** macros so that test stubs (to begin with) can be identified for each functional requirement. A Framemaker interface that uses Maker Interchange File Format (MIFF) macros for functional requirements that are written using Frame also exists.

Many other techniques are available for measuring test coverage. More will be said about test coverage in the test tools chapter. Incorrect fixes or regressions due to poor regression testing are some of the more well known areas that are measured by most QA functions today. This is another critical metric that must always be considered for measurement because it can have a great impact on customer satisfaction(quality).

Table 6.2

Mapping Functions to Test Conditions		
Function or Operation	Condition 1	Condition 2
Read Graphic File	small image	large image
Write Print File	text file	graphic file
Print Edit File	large file	empty file
Edit Special File	binary file	linked file

6.7   Bad Fixes (Regressions)

When a resolution to correct a defect is incorporated into a product release, a feature that was working prior to the upgrade often suddenly stops working. Post-resolution of functional failures is the primary requirement of regression test suites; however, often regression test suites do not and cannot provide coverage for every function. This is one of the common traps that many development and quality engineers fall into by attempting to automate the testing process without any regard to functional test coverage. Several methods, however, can be used to effectively deal with source code modifications. One approach is to use testability metrics to determine the level of testing difficulty associated with a source code change.

In general, *testability* provides an estimate of how difficult it will be to test a specific function. One model of testability was developed by Dr. Jeff Voas. It is known as: "Propagation, Infection and Execution". This method is also known as PIE. A product called PiSCES is provided by Reliable Software Technologies (RST) and is discussed in the test tools chapter. Complexity metrics can also be used to make assessments regarding bug fixes that may end up as *bad fixes*.

Use of a system or process whereby the changes that are made to a source code module (file) are always globally advertised to the project team is a good method to improve communication. Two technologies to improve communications between members of the project team are the UNIX **news** utility and **mosaic**. Test harness, management, and capture/playback tools can all be used to perform automated regression testing.

6.8   Change History

One of the best metrics for source code inspection, walk through, code coverage testing and other evaluation techniques is the frequency of change per file. Usually, when there are many changes being made to a single function or module, many problems will continue to result even after further changes are made. The UNIX Revision Control System (RCS) and Source Code Control System (SCCS) both provide the ability to evaluate change requests made to each source file. With RCS, this is accomplished using the **rlog** command. Each module will contain a text message describing each revision, hopefully, assuming the engineer entered a useful message when the module was checked into the product tree using the **ci** command. It is often helpful to add a standard template for commentary text when changes are made to a file under CM control. This template can provide various report data such as:

• A problem report number
• Product requirement document reference location

- Names for associated unit test programs for regression testing
- Where in the software development process the problem was introduced
- Files or functions that may also be affected
- Comments on how the problem could have been avoided, or root cause analysis

A front-end shell script to the UNIX RCS **ci** command can provide this information prior to checking the code into the master source tree. All that is required for such a mechanism is a prompt for user input and a means of storing the responses in shell variables that are then passed as input to the **ci** command. Several commercial defect tracking systems can be integrated with the CM system. See the chapter on test tools for more details. Many commercial CM products provide these and other even more advanced methods of change control and management of software.

6.9   Size, Cost and Effort

Lines Of Code (LOC) was an early accepted measurement for both productivity and schedule. Unfortunately, the indiscriminate use of this metric often produced indiscernible results. For example, programmers would pad the source code with more comments and use heavy indentation to increase line counts and meet management objectives. This, in turn, has negative implications such as requiring more storage space for program installation and execution because more instructions are required to complete a function. In general, NLOC and LOC are still commonly-used metrics, however, they must always be carefully considered in the context in which they are used. A more specific measure of productivity can be assessed using function point metrics [PRE92]. This provides a clear product requirements document for the source code under development. Several key criteria must be included for each function point. The number of expected inputs and outputs is an important factor for measurement. This includes processing operations that can be performed based on various user inputs. Expected performance goals must also be stated. [PRE92] states that function points are computed by providing data for a table with five information domain characteristics. These characteristics include:

1 Number of user inputs
2 Number of user outputs
3 Number of user inquiries
4 Number of files
5 Number of external interfaces

In the case of a UNIX device driver or system process that runs in the background, the number of files and interfaces utilized would be more appropriate for analysis than user inputs. Normally, however, a count or quantity is usually assigned to each of the above categories. A multiplication factor is based on whether a function is simple, average or complex. Complex measurement parameters have a higher weight than average or simple parameters. Another way to determine complexity is by noting the contents of the on-line UNIX **man** (manual) pages. For example, the SunOS 4.1.3 C compiler **cc** has approximately 40 command line arguments that can quickly be identified from the synopsis section of its **man** page. This command will obviously require significantly more effort, cost, resources, time, etc. to test than the UNIX **echo** command that has only two arguments. The metric for documentation is often ignored; however, it can be as critical as any other metric used for code evaluation. CodePlan provides the ability to perform planning and estimation based on size, cost, and other attributes.

6.10 Documentation Problems

Unfortunately, product documentation, along with testing, is often the last activity to be considered in the software development life-cycle. This end-of-life-cycle attention usually results in either incomplete or inaccurate documentation. If product specifications are developed early in the design process and maintained throughout the product life-cycle, this will insure a more accurate source of information for technical publications personnel, who can use the specifications to complete user documentation. Requirements Based Testing (RBT) or functional testing can be performed when product requirements are used to provide input to test case generation and execution using tagging and cross reference mapping. Products such as VERITAS' VistaTRACK and QASE's MCman provide this capability today using Frame, **nroff**, plain text and other documentation facilities.

Another common documentation problem is using examples that are incorrect, incomplete, inefficient or untested. One method to automate this process is to not only use requirements based testing or formal requirements testing methods, but to simply capture text examples and execute a program using a standard test harness. Extraction of example text from on-line documentation **man** pages is fairly simple, yet how many times have you seen examples that just plain do not work?

Product interoperability can also be tested using documentation, especially when several individual products will be used together by a customer. Documentation metrics measurements are also closely related to usability metrics, because the lack of documentation usually results in measurably more difficult-to-use products (this includes both hard copy and/or on-line documentation).

6.11 Usability

Usability metrics provide measurements of the ability of users to learn and utilize product features, including documentation readability, status and error messages, etc. Video-taping new users attempting to learn and use new products can provide valuable input for new user interface design concepts.

UNIX has always been considered one of the more hostile user interface systems around, which can be attributed to its roots. It was initially designed by software developers for software developers. Portability was also a primary objective. Then, other factors increased in importance; for example, performance. Performance characteristics can affect product usability metrics and must also be combined with user requirements characteristics when possible. For example, what is the average response time for an average function during user execution?

Developing a set of scores and weighting factors can be helpful; however, this may be very difficult for quantifying ease-of-use or ease-of-learning for a particular product. One approach to minimize this difficulty is to set style guidelines and monitor violation limits. An example of how to measure ease-of-use or ease-of-learning is having more that 20 windows open to complete a function. Also, error and warning messages must be scrutinized during detailed design (for customer usability in use and learning). These and many other items can be selected for review and analysis early in the development process. Visual perception, cognitive psychology of reading, human memory and deductive and inductive reading are a few methods that can be used early in the requirements and design process. The following can be used to assess product usability metrics:

1 Has an external group completed a task analysis for the product under test? (Steps a, b, c, and d.)

2 Has a prototype for the product concept been completed based on the concept specification? (Paper prototypes are recommended.)

   A. Only with 100% throw-away code (cannot be used in final production release)
   B. Using the previous release base
   C. Only part developed as a prototype (what percentage?)
   D. Only part is throw away (what percentage?)

3 Has a usability test on the prototype been completed?

   A. Less than six subjects or members participated
   B. More than six subjects or members participated (how many?)

4 How many of the recommended changes have been made?

   A. All the mandatory changes have been made
   B. 50% of the mandatory changes have been made

C. Less than 50% of the mandatory changes have been made

D. All requested changes (non-mandatory) completed

E. At least half of the requested changes (non-mandatory) completed

No tools are known to exist which collect usability metrics during testing.

6.12 Mean Time Between Failure (MTBF)

This is one of the most critical metrics available. If a product has a short MTBF or Mean Time To Failure (MTTF), it will be rendered useless regardless of how new or improved. An MTBF can be obtained using historical information contained in journal files that could be provided by the test environment or harness; however, it is often difficult to discern the benefit of MTBF information without specific supporting cause-and-effect data. One suggestion would be to build a daemon (UNIX process) that monitors core files created when programs abort due to a memory access violation. Next, the daemon must be modified to record the frequency of core file creation and, if possible, include the program that generated the core file. Also, it would be useful to automatically email (electronic **mail**) the contents of the core file for the failed program to the software or hardware vendor for analysis and debugging. Few tools are known to provide this capability, however, several companies such as SunSoft provide libraries for their own internal tracking of beta test customers.

MTBF and MTTF metrics require ongoing data collection. This then requires the ability to record specific events over the course of hours or days and may require significant system resources to perform the data collection for MTBF or MTTF metrics.

Operational profiles, on the other hand, define the expected usage, usually by function, over the product's expected or anticipated lifetime. Selection of tests can also be designed using the proportion of system usage. For example, if a function consumes 20% of system usage, then at least 20% of the test cases must test that specific function. There are three approaches to predicting system defects and anomalies:

• Actual (can never fully see all of the failures)
• Estimated (from testing and is usually approximated)
• Predicted (from sensitivity analysis to identify failure relationships either joined or separated)

6.13 Call Entry and Exit Coverage with Interfaces

It is usually considered high risk if a function has many other modules, functions or products dependent upon it for success. Therefore, these functions must be considered for more rigorous interface testing. More about instrumentation and technology for call entry and exit test coverage and reporting will be discussed in the chapter on test tools. This metric is also the fundamental premise upon which functional or requirements testing is based. If all function call entry and exit points have not been exercised, then this must be considered as a critical or must category requirement for starting all new test development.

Requirements are often categorized as *must, should* or *could* based on company priority as identified by product marketing and sales. Call entry and exit test coverage criteria, as defined in the system test plan, must include call coverage metrics. Project completion time is often directly impacted by call entry and exit coverage, as failures with modules that are highly used have enormous impact on multiple areas of test and development. If external functions are not available for call entry and exit testing, simulation libraries and stub files are defined and used as follows (available with ViSTA and MCsim):

- **Simulation** is when a program that behaves or operates like a given system is used for testing. Simulation libraries are a collection of stub files (in object file format).
- A **stub** is a skeletal or special-purpose implementation of a program. These files can be used to help develop the foundation for a function using only skeleton logic (error and exception conditions). Stub files are useful for testing interface functions prior to completion.

With simulation or stub libraries, basic functional interface hooks are provided for testing purposes so that a function such as the UNIX **malloc** library call can return the error ENOMEM, which is often difficult to accomplish in the normal operating environment. One of the other benefits of simulation libraries is that a function may be replaced or completed at a later date. Therefore, stubs and simulation libraries are useful for interface and integration testing and can be developed during the design phase of the product life-cycle. More about simulation tools and technology will be provided in the chapter on test tools. (See the section on ViSTA.)

6.14 Project Completion Time

The project schedule time as a metric is usually the most important for management. Unfortunately, this measurement is usually a trailing indicator of several other factors and metrics as was previously discussed. That is not to say that this metric is not useful. Data from previous products and release baselines can be used to better estimate product completion. Project planning and project estimation tools are useful for determining completion time. However, they require baseline values such as reliability goals, to be useful. This can only be provided with collected data (i.e., defect density, containment, etc.). (See the section on CodePlan.)

Now that we have covered some of many possible metrics for measurement, you are probably wondering which metrics you must consider for use in your company?

6.15 No Single Metric

In general, no single metric can satisfy all possible quality and reliability measurement requirements. It would be very difficult to attempt to collect data for all metrics at the same time and then try to make some rational judgement. It would be very difficult to determine from all available information what decision must be made.

Several suggestions can be made to determine which metrics to use initially. It depends upon several factors, including and not limited to the following:

- People (expertise and skills, quantity, etc.)
- Time
- Cost
- Priorities
- Products
- Competitors
- Customer requirements

Always begin with the end-in-mind or a picture of the final result when attempting to set any metrics goals. Another way of saying this is to ask what is the purpose and objective of collecting metrics data? Senior management may desire an increase in product revenue and reduction in expenses (i.e., working smarter and harder). Technical support would always like to put themselves out of business with fewer phone calls regarding usability or functionality errors. Engineering often wants to create and add new functionality without having to support existing products that have unit test failures, performance or other problems. QA would like the customer to be happy and the marketing and sales organizations always want more products to sell ahead of the competition. With this much diversity within most organizations it is no wonder that most companies have no consensus of where to begin when it comes to establishing and maintaining a metrics program for software development.

In general, all metrics must always be evaluated as to whether they will provide the added value or benefit of new or existing competitive products or services without failures to customers within schedule. These factors usually affect profitability and revenue. One approach to metrics is to compare product functionality complexity increases, while comparing defect containment rates with previous product results. If failures are increasing, the trade-off between feature content and quality metrics must be carefully analyzed. In addition, it is important to assess the scale of customer expectation and satisfaction with previous production releases. Customer expectations can usually include no major loss of functionality or data corruption and only a small number of problems with a difficult-to-use work-around. Obviously these expectations will change with product complexity, cost, maturity, etc. The end result must always be if any problems are found, only a minor loss of functionality must be experienced and a well-defined (documented) work-around must be realized.

When classifying problems, it is important to distinguish between company *priority* and customer *severity*. What might be a high severity problem to the customer often is considered a low priority to an engineer supporting the product. It is important that the QA function act as the customer advocate to resolve these and other conflicts between the company and the customer. The old saying "The customer is always right" must never grow old. This leads us to the next metric— the quality of the metrics data and process used to collect the data must be accurate and also measured.

6.16 Garbage In Garbage Out (GIGO)

Metrics data must be carefully analyzed prior to use. There must always be a sound basis for decisions based on metrics measurements. The qualitative aspects of the data must always be questioned prior to making any decision. Also, negative implications such as finger-pointing and destructive criticism must not be the result of a measurement. In fact, if you were to survey most individuals in your company, I believe that most people would not like metrics because they naturally feel that they are going to be unfairly judged. Blaming poor products (garbage out) on poor inputs (garbage in) does not improve customer satisfaction or decrease the cost of rework and maintenance. However, using metrics to increase peer pressure for the production of higher-quality products is strongly recommended.

Another approach to the development of best practices for metrics implementation that can be helpful to the establishment of any new metrics program is to acknowledge people doing the right things at the right time. One of the primary objectives of the ISO 9000 Total Quality Management (TQM) standard is to implement and assure the operational discipline that quality is a management function [ISO91]. Processes must be blamed and never people. There are of course exceptions, whereby individuals will need training, coaching and finally counseling to hasten desired improvements. An important factor in the acquisition of any metrics data is the skill and knowledge of the individuals responsible for collection and interpretation.

6.17 Who is Involved?

It is important to determine the individuals and organizations that will be responsible for metrics collection, reporting and usage. Again, an executive sponsor and champion will be required to maintain momentum with any metrics measurement program. Mapping a milestone to a metric can ensure proper measurement in the product life-cycle. A product release team can then use metrics results to determine if the milestone is complete before proceeding to the next development phase and set of milestones (this is also known as phase containment). Including a purpose and definition for each metric is also important. A quality handbook or manual can be useful to document and preserve the process when metrics definitions and usage are described for use by other product and project teams.

It is critical to explore concerns with internal customers and providers of the metrics measurement program. Evaluation of the Return On Investment (ROI) can help determine the value added by a particular measurement. When the cost of a problem is first determined, the ROI factor can be used to determine the relative benefit when one metric discovers and locates a problem that results in a reduction in development or maintenance costs. More often than not, current procedures can be slightly enhanced without adding more bureaucracy. For example, test files and programs can be organized within the CM system rather than just scattered everywhere. This can help in the execution of unit and function tests based on product changes. Structural test metrics (call entry and exit coverage, decision test coverage, etc.) are then used for comprehensive testing after test modules have been identified. Make sure that the roles and responsibilities of all members of the project team are clearly defined, especially when it comes to metrics!

6.18 Other Metrics for Measurement

Several other metrics may be used for measuring product quality. Some of the many possibilities include:

- Statement, decision or branch test coverage
- Memory access violation and memory leak analysis
- Testability analysis (identify difficult-to-test source code)
- Data flow (transformations and transactions for state changes)

Many other metrics are available to determine how reliable, testable, readable and maintainable a software function, module or system can be considered. It is important that complex functions and code be determined; however, trying to reduce code size can often make a function more difficult to maintain or test. Even if the intent is to reduce code size so there will be less lines of code with fewer errors, this can make it more difficult to maintain, test and support. As is often the case with software tools, software engineering management is cautioned to be careful and not allow the metrics or tools to manage the project. Instead, the engineer must manage the tools. Unfortunately, the documentation associated with many software development and test tools requires weeks of training. A note to the software test tools vendors—we need simple tools! Of course, manual techniques can always be used (test plans/matrices) before any tool is used.

Many potential problems are associated with metrics and the following list is just a sample of many cautions when using software metrics:

- Metrics are introduced for the benefit of others (e.g., corporate and management use only)
- Metrics data will be used against employees
- Most software developers thrive on creativity, i.e., "Don't bother me with process related metrics!" and "We are a technology driven company!"
- Individual metrics create a narrow focus that is not useful
- Metrics can measure the wrong things (poor management)
- Collecting metrics data will distract from development activities
- Individual goals and objectives are not tied to metrics (poor management)
- Project schedules are not built on metrics (poor management)
- Lack of automated tools for metrics collection
- Training in the proper collection and analysis of metrics is missing
- I don't have time for testing and metrics

6.19 Conclusions

- We make time for the things that are priority.
- Software developers must be the primary responsible party for unit test and measurement. If a schedule has not provided adequate time for complexity and test coverage metrics completion, but the code compiles, what do you think will usually happen? Unfortunately, more often than not, the code will just get checked in and some poor quality engineer will be left to blindly unit test a function instead of measuring system and interface function and structural test coverage, as was originally sched-

uled. The end result will either be schedule slips or a poor-quality product that usually fails customer acceptance or beta testing.

- All the defect prevention, detection and containment metrics combined (testing) can never compensate for poor product planning and lack of complete customer requirements documents.
- Metrics are critical to revealing product phase defects and must be used during all phases of product development and test. The results of metrics provide valuable input as a feedback loop for future projects.
- Metrics data help improve planning aspects prior to or during product development. One of many metrics to consider is the number of positive or clean tests to negative tests. (What is the ratio at your company?)
- Metrics data must always be used collectively to improve management decisions that result in improved customer satisfaction and reduced defect repair.
- The following common list of metrics was presented in this chapter; however, many other measurements are possible:

  Bug categories
  Defect density and containment
  Test coverage
  Bad fixes (regressions)
  Change history
  Size, cost and product effort
  Documentation problems
  Usability
  Mean Time Between Failure (MTBF)
  Call entry and exit coverage with interfaces
  Project completion time

- Many of the tools listed in the test tools and test harnesses chapters can be used to generate a functional, structural, reliability or regression test metric.
- Make metrics and testing a priority up front to save time at the end of the release cycle.

CHAPTER 7

Load and Stress Testing

Load and stress testing is one of the most complex and difficult aspects of function and system testing, especially in the UNIX multi-user and multi-tasking environment. UNIX has progressed from crashing or hanging when common problems are encountered such as unavailable processes or virtual memory. Now, it is a highly commercial, fault-tolerant, highly available operating system used in a variety of applications. However, this has been a painful process for many engineers because little or no industry standard test suites or official documents were used to define the process or technology used for stress and load testing. As such, there are several different interpretations of stress and load testing. In this chapter the following will be discussed:

- Stress testing (strategies and approaches)
- Modular stress tests
- Exercisers as stress tests
- User and device exercisers for stress and load testing

7.1   Introduction to Load and Stress Testing

Load and stress testing falls under the category of functionality, reliability and regression testing. Many people also often confuse load and stress testing with performance testing.

7.2   Stress Testing Definitions

Stress testing has several possible definitions. One general definition is any test or test suite that results in system activity that is used to to identify the critical load conditions at which the system fails to continue to perform basic functions. Another definition is to focus on exhausting all reasonable resource limits of a system. For example, all available pages in memory or disk blocks during stress testing might be depleted. Another example is to create a high spike of system activity, followed by a short valley of idle time and then cycle back to a high spike of activity. All of these definitions are appropriate depending upon the specific application. The keyword associated with stress and load testing is *fail*, as stress tests often measure how *robust* a program has been designed by pushing it beyond its defined limits. For any stress test to be successful two critical attributes must be present:

1 The author must have an objective/unbiased attitude toward the product under test
2 Proper understanding of the program's limits (e.g., high and low water marks or boundary values)

7.3   Difficulties with Stress Testing

Discovering limits and boundaries for a program is a challenge that is often left to a third party; but hopefully, not the customer. However, that is not to say that mature software developers can not and must not be able to write stress and load tests for their code, especially tests that include interfaces to other functions. One of many problems I have encountered with application and operating system software can be attributed to lack of stress testing with customer data and operations using appropriate system and network configurations. In case you didn't notice, the last statement listed many variables. Many times, benchmarks or test suites fall short of real-life application stress tests. Therefore, it is imperative to determine worst case and extreme situations, or *corner cases* for stress testing up front before a product is released. A corner case test includes data and procedures that are strategically located at extreme boundaries within the universal set of testing conditions and data values. The ability to quickly isolate the vital few from the trivial many using the Pareto 80/20 rule is critical during the development of stress tests (or any test), as they can expand to be unnecessarily large.

7.4   UNIX Commands for Measuring System Stress and Load

A common solution for many multi-user or multi-tasking failures is to request the customer to size the system hardware and software according to the needs of each user. For example, a rule of thumb with several multi-user/multi-tasking systems in the early 1980's was to configure a system with a minimum of 512k (your mileage may vary) of memory for each user or application product. This was primarily for performance reasons to eliminate swapping and thrashing.[*] However, it also ensured a consistent minimum hardware configuration. Today one would need much more memory per user depending upon the application. For example, some applications require 64mb of memory, or greater per user depending upon the product's complexity and size.

The **sar** command provided with UNIX System V Release 4 (SVR4) has consolidated all of the tools for monitoring critical system resources (i.e., memory, disk, paging, swapping, etc.). The reader is encouraged to use the SVR4 facilities of **sar** or the BSD commands: **iostat**, **vmstat**, and **fstat** to help monitor and better determine how close to the edge to push a system during stress and load testing. UNIX SVR4 also provides the kernel profiling tool **prfld** to monitor the operating system kernel activity. These and other tools are extremely useful in the development (debugging of tests) and execution analysis of stress and load tests for UNIX.

7.5   Time and Resource Requirements of Stress Tests

Another problem with thorough stress testing occurs when tests are difficult to successfully complete. Testing then often becomes impractical. Suppose you have a disk, memory and other device exercisers that consume all available memory and disk resources, running concurrently in the background. It is then useless to attempt to stress test any other subsystem such as graphics or serial communications at the same time. Therefore, you must always design specific ensembles of stress tests for load testing.

Unit tests must be used to build functional tests. Unit and functional tests must also be modular and well structured for successful load and stress testing. This is because stress and load testing introduces much more complexity into the maintenance and enhancement process than unit and function level testing. Test reuse is very important!

---

[*] Swapping occurs when the entire process context working set in memory is swapped or exchanged with auxiliary storage (e.g., hard disk). Thrashing is when most or all system resources are consumed on overhead operations (e.g., swapping data and programs between main and auxiliary storage, rather than on intended computing functions).

7.6   Modular Tests

A modular or structured approach to code development applies to stress and load tests as well. This approach is based on the premise of structured design methods and is defined as:

> **Modularity** is the degree to which a program is composed of independent components such that a change to one component has minimal impact on other components.

This approach to stress test development must be carefully considered during product development rather than the accidental evolution of a single large test program that becomes impossible to maintain. Some software development methodologies have moved from a structured to an *object-oriented* approach to product and test development. Object-oriented approaches provide several benefits by increasing reuse and, when combined with modeling technology, providing early prototypes for testing and analysis. However, testability or the level of testing difficulty will often times increase. Use standard templates provided with the test harness to ensure modular tests.

A modular stress test for a floppy or tape device will provide standard write and read verify tests as subroutine functions that use predefined block sizes, data patterns, media types and record sizes. These standard functions can be used by other storage devices for stress testing a CD-ROM, Write Once Read Many (WORM), Magneto Optical (MO) and other random access storage devices. Also, it is important to first localize and execute subsystem stress points prior to full system stress testing. This in turn will provide more manageable diagnostic data for easy failure reproduction. Resolution of problems will also be easier when device driver-level stress and load tests are performed prior to testing other commands such as **tar, cpio,** and **dd,** for example. Tape and floppy exercisers will now provide examples of modular load and stress tests that can be integrated into full system exercisers and diagnostics.

7.7   Tape and Floppy Exercisers

Pseudo-code or skeleton logic for stress testing tape and floppy devices is shown in Illustration 7.1. This test individually would be considered more of an exerciser than a stress test (see devices exercisers below), and would require execution in parallel with multiple devices to be considered a successful stress test.

A floppy or tape exerciser would use the following variables: data blocks, pattern, record size and device name. It would cycle through each of many possible values for each of these variables. The following are suggested data patterns for floppy and tape device stress testing because they help identify common read or write operation failures at the bit and byte level (the call also uses a "walking ones" pattern):

```
0x00000000
0x55555555
0xaaaaaaaa
0xffffffff
0x01010101
0x11110000
0x11001100
0x00011101
```

A record size variable could contain one or more of the following values (where a record is the amount of data to read or write): 512, 1024, 2048, 4096, 8192, 10240. The file size variable could be one of the following (where the file size is equal to the actual size of the buffer used to read or write to the device): 1, 10, 100, 500.

Both rewind or non-rewind devices can be used for each tape device with various densities. This type of framework does not have to be limited to tape or floppy devices. Testing of other sequential or random access storage devices can benefit from the above framework. Complete source code details of the exerciser are provided in Appendix A. Now that the fundamentals of stress testing have been discussed, load testing can be described as a super-set of stress testing.

```
pattern[] = { 0x00000000, 0x55555555,
0xaaaaaaaa, 0xffffffff };
record_size[] = { 512, 1024, 2048, 4096,
8192, 10240 };
file_size[] = {1, 10, 100 };
#define major_number      some_structure   /*
for various media */
#define minor_number      some_structure   /*
for various media */
start_program
for starting_file_size to maximum_file_size
loop_increment
     for starting_block_size to maximum_-bock_size loop_increment

         for starting_pattern to maximum_-data_pattern loop_increment

                 write
                 read_and_compare
                 log results
         end_loop
      end_loop
   end_loop
   end_program
```

Illustration 7.1

7.8   Load Testing

Load testing has several interpretations or definitions. Some people think of load testing as volume testing. The usual approach to load testing is to determine if the system can continue to operate at *red line,* or at the point when all or most all system resources are depleted over long periods of time (usually days). Volume tests, stress tests and storage tests all evaluate the program at its limits. Load testing brings many advantages and disadvantages. Some of the advantages include the ability to simulate worst-case scenarios or boundary conditions. This occurs when the demands placed upon a program, system or both generally exceed the capabilities of the original design.

It is also important to incrementally or simultaneously exhaust all available system resources. This includes memory, disk and other hardware resources, as well as software resources such as locks, processes and files. One of the many disadvantages (difficulties) associated with load testing is when failure reproduction is difficult due to execution order complexity (i.e., what combination of tests caused the failure?). Therefore, it is recommended that a journal or audit trail log for failure reproduction be maintained and included as part of test execution (see the chapter on test harnesses for details). The UNIX **script** command, for example, records input, output and error messages to a **typescript** file by default. Illustration 7.2 shows how to use the **script** command to save both input and output to a disk file called **typescript** (default).

If we display the contents of the disk file **typescript** we will see the following data as listed in Illustration 7.3.

Computer Automated Software Test (CAST) which is used in regression testing, can be very useful in creating both text and graphics audit trail and journal

---

Example of UNIX **script** Command

518 % **script**
Script started, file is typescript
my_system> **whoami**
rodney
my_system> **pwd**
/usr/mnt/rodney
my_system> **date**
Tue Nov 30 15:51:56 PST 1993
my_system> **exit**
my_system> Script done, file is typescript
519 %

Illustration 7.2

```
Results of UNIX script Command

519 % cat typescript
Script started on Tue Nov 30 15:51:43 1993
my_system> whoami
rodney
my_system> pwd
/usr/mnt/rodney
my_system> date
Tue Nov 30 15:51:56 PST 1993
my_system> exit
script done on Tue Nov 30 15:51:58 1993
520 %
```

Illustration 7.3

files. These tools will be discussed in the chapter on test tools[*]. Test time is a critical resource and must be carefully managed as part of load and volume testing.

7.9   Ensembles of Tests

Load testing must consider various combinations (ensembles) of tests. Devices and programs must be tested to their limits. Some of many device tests that can accomplish this include full disk, printer out of paper or off-line, minimum memory and others. It is a good idea to use a minimum configuration for stress and load testing. This will help push the system past the limit much sooner (e.g., out of disk and memory situations). Some of the many other tricks that can be useful and that most people learn over time (error guessing) from experience include broken or short tape media that produce failures for tape devices and broken or corrupt floppy disks. Load testing is different from catastrophe testing, which can be as severe as powering off the machine.

All sorts of destructive tests can be directed at various device media; however, good judgement is still required. Breaking or destroying an expensive hard disk drive will probably not be viewed as a good investment by management for the sake of stress and load testing; however, in some cases this may also be con-

---

[*]Sometimes this is also called Computer-Aided S

sidered inexpensive and necessary insurance when compared to potential revenue loss from an angry customer. This all proves the point that regardless of the amount of unit and integration testing performed by a software developer, independent verification and validation is still required.

7.10 Fighting the Clock

Several days may be necessary before a load test completes. Therefore, both system and employee resources may be expended waiting for test completion after several days, rather than hours or minutes as is the case with a stress test. The solution is to complete individual stress tests prior to load testing. Ideally, load testing will consist of test ensembles (devices, programs, data, libraries, etc.) of stress tests organized according to the goals identified prior to testing.

It is important to include customer requirements during the definition and development of load and volume tests. The Electronic Design Automation (EDA) market uses the terms *design* or *solution flow* to encompass the integrated usage of many products by a customer to complete a product design. Most customer models or usage flows must be incorporated as a critical aspect of load and volume testing.

False alarms must be planned for or expected, because the amount of time to complete volume or load testing may be on the order of days or even weeks, dependent upon the application under test.

7.11 False Alarms

False alarms can also occur several days after test initiation. Some potential false failures may include:

- Power failure
- Premature resource exhaustion
- Foreign process interference
- Hardware failure
- Incorrect system configuration
- General environment change (temperature, humidity)

Each failure, regardless of cause, requires the test to be restarted from the beginning. It is recommended that system-level diagnostics be successfully completed prior to any stress or load testing.

One common problem with load and stress testing is the level of difficulty required for both execution and analysis. It may take substantial training for the proper execution of load tests and several senior engineers assigned may be to analyze the results. In other words, resource costs for both equipment and personnel can become a costly problem associated with load testing. Test personnel may want to have at least minimum, maximum and default system configurations available for system load testing. Also, with careful consideration, performance characterization using load tests can be conducted in parallel. For example, hardware configurations can be documented as well as compiler options, library versions and other critical software configuration options. There is often a tendency to end up with everything including the kitchen sink as part of stress and load test validation suites. It is important, however, to understand which tests are no longer adding value and must be retired. Also, organize the tests so that one failure will not impact the results of continued testing.

7.12 The Kitchen Sink Approach - NOT!

A common historical approach for load testing was to use all of the available tests from regression, function and integration test suites. This is better known as the kitchen sink approach. The problem with this approach is that the software quality engineer will have a very difficult time reproducing and resolving any load test failures. Therefore, it is imperative to provide a sufficient level of system testing while keeping the total build and execution time required under 48 to 72 hours. This will provide several benefits, one of which is the ability to rebuild and execute tests over the weekend and return to work Monday morning with results ready for analysis. Tests that are first compiled and then subsequently executed are always preferred to testing with binary executable files only. (These tests are often termed "quick" or touch tests.)

Dynamic functional and structural code coverage metrics are used to carefully evaluate the value added by each unit, function, subsystem and system test. If no obvious measured value is added, the test must be considered for retirement.

One approach used in the operating system world for library function standards is to publish calls at Level 2 for several years before finally retiring a function. The System V Interface Definition (SVID) defines two levels for functions. Therefore, Level 2 functions must always be tested after Level 1 functions, because they may be eliminated in the future and replaced by a new feature.

7.13 Source Code Control and CM

One approach for load test and product development is to have a parallel test case tree for each product source code tree. Each product module change must also require a complementary test case that will be activated for load testing. For each new or modified module, a corresponding test program must be referenced using a source code revision control system. For example, with the UNIX Revision Control System (RCS), when a module is checked into the product tree from a working directory using the **ci** command, text is solicited for commentary. A simple package (shell script) can be written that will prompt for specific attributes (test module name and revision), among other things. CM and control of test cases will also help alleviate problems of redundant test cases. *Coverage partitioning* will also be discussed in the chapter on test tools to help eliminate redundant test cases. Combining this method of structural testing (instrument specific code segments with the intent to measure test coverage for each test programs) with CM changes can greatly increase the performance of load testing.

7.14 Performance Metrics and Load Testing

Integration and performance testing must be considered prerequisites to stress and load testing. Performance metrics and goals must also be included in product requirements specifications and must be measured early in the development process during unit testing, even if stub routines are used for incomplete modules used later during system integration and test. Also, performance and regression testing should be performed simultaneously.

A common mistake system and application vendors make with regression testing is to analyze execution results only. Often they completely disregard any performance degradation for both test compilation and execution processes. To eliminate this mistake, the UNIX **time** command can simply be added at the start of a build or regression test execution process.

Load tests will have to be built and executed in a consistent environment for performance results to be meaningful. On the other hand, it may be desirable to provide a **scramble** option to the load test driver to randomize the execution of individual load test modules for even better test interface and system test coverage. However, the amount of build and execution time must not change. A good test harness will provide the option to randomize the order of test construction and execution. This has been accomplished by customizing the perennial *driver* program.

7.15 Exercisers vs. Functional Tests

It is important to distinguish between exercisers and functional tests. For example, a floppy disk driver functional test may check that proper error codes are returned for every possible exception condition using most all available unit tests. Conversely, an exerciser would provide rudimentary testing of the device in a recursive or repetitive manner for load and reliability measurements. Exercisers are less focused on the source code exercised and more interested in the usage of a device over a long period of time. In general, 100% coverage using structural testing methods is outside the scope of an exerciser. That is not to say that exercisers must exclude call coverage by way of call tree or call graph touch tests. This basic requirement insures that at least basic fundamental operations are conducted and exercised by the tests. These tests are also sometimes called "wiggle" tests. They touch or exercise a function to ensure that it is still alive (able to move).

The purpose of an *exerciser* is to execute a system (hardware and software) using a series of rudimentary tests as a method of system reliability and regression testing. Exercisers are not really designed to be functional (comprehensive), performance, conformance or unit tests. They can, however, be useful tools for manufacturing and incoming quality personnel, as life or reliability tests for various device subsystems. Someday, exercisers will be available for inspecting new software parts just as benchmarks are often used for new system peripherals. In the future, most software users will require more customized software. This will require installation, configuration, and power-on tests to be included with the product release. Exercisers are important tools to help provide these and other critical services.

7.16 Software Resource Exhaustion Tests

Software resources can be depleted individually for better boundary and exception testing and debugging. Resource tests focus only on critical system resources. For example,

- Available system memory (**malloc** library call for example)
- Swap space
- Physical disk space
- CPU performance
- Floating point
- Graphics performance
- Multimedia
- Others

UNIX resource evaluation tests focus on kernel resources (inodes, locks, files, etc.). Specific tests for kernel limits can often be developed while library assertions are written. For example, test assertions for UNIX **libc** function calls (i.e., *fork*, *unlink*, etc.) can also provide the basis for resource boundary and exhaustion tests.

7.17 System Exercisers

System exercisers are excellent diagnostic tools for new hardware, system software or both. They are equivalent to many tests commonly found in hardware diagnostics. The main advantage of system exercisers is that they execute under the control of the operating system, whereas stand-alone diagnostics do not. Diagnostics usually execute under the control of a firmware monitor or mini-executive operating system. Power On Diagnostics (PODs) are different from stand-alone diagnostics and usually are always executed prior to booting the operating system. POD tests are usually a subset of stand-alone diagnostics and are always required prior to system usage.

It is helpful to run stand-alone diagnostics on hardware that may readily fail. Run stand-alone diagnostics prior to loading the operating system and before performing any kind of stress and load testing. For example, a hard disk drive that has developed defective sectors that must be mapped out to a spares area and formatted must be evaluated by way of stand-alone diagnostics. System exercisers usually operate on the following functions:

- Memory march
- Disk read/write
- Serial I/O
- Network I/O
- Parallel port I/O
- Keyboard, mouse, etc.

Device exercisers are good building blocks or prerequisites to system exercisers. Again, these tests are also valuable for life or reliability testing and can be used in the manufacturing process for either software or hardware. Good system exercisers will keep each device busy in the hardware system without allowing one exerciser to dominate all available system resources. It is recommended that your system hardware first pass power-on and then stand-alone diagnostics prior to exposure to any of the above exercisers or tests.

Note that symmetrical multiprocessing tests can be developed using user- or system-level exercisers. These tests must evenly distribute system load across multiple processors. Also, multiprocessor exercisers must check for gross failures, as well as performance degradation based on load increases. These exercisers can be built using record- or file-locking mechanisms for multiple processes executing on multiple CPUs. Shared memory, messages, semaphores, signals and other Inter-Process Communication (IPC) mechanisms can provide excellent frameworks from which to build multiprocessor exercisers. Some of the many possible combinations for multiprocessor exercisers include (a table is recommended):

- Multiple small processes (text and data) with parallel execution
- Both small and large processes (text and data) with parallel execution
- Multiple large processes (text and data) with parallel execution

The above combinations can also include processes that are:

- CPU-intensive
- Floating point intensive
- Network- and parallel/serial communication-oriented
- Disk and storage intensive

7.18 User Exercisers

User exercisers simulate actual or expected user activity on a system. Several benchmarks are available to provide user simulations. Some of many popular UNIX products include:

- AIM Technology Suite 3, 5 and Milestone
- SPEC's (System Performance Evaluation Cooperative) SDM (Software Development Multi-tasking)
- Kenbus (also known as Musbus from Monash University)
- Gaede from AT&T

These benchmarks attempt to create a typical user load using shell commands and C programs. The SDM benchmark generates a metric for the number of scripts per hour, where a script is equivalent to one user.

An appropriate amount of time for user exercisers is between 48 and 72 hours. After four days, greater than 50% of all failures (from the author's experience) are a result of resource exhaustion or lack of ability for the benchmark to progress to the next higher user level. For example, the AIM Suite 3 benchmark continues to increment user load until the system is unable to complete the job mix for the total number of requested users. User exercisers and benchmarks are appropriate prerequisites to customer acceptance testing or as the final stress and load test.

7.19 Final Stress and Load Test Tips

Customer acceptance tests often contain the best stress and load tests available. Customers manage to discover ways of pushing system software and hardware limits and resources in ways no one in engineering and QA ever expect or can simulate using functional tests. Some of my favorite examples of these tests include starting multiple copies of a large data base **query, update,** and **delete** simultaneously for each workstation and multiple X or dumb terminals connected to a server over an ethernet local area network. Another example is to simultaneously recalculate and repaginate (calculate new page numbers) using large data files for each user or client connected to a server. These operations can usually beat, bash or stress memory (buffer cache) the hardest and therefore provide excellent stress and load tests.

Locking tests for multiprocessing, multi-user, multi-tasking operations are also very useful stress and load tests. Operations such as **open, lock, write, unlock, wait, reopen, lock, read, check, unlock, unlink** and **exit** between two processes provide excellent stress conditions. Most database management companies will love you for testing these functions before providing an operating system, application, or computer system for porting and testing.

IPC testing using shared memory and semaphore operations to read by user, alter by user, read/alter by group, and read/alter by others are also valuable. Raw disk input and output using the UNIX **dd** command or a small C program (e.g., adapted version of a floppy exerciser) can be very useful in stress testing.[*] The many other possibilities include CPU, floating point co-processor, serial input and output, ethernet, synchronous serial ports, parallel printing, file system tests and more. If possible, customer acceptance tests must be selectively added to a well-profiled regression test system.

7.20 Conclusions

- A well-defined software development and test process must be established prior to the execution of any stress or load tests, as quality must be planned, designed and embedded into software. It cannot be tested into the product.
- Unit-level tests that provide at least 80% code coverage (branch is preferred over statement) witnessed by instrumentation tools must be completed prior to stress or load testing.[†]
- After unit testing is complete, stress, device, system and user level exercisers can be executed using tests described in this chapter (system test phase).
- Stress tests must be completed prior to formal beta testing and customer acceptance testing.
- See the chapter on stress tests for example programs that can be used for stress testing.
- Unfortunately, very few tools exist today to perform any type of scientific stress and load testing. Several tools exist; however, to measure the performance of the system during testing. For example LoadRunner from Mercury Interactive.
- Selecting load and stress tests that will provide the greatest ROI is and will continue to be the greatest challenge for most organizations.

---

[*]Raw disk devices do not have a UNIX files system; however, many database vendors perform their own physical input and output operations for performance reasons with the raw disk device.

[†]Many caveats apply here. Products that are integrated with third-party software where source is not available may not be able to achieve this goal. A reasonable and measurable goal must be established prior to product release.

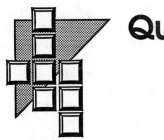 # Quality Assurance

Teamwork is probably the best word to describe the most critical element for a successful working relationship between engineers and QA professionals. This chapter will discuss the following critical topics associated with the QA function:

- Software QA
- QA responsibilities
- Benefits associated with being a member of the QA function
- Difficulties associated with being a member of the QA function
- How to implement testing and benchmarking as a member of the technical staff (project team)

8.1   Introduction to QA

Many companies use advanced information management or Management Information Systems (MIS) technology to translate raw data into useful information with which to make important business decisions. However, most of the time, information is based only on financial results and rarely considers the results of product quality measurements. This usually results in a more tactical, or reactive, and less proactive, progressive and strategic approach to business operations. Quality indicators are usually not noticed by executive management other than problem report data from critical accounts that continue to contact executive management. For example, test coverage statistics, revision history, function point complexity and mapping functional tests to product specifications must be considered critical to any employee bonus program. Consequently, engineers are often only reviewed based on meeting scheduled delivery dates and reducing problem incidents, rather than on producing products that satisfy customer product requirements. Monitoring field defects usually results in a more tactical/reactive, and less progressive or strategic approach to business operations.

For the mature planning approach to work (instead of the standard seat-of-the-pants method), a solid product plan must first be established that will remain fairly consistent throughout product development. Otherwise, if product requirements continue to change, quality will suffer as will employee morale. One approach to the development of a three- to five-year product plan would be to identify the customers in your market and survey their needs as input to the plan. It is then the executive staff's responsibility to ensure that the plan changes as little as possible.

8.2   The Need For Quality Data

Processing quality data is a critical factor in the generation of product revenue, as poor-quality products are either late or returned by dissatisfied customers. Unfortunately, most raw data on software quality is usually buried in engineering or customer service databases and is rarely noticed at the executive level. A favorite statement that someone once said is quite true: "If most companies managed their money the way they manage their product quality, they would probably be arrested and put in jail by the IRS". Such problems can be greatly alleviated through the use of testing metrics based on the functional, structural, reliability and regression testing strategies explained in this book. These test methods will help provide a framework, strategy and standard set of terms from which to build quality goals; however, proper management of these quality systems is still necessary for success.

Rarely do people in quality circles mention the term *zero defects* anymore. Instead the terms *continuous quality improvement* or Total Quality Management (TQM), are used. In other words, instead of setting the bar or goal to jump one million miles up into the air, it is simply set an inch or some reasonable distance above the current position. The ultimate goal of continuous improvement is usually either customer or employee satisfaction and cost control. Developing a measurement system is critical to success for the proper analysis and monitoring of satisfaction. It is time for senior management to awake to the call of their customers for the delivery of quality products. In the 1980's, the software QA function was considered responsible for making sure that quality products were released to customers, or the achievement rather than assessment of quality factors. This has slowly changed to include the entire organization, as must have always been the case. After all, in a manufacturing operation each employee is responsible for his/ her piece of the process; however, software development processes are usually not documented. Therefore, it is difficult to provide the same level of accountability when an *ad-hoc* process is used. Inspection is the responsibility of each employee.

8.3 Feature Content, Schedule, People, Equipment and Quality

In general, four factors are commonly used to manage the product development life-cycle and release model. They are often re-evaluated during the implementation and test phases and include the following:

1 Product feature content
2 Schedule (time)
3 People and equipment
4 Quality

Usually, the product content or feature set is the first area of sacrifice after testing has uncovered product failures. This element has the least amount of risk of the four factors. However, competition can quickly take customers away from an existing installation base as a result of not providing necessary features and support. Changing any of the other variables will also have a negative impact. Therefore, proper planning and estimation tools must be used to provide accurate and realistic software verification and validation schedules. CodePlan from Azor, Inc. will be discussed in a later chapter. This tool helps to balance key resource areas such as time, people and product features. The end result is that when verification and validation metrics and goals are first established as part of the software life-cycle, engineers will be able to better determine and build an accurate schedule.

8.4 Software QA and Quality Control

Software Quality Assurance (QA) may be defined as not only the satisfaction of both internal and external requirements using advanced quality control test measurement technology, but more importantly, *constant measurable improvement in quality*. Software quality control is the execution of a process whereby QA goals are monitored and measured. By focusing on the rewards of continuous quality control improvement a much more positive framework within which to work is created. This is opposed to only the narrower search for and measurement of negative quality indicators such as defects, errors and mistakes. One of the approaches used is for QA and QC to perform reviews. These are less intrusive than the term "test". The term "bug" can also be described as rework or spoilage. Bugs often times represent things that have legs and can move based upon their own free will. However, this is not the case for software failures. Errors, faults, failures, defects or spoilage are not innocent, cute little things that can crawl around in software. They are the result of errors usually introduced during the requirements and other development processes.

It is important to understand the quality organization's responsibilities in more detail before proceeding to a discussion concerning tools for functional, structural, reliability and regression testing.

8.5   Quality Group Responsibilities

Software quality function responsibilities are continually changing to include not only *program management* functions, but also test development and implementation. Program management responsibilities often include management of the release content, schedule, quality goals and metrics in a matrix management presentation. This often means that individuals from quality, engineering, support, marketing, publications and manufacturing are assigned as members of a release team with the program manager acting as the leader.

Integration and system-level functional and structural testing are functions that have been without an official owner for years, leaving the customer to test whether or not all independent modules can co-exist. Engineering is often expected to write unit or structural tests during the coding phase; however, test development usually doesn't happen. Usually, the quality or test group often ends up trying to perform manual unit testing, often times with a less than adequate understanding of the implementation details or failure modes associated with the product under test. This case is common place, because software engineers are not trained in state-of-the-practice test methodology. The gap between product and test development is now being closed with professional technical software engineers that understand not only software development, but all associated and available technologies and processes to deliver quality software products ahead of the competition.

Quality tools and technologies developed by QA for engineering must be developed with the intent of bringing these programs to market as products. One example of this is to have QA be responsible for the delivery of the tests (documentation, installation, source code, data, etc.) used for customer acceptance tests. These tests must be viewed as a separate product deliverable for CM, used for customer/employee training, demonstrations, compatibility and regression testing strategies and techniques.

Several other quality responsibilities include training and expertise in software quality, inspections, reviews, audits and measurement using modern day metrics. These all provide benefits to development engineers and must be included in the software development plan.

8.6 Benefits Associated with Software QA

Several benefits are available to members of software and hardware engineering and QA functions. Some of the many possible benefits are explored below. The purpose of the following section is to help both the engineer and manager better understand what areas are available to engineers either seeking or developing a career in hardware or software QA or engineering. Management can also help engineers to cultivate fairly marketable skills as a result of the following discussion.

Shortage of Professionals with Experience in the Area

As the software industry matures, skilled professionals will be required to establish a more well-defined and organized process for the development, integration, test and maintenance of software systems. Quality engineers with the experience of bringing high-quality products to market on time will continue to be in great demand as the time-to-market shrinks along with profit margins for most computer and software companies. This is especially true as the complexity and size of software continue to increase. As user demands continue to push modern-day software development tools and processes to their limits, new standards and practices for the design and development of high-quality and reliable software systems will be required. Experienced professionals will be required to assist companies to meet these and many other customer demands for the next several years. As a result of the increased demand by companies for experienced quality professionals and engineers, compensation for test developers will continue to increase.

Salaries of Engineers and Quality Professionals

Compensation for test engineers in the past has been lower than that of development engineers; however, times have changed and are still changing. To attract good software QA and test engineers, competitive compensation packages and salaries must be offered. In the past, quality engineering departments were often comprised of junior software engineers right out of school or with little relevant job experience. Quality or test personnel may often have been transferred from the technical support group, marketing or non-technical engineering functions. In the past, test engineers were often considered not good enough for the development organization. However, quality and software test engineers were told that if they were successful in learning product technology, they might be able to transfer to the development or research and development group. There is nothing wrong with this approach. It is often advised that every engineer rotate through the technical support, engineering, marketing or QA groups to better understand how other groups operate, as well as, to learn how products are used by customers.

The impact of poor-quality products must be shared by all. In general, however, engineers graduate from school and are often assigned new product development or maintenance without any formal training in testing strategies or methodologies.* It is no surprise that the current quality standard for the computer industry is very low and that system crashes and data corruption are often accepted by users. Many quality professionals are now able to teach the development staff proper software development procedures and methodologies. They are also able to identify best methods and practices and champion new approaches throughout the company. This, in turn, facilitates the proper design and development of software products, rather than the old way, which has led only to failure (fix it later).

Improving quality through testing has not worked in the past, and will continue to fail in the future. Testing can only provide measurement data by comparing the software under test to the specification, test plan or both. This implies an assessment rather than achievement function. That is not to say that testing is not an important tool for defect detection and containment and the achievement of quality products. In general, whenever more testing is required, it is a sign that there are more quality problems in the requirements, design and implementation phases of the product development life-cycle than in the final validation phase. QA engineers must help train others in the use of successful development methods (including test design and development). Another major benefit for engineers is the ability to explore new product technology offered by the company, either early or late in their career.

Increased Exposure

One of the most common advantages quality engineers often have at their disposal is the ability to pick and choose among product technologies. When any one area of interest is identified, that particular area can be explored by comparing an actual product deliverable with the expected functionality as defined in the requirements specification. Internal product requirement specifications or user documentation can be used to learn about product features. Source code can also be freely studied.

One of the primary disadvantages quality and test engineers often face is that they can only report problems and rarely have the opportunity or time to actually resolve problems. This has been one of the major contributors to poor employee morale and perception by engineering peers. However, this doesn't have

*See the 1991 CAST report for details [GRA93].

to be the case. Software quality and test engineers must be given the opportunity to not only report problems, but also to research product failures and provide alternative solutions (root cause analysis). This of course needs to be included as part of the scheduling and estimation process. Root cause analysis is not usually performed by engineers and can be an excellent method whereby QA engineers learn more about the depth of various products, or at least train engineers in the process.

The ability of software test engineers to focus on product breadth by performing functional, structural and system testing also enables the engineers to obtain greater experience. Because product breadth can be explored through interaction with members of the company and customers, increased knowledge and technical skills often result for quality engineers. Also resulting is the fact that any software test and quality engineering professionals are in great demand and therefore are receiving significant rewards as either contractors or consultants. Product delivery of complex software products will continue to require skilled individuals (including QA) for success.

Diversified Interaction

QA and software test engineers often take on a program management responsibility using matrix management. This means that they are able to work with various individuals within the company including marketing, sales, technical support, engineering and others. This allows them to monitor quality goals from a global company standpoint. QA often then becomes the glue that holds the development process together as raw technology migrates from the concept phase to a finished product. There are several other areas where QA and software test engineers are provided unique opportunities; however, it is also important to understand the common areas of difficulty for members of the quality group. Being able to overcome these challenges will benefit both you and your company.

8.7   Difficulties Associated with Software QA

Missing Technical Skills

Some people argue that because QA personnel and software test engineers never take full ownership and responsibility for any specific products, they often are not able to develop the necessary or equivalent skills of a successful software development or engineering professional. This may or may not be the case. However, it may also be like comparing a manager to an engineer. Each has responsibilities that have specific requirements and both are critical to the success of a company. The manager must have a good high-level perspective of business operations. The engineer, on the other hand, is expected to have detail knowledge of a specific area of responsibility. Another analogy may be for your foot to say to your hand, "I really do not need you, I can walk just fine without you." This may seem silly since we know that both are important and are critical parts of the body. However, each has a specific purpose.

Another common problem for the QA and software test employee, and others for that matter, is that they are not always recognized for the tasks they perform. General managers and executive managers must always recognize and understand that employees thrive on recognition!

Please Don't Shoot the Messenger!

Often times QA and software testing personnel are the messengers of bad news. This often does not make them the most popular individuals in a company. However, if you ask senior management what is one of the most critical functions within the company they will often cite the ability to provide quality products to customers that avoid rework, returns and a high cost structure for development. This is often referred to as spoilage in Japan. Imagine the productivity increase for customers with products that currently force them to spend a third or more of their total time dealing with defects and rework.[*] If just half of this time were available for product development rather than dealing with software problems, many more products could be brought to market ahead of time. Think of the impact of this on the Gross National Product (GNP). How about morale in general?

As an example of how thankless and difficult a job in QA and software integration and testing can be, the following is provided. This of course can be said of any job. The following statement made by the vice president of engineering after my second day of work, is still very clear to me, even though it happened over ten years ago. He said, "I can't trust my QA department!" I had just been hired and was responsible for validation testing of all products including operating systems, applications, networking and languages. This also meant testing all software products on a variety of hardware configurations. It is often the case that the quality and software test group assumes the guilt of not properly testing software or hardware prior to shipment, even though they didn't put the bugs in the software in the first place. This is one of the most basic problems most QA groups must be able to contend with—accepting accountability without having the responsibility. Quality is an umbrella activity that must encompass all groups within the organization. This is basically the major concept behind TQM. QA is the customer advocate! Every company must have a customer advocate group, or they will lose whatever customers they currently have.

---

[*]From my root cause analysis this is typical.

Humble Pie (Always Think Win—Win!)

A difficult, yet valuable learning experience occurred to me many years ago. The director of engineering requested that I interview a candidate for the software integration and test group. The individual that I was looking for was going to be responsible for developing automated system validation tests for a multi-threaded operating system running on a moderately parallel super-computer (a very large task for such a small group of engineers). The candidate was already in the process of interviewing for another product development position in engineering. Toward the end of the interview, I was asked to interview the candidate for the QA group instead of engineering. As I entered the conference room to interview the candidate, the engineering manager had apparently just finished telling the candidate that I would now be interviewing him for a position in software testing instead of development. I will never forget the job candidate's response as I entered the room. "If I get real hungry maybe I will come back and talk to you." My brain immediately starting thinking several things as he stormed out of the building. First, there is a notion that quality engineers are beneath or inferior to development engineers. Therefore, how can any company ever expect to produce quality software products if the employees that are responsible for measuring quality are inferior, despised and looked down on by their development peers? This guy hates me and I have not even had a chance to talk to him. However, it is also important not to place all the blame on others. Maybe this guy worked with some really terrible QA people at his last job. The value provided by some quality groups often has been more detrimental than useful because it has been staffed with poorly trained individuals with very low morale.

Providing test tools and programs for better automated testing improves the consistency, accuracy and efficiency of testing. This can make the difference between the quality group and company products thriving or decaying. This leads to a very important activity that must occur for any software company to be successful.

The organization (management) must break down the walls between engineering and QA. It is also the responsibility of each and every employee to combat the problem of employee turnover and low morale. [DEM87] states: "only a few reason account for most departures:

- A just-passing-through mentality: Co-workers engender no feelings of long-term involvement in the job.
- A feeling of disposability: Management can only think of its workers as interchangeable parts (since turnover is so high, nobody is indispensable).
- A sense that loyalty would be ludicrous: Who could be loyal to an organization that views its people as parts?"

Breaking Down the Wall

Unfortunately, in the past many walls were built between engineering and the QA or software integration and test groups. Many companies now use release or project teams to monitor and manage the development life-cycle from the concept or requirements phase to product shipment. This provides better teamwork than simply having development throw a tape over the wall to the quality group for testing. Instead, engineering, quality, software test, technical support and marketing must always work together to solve issues during the integration and testing phases prior to manufacturing production release. A team environment can also help resolve the next most common problem, the lack of recognition and promotion opportunities. Have the quality engineers and managers rotate as project leaders. Teamwork is a stakeholder to success!

Recognition and Promotion

Often there is a misconception that QA engineers and managers will not be promoted and that engineering, marketing or sales employees will have a better chance at obtaining executive staff positions. Some people that don't aspire to senior management positions may actually see this as a benefit. Several software companies live or die on product quality because of increased competition. If a product does not provide the required functionality properly, and the problem doesn't get fixed quickly, many customers will simply return the product and buy a competitor's product. Another classic obstacle for software test and QA is the definition of a tangible deliverable.

A Clear Deliverable

QA engineers often have difficulty in identifying a clear tangible deliverable as a result of their effort. Engineering is usually responsible for delivering a product to manufacturing. Manufacturing is responsible for providing a CD-ROM, cartridge tape, documentation and other Bill Of Material (BOM) items. Marketing must provide data sheets and product literature to sales. Sales must provide customer orders for the company to generate revenue. Unfortunately, quality usually provides the process, and sometimes technology glue, to make sure that all other groups within the organization are successful. This includes milestones, metrics, test automation tools, build and integration environments and other tools of the trade. We all need to realize that each deliverable is critical to company success (and can result in recognition and promotion).

A software developer can always point to some flashy screen and claim that his program works, and it takes work to disprove that assertion. A QA engineer has to work hard to make his product (usually the process) visible in the first place. QA tasks are often invisible and are harder to feel good about. Finally, QA tasks are much like that of engineering management (more people and process-oriented).

The next difficulty is often true for any position and it is management's responsibility to resolve jointly with the employee.

Technical Challenges

In the past, it has often been the case that software quality and test was more reactive than proactive to problem flows. This involved *fire fighting* and trying to catch any type of *pollution* before it continued downstream to the customer. Unfortunately, this process did not include going back to the source of the problem or performing root cause analysis. However, the modern-day QA organization must be proactive in the design and development of software using state-of-the-practice software methodologies and technologies. The following list is just a few of many possibilities:

- Static source code test coverage metrics (structural analysis)
- Dynamic source code test coverage metrics (structural testing)
- Memory management debuggers
- Source code standards analysis
- Object-oriented testing approaches
- Software safety analysis
- Static and dynamic testability analysis

Software, like anything else, must be designed with quality in mind. Functionality, structural integrity, reliability and stability (no regressions) can never be tested into a product. The development of a technology that exceeds a company's quality standard must be the greatest technical challenge available (in my opinion). We must all accept this challenge!

8.8 Conclusions

- It is critical to understand both the strengths and weaknesses associated with any employment position. It is important not only for individuals looking to make a change or starting a career, but also for management.
- The role of testing is to find problems and make sure they are fixed. This, by definition is the role of QA, better known as defect detection and containment. However, modern day QA must provide prevention training and services as well.
- Features, schedule, resources and quality must always be balanced.
- Software development tools used by developers and engineering can help in the early detection of problems. However, independent product assessment must be performed by the QA group to contain defects and product failures prior to customer release.

- The QA group, by definition, must always act as a customer advocate. The customer is always right.
- The evolution to reliable software systems requires skilled software quality professionals to help in the development of unit tested modules that can be reused for highly reliable integrated systems.
- Test plans, matrices and unit and functional testing are the foundations upon which reliable systems must be built. QA must identify solutions for process improvement.
- Bug rewards, using cash, dinners and trips can save companies thousands of dollars in rework and maintenance costs. Other incentives can include providing engineers with customer contact.
- Consider having developers that continue to turn out poor quality products rotated through the technical support/phone support function. Not as punishment, but as training.
- Ask developers if they will carry beepers to answer calls from customers for just one month. The good employees will cooperate and the bad ones will leave, hopefully.
- Employees have needs that must be balanced with the customer's requirements. Quality engineers and developers both want to feel that their contributions are significant to the success and future of the company.
- The QA team members need to continue to challenge and help others by providing sensing metrics for product and process improvement. This means they must provide training as to how to use each method, tool and metric. This will help the company and individuals grow as a result.
- Always remember to try and have a proactive attitude!

Finally, software quality and test professionals will have highly marketable skills that will be a primary weapon against an economy suffering from depression or hyperinflation. If you can become highly proficient and technically skilled (e.g., how to successfully develop and test software), you will rarely be without a source of income [BUR91]. QA and engineering professionals with experience in bringing quality products to market will continue to be in great demand for many years. However, this will take both personal initiative as well as professional maturity and effective habits to move the development and quality organizations from independence to interdependence. [COV89] states: *"Independence* is the paradigm of *I—I* can do it; *I* am responsible; *I* am self-reliant; *I* can choose. *Interdependence* is the paradigm of *we—we* can do it; *we* can cooperate; *we* can combine our talents and abilities and create something greater together." The organizations of the future that will succeed will be highly interdependent. (Interfaces are one of the most complex aspects of software design. By definition, they require project team interdependence.)

It is the quality engineer's responsibility for training other engineering staff in the methods and tools used for state-of-the-practice software development and test. If the quality engineers can find just a few developers that are willing to use the methods and tools of functional, structural, reliability and regression testing, continuous improvement is inevitable. Once a few engineers start using new methods and tools (a consistent process), their products will increase in customer satisfaction and decrease in rework. They will be able to move on to new development, while their peers are left resolving the next new functional or structural defect.

Most companies spend approximately 50% or more of the engineering development budget and time fixing customer defects and making product enhancements. It is amazing to think about the productivity increases for both developers, as well as end users once this problem is reduced. Having your peers move on to new assignments, because they have used a mature process accompanied by automated technology, is the best thing that can happen to a company. Your job in QA is to make the team and others successful!

The next chapter describes a series of standards conformance test suites for the UNIX operating system. These standards provide examples, as well as real life tools for increasing functional testing in the system and application software environment.

CHAPTER 9

Standards Conformance Test Suites

The main purpose of standards conformance test suites is to verify documented standards with test assertions, usually written in the C programming language. This chapter will discuss the following:

- The System V Verification Suite (SVVS) test suite
- The Verification Suite for XPG (VSX) test suite
- The generic Application Binary Interface (gABI) test suite
- The POSIX Conformance Test Suite (PCTS)

9.1 Introduction to Standards Conformance Test Suites

The standards conformance test suites discussed in this chapter will deal exclusively with operating system services, usually provided by the UNIX kernel. Some of these tests also examine UNIX utilities and commands as well. These tests are not considered static structural analysis checkers for compiler-generated code.[*] The products that are discussed are functional conformance verification and validation tests for the general behavior of UNIX according to each published standard. For example, the System V Interface Definition (SVID) from Novell defines the behavior of the **open** system call or kernel service. One of many possible error behaviors for **open** might be EACCESS. For example, when the search permission to the path that is passed as an argument to the function has an error, it must return EACCESS. This is a test for a specific type of behavior known as a *test assertion*. This chapter is important and is for use by both application and system software vendors to realize the importance of standards conformance testing!

9.2 Industry Standards, QA and Strategic Planning

An important attribute for successful companies today is the maintenance of a proper balance between the development of competitive products based on industry standards and validation technology to certify compliance. Computer, software and other related companies can no longer afford to provide proprietary or non-standard products and expect to gain developer and/or end user customer loyalty. This is because investment protection is a critical requirement for most software and computer system purchases. This is especially true considering the number of companies that have gone out of business over the last ten years because of poor quality products and services.

The continuing evolution of verification and validation testing strategies for system software and application integration environments must be a high priority for business success. This is because price, performance and quality are all equally important factors to business success. The software industry has moved quickly to a commodity-based marketing strategy and away from more specialized or proprietary systems. Add to this the fact that volume shipments often create standards by themselves, without the need for an official standards body. For example, the Network File System (NFS) introduced by Sun Microsystems in 1985 has become a *de facto* standard in the UNIX industry for transparent access to remote disk resources [STE91].

A major difficulty associated with most *de facto* standards is that standards documentation and test suites rarely exist for compliance and conformance testing to the standard. However, in this case, SunSoft has sponsored an annual event called "Connectathon" which concentrates on NFS testing. The XNFS test suite is also now available for testing the NFS network protocol. See the chapter on validation suites for more information on the connectathon test suite.

In most cases, without standards conformance test suites, the developer must often guess if the port of a product is successful or compliant with the standard. As always, guesswork creates less-than-optimal circumstances for everyone involved, including system and software vendors and of course, the poor customer and end user.

---

*UNIX provides the **lint** utility to perform static analysis of C source code and this must be considered an important metric for evaluation. However, many UNIX utilities, such as the shell, will not pass **lint**'s evaluation. One of many features of **lint** is to identify unreachable sections of code. This tool is not available for C++ programs.

Until better standards are available, the software factory dream, as described by Walter Utz [UTZ92], is an approach to development that will continue to be just a dream. Because interoperability standards are non-existent for function and code reuse, software continues to be quite different from hardware in terms of manufacturing reuse. Usually, software functions are not available off-the-shelf the way parts such as transistors, resistors, transformers and other devices are often purchased. Therefore, the need to develop a standard development and test process is critical to the success of most companies in business today. Code reuse must not be limited to just products, but must also include tests as well.

A verification and validation process that includes development and execution of functional, structural, reliability and regression tests is proposed as the standard framework. The end result of this strategy is improvement in the production of high-quality and reliable (customer satisfaction) software products. Also, reduction in the cost of maintenance and support through defect prevention and detection methods that are integrated into the process can be used to create a final product with greater productivity.

One of the most important breakthroughs in the area of testing and benchmarks of both hardware and system software has been the use of standards technology for function, system and stress testing. Unfortunately, standards take a long time to evolve, go to ballot and finally become approved. The general standards development process typically takes years rather than months, therefore, because standards can take a long time to evolve, standards conformance test suites are difficult to find and usually do not exist. One major standards effort in the UNIX industry is a model by which more standards must evolve in the future. This effort was coined as UNIX unification.

9.3   UNIX Unification

The Application Programming Interface (API) standard was released on September 1, 1993 after several years of research by many UNIX engineers. This standard for Independent Software Vendors (ISVs), hardware manufacturers and end users allows a single set of source code files to be re-compiled on various UNIX systems without conditional compilation of standard system services, as is the current practice. The customer also benefits from the standard because code sizes are shrinking (it is no longer necessary to have "#ifdef" statements throughout the source code for each flavor of UNIX). Performance and reliability are increasing as well as a result of smaller (single) sources being developed by application software vendors.

The API standard is really the integration of three standards (XPG4, SVID3 and OSF's Application Environment Specification with some *de facto* standards from application vendors for various system services).

9.4   API and ABI Standards Testing

Both negative and positive tests are used for testing either Application Programming Interface (API) or Application Binary Interface (ABI) standards. API standards are concerned only with product source code compliance to the interface standard. ABI standards, on the other hand, define how executable files (binaries) look following source code compilation. ABI standards are very helpful in both increasing the breadth of functional test coverage, as well as reducing the amount of code to test in the UNIX environment. The coverage of testing by ABI test suites help to exercise both the function under test and the environment required for binary portability. This includes facilities such as the run-time loader that resolves symbol references during execution for programs that are compiled and linked using dynamic shared objects. Having binary portability is nothing really new; rather, it is something that has been enjoyed in the PC marketplace for several years now.*

9.5   ABI Standards Testing (A Reference Platform)

The primary purpose for ABI standards is to provide shrink-wrapped binary or pre-compiled software that can execute on similar processor architectures without re-compilation. For example, a binary or executable program compiled on one system vendor's machine executes on another system from a different manufacturer, providing the greatest investment protection to the user possible. There are some potential drawbacks associated with ABI standards that are relevant to functional testing. If a single reference platform exists where all binaries or executable programs are generated, all other systems that intend to execute those binaries must be failure-compatible with the reference platform (this also referred to as back-to-back testing). Notice that I used the term failure, not fault. The end result must be the same or the internal workings (source code) could be different between systems. To minimize risk the source code bases for libraries, files and directories located in **/usr/include** and other system directories must be identical between potentially competitive system vendors. Now, you are essentially back to one single source code provider, that prevents each vendor from adding competitive value.

The **/usr/include** files that are often used by the C compiler's preprocessor to expand macro definitions for variables during program compilation can be standardized. For example, the size of various system defined variables can be determined by a file located in the **/usr/include** directory rather than hard coding parameters in the C program. This provides portability across various system

---

*This is primarily because the PC marketplace has often had one dominant software vendor, Microsoft, as its primary operating system provider.

architectures that may include either 16-bit, 32-bit or 64-bit word processing capability.[*] Unfortunately, this process is still only somewhat a reactive rather than proactive approach to verification and validation testing. Test suites and applications must be used for the following:

- **Compliance testing,** which is functional testing to a published standard
- **Compatibility testing** is the ability of two or more systems or programs to perform their required functions while sharing the same hardware or software resources and/or environment

Both compliance and compatibility testing must occur prior to reference and non-reference platform operating system product release. This means that each operating system is in compliance with the standard and is compatible with other systems based on test compilation and execution results analysis. (The same concept applies to application software modules.) The subject of debate among many groups has been that if the test suite is complete, the need for a single reference platform is eliminated. The problem is that no one person today (that I know of) believes that any test suite is ever complete or fully comprehensive. Thus, a single reference platform provides the "tie-breaker" vote in situations where a problem occurs and the standard documentation definition is ambiguous as to the correct behavior for a particular function. A reference platform is always a good strategy for system-level functional testing. *System testing* considers other aspects of testing not normally considered during unit and integration testing. For example, system testing considers the operating system, networking, graphics and other software and hardware system components.

ABI standards greatly benefit testing since only one binary is used for testing on multiple systems. With ABI standards, the binary image remains the same, making the core functionality of the program the same, even though the interfaces to the system (externally) may be different. This allows the binary program provider to focus only on the core functionality and test on a single reference platform. In general, standards conformance tests can provide many benefits, especially when binary compatibility standards are used to reduce the number of binary versions to test (e.g., from several to just one). Therefore, the priority of functional testing (standards conformance using binary and source level standards) must be considered the highest priority for any system or applications software vendor.

Having access to source code is really a double-edged sword. On one hand, it provides the benefit of allowing the software vendor to improve performance and add functionality to be more competitive. On the other hand, it comes with the added challenge of compatibility. This challenge can be removed when only one

---

[*]There has been great debate over how to size various standard variable types such as **int**, **long** and **word** as used by the C programming language when larger 64-bit processors are used.

technology provider is used, but it is accompanied by a significant penalty in competitiveness.

9.6 Testing and Standards Conformance Conflicts

Standards conformance tests are usually selected over any other functional-level tests (if they exist). This is due to continual demands and increased market pressures for both non-proprietary systems and shrink-wrapped[*] software. Standards conformance tests also provide a more level or equal playing field for product quality comparisons between vendors; however, waivers can often distort the meaning of the term conformance or its value to the test engineer and customer. Today, most test suite waivers are managed by both the test suite vendor and standards or specification body for which the test suite was developed. One common reason for waivers is that one standard may be in conflict with another. This means that if the developer resolves a test assertion problem (e.g., unit test program) for one standards test suite, other test suites may now fail.

Another common problem with standards-based tests suites is that for all product providers to be compliant or provide conformance, the standard often must be boiled down to its lowest common denominator. The end result is often a standard that is almost useless by itself. A possible solution to standards fixes breaking other standards is to use a testability metric to identify other interfaces of impact as a result of the change. Testability analysis also provides information regarding how difficult the change will be to test. See the chapter on test tools for more information on complexity and testability analysis metrics and tools.

9.7 Hardware and Software Certification

It is interesting to note in this section on functional testing based on standards conformance that computer hardware certification by the Federal Communication Commission (FCC) and Underwriters Laboratories (UL) has been available long before software certification. Only since the early 1990's have seven companies been approved by the National Institute of Standards and Technology (NIST) under the National Voluntary Laboratory Accreditation Program (NVLAP) for POSIX compliance certification. Incentives for certification (or at least passing tests) were identified as an important aspect of standards compliance. Therefore, UNIX system vendors would receive reduced royalties for compliance to some standards; for example, the X/Open Portability Guide XPG/3 and XPG/4 specifications.

---

[*]Term often used to describe software that is available for mass consumption. For example, PC-based application software.

Many people may think of a coding style checker when the term standards conformance testing is used. The UNIX utility **lint**, a C program verifier, may be considered one specific type of standards conformance test tool. However, the full semantic functional behavior of an operating system service is not considered by this type of static source code checker. Instead, a standards conformance test suite is required. Other tools such as TenDRA from X/Open and QA C from ASTA, Inc., provide the ability to statically analyze C programs for compliance and conformance with a standard (i.e., ANSI-C guidelines, etc.). As you will see in a later chapter, test suites must be used to validate functional conformance for syntax, as well as semantic behavior of operating system services, commands and libraries.

9.8   Branding and Certification

Some of the most significant increases in code coverage have been facilitated through the use of written test assertions based on published and approved standards documents. Standards conformance test suites have become the greatest off-the-shelf tool available for system and application software QA departments (when they are available). These test suites can be used for functional, system and regression testing. It is often less expensive to purchase rather than develop software, including test suites. Use of standards test suites has now evolved to the point where National Accredited Verification LAbs Programs (NAV-LAP) are also available for the testing and certification of various standards. Formal certification and branding usually requires an accredited lab to either come on-site or perform testing in a branding lab. Certification comes with a fairly expensive price tag; however, to do business with the U.S. government, all testing must be successfully completed using an accredited lab prior to procurement.

Unfortunately, the return on investment for the development of standards conformance test suites has not made it a booming business. Several attempts to make testing financially rewarding have proved unsuccessful. Many of these products are as complex and sometimes more complicated than the operating system software product they are testing, thus making development, test and support costs extremely high.

Both application vendors and end users must understand if that platform (operating system software and hardware) is compliant with industry standards, this will provide a baseline for comparison prior to application porting and end user purchase. It is a process that is similar to purchasing an automobile using *Consumer Reports*. X/Open provides reports regarding systems that have been officially branded. Another significant standards conformance test suite for the UNIX operating system is called SVVS4.

9.9   System V Verification Suite (SVVS4)

The System V Verification Suite is only available from Novell. The purpose of the SVVS4 conformance test suite is to provide System V Interface Definition (SVID) Issue 3 compliance testing for system software vendors that have ported System V Release 4 (SVR4) to a specific platform. The test suite is broken into two main categories: BAsic (BA) and Kernel Extensions (KE). The BA section has subsection tests for the operating system (OS), libraries (LIB), environment (ENV), and devices (DEV). The kernel section (KE) has tests for the environment (ENV) and operating system (OS).

Two different versions of SVVS exist: one for UNIX System 5.3 (SVVS3) and one for System 5.4 (SVVS4). It is important to note that UNIX 5.3 is based on SVID Issue 2 and UNIX SVR4 is based on SVID Issue 3. SVVS was used as an SVID compatibility test as part of the common API testing for the Open Software Foundation (OSF) members with Application Environment Specification-(AES) based operating system technology. This is a perfect example of why standards conformance tests must be available along with standards documentation for proof of compliance. This is one of few realities available today for open systems. Most people will admit that the term open has been used and abused to the point that it now often has a negative connotation.

Device Driver Considerations

The engineer is required to add streams kernel device drivers to the operating system under test prior to executing several SVVS4 tests. The following four pseudo device drivers are needed:

- **lo** (loop back)
- **tmux** (Transport Layer Interface (TLI) - multiplexer)
- **tidg** (TLI datagram)
- **tivc** (TLI virtual circuit)

The **poll** test provided by SVVS may hang or become suspended during execution unless the above kernel streams drivers have been successfully installed and the system has been rebooted. Also, several other tests will fail when these drivers are not present including:

- **ioctl** - input and output control
- **streams** - TLI streams network test driver
- **t_accept** - TLI streams network test driver
- **t_bind** - TLI streams-based network test driver
- **t_close** - TLI streams-based network test driver

SVVS4 is an assertion-based test suite completely written in the C programming language. Functional failures are tested by checking for the proper error number, return code or both with an expected value as defined by SVID standard documentation. If a test case or assertion does not generate the expected error number **errno** and **return code**, a failure is reported. Results are stored in journal files located in the **adm** directory for each test assertion. The **report** program is used to provide results and perform test execution analysis.

Administration and Configuration Issues

SVVS4 requires the engineer to add streams kernel device drivers to the operating system under test prior to executing several tests. Streams provide a *flexible* interface for pushing and popping streams modules for various network system services. Usually there is a stream head and tail, however, many modules can be pushed or popped into the stream. Also, approximately 50mb of hard disk space and a file system partition are required for use as a scratch area for several tests. An NFS[*] mounted file system partition can be used if a local disk is unavailable, however, the file system must first be shared using the **share** command and mounted for read/write access. Some tests that require the file system to be a local mount may fail. Also, you will need to use the **anon=0** option in the **/etc/dfs/ dfstab** file for sharing root access to the remote NFS-mounted file system. For more information on the **share** command, refer to the UNIX **man** pages.

Programs are also provided to set and clear access permissions (**setaccess/clraccess**) for work files used during testing. These files are located in the **data** subdirectory for each test section. It is extremely important that these files be available for various operations and therefore proper file and directory ownership and permissions are set prior to execution of SVVS. Special care must be taken if the entire SVVS4 binary tree is copied to tape or another disk, as this could change the ownership and/or permission of these critical data files.

Prior to test execution, the engineer must carefully review all definitions in the SVVS4 include sub-directory, especially the values contained in the **config** file. This file contains definitions such as the block device name for a scratch file system and the file system type. For example,

- UFS[†]
- NFS
- S5[‡]

---

[*] NFS is a trademark of Sun Microsystems. It provides transparent access to remote disk resources (file systems).

[†] UNIX File System, or the Berkeley Fast File System.

[‡] System 5 File System from Novell. Most UNIX System V.4 installations do not support the S5 file system.

SVVS4 contains approximately 2779 test assertions in the BA section and 249 in the KE section for a total of 3028 test assertions.

9.10 Application Binary Interface (ABI) Compatibility

SVVS4 has also been used successfully for Application Binary Interface (ABI) compatibility testing. A major caveat is that Novell must provide written approval before either source or binaries may be distributed from one license to another. There are several areas of complexity and difficulty using SVVS for binary compatibility testing. For example, configuration parameters must be either identical to the build system or modified prior to execution.

Interactive shell scripts can be built to modify parameters such as userid's and groupid's in the **/etc/passwd** and **/etc/group** files prior to execution. SVVS4 provides unique tests for generic ABI library (**libc**) testing.

The ABI consists of specifications for the following:

- gABI[*]
- psBI[†]
- Black Book, or implementation guide

The gABI is an architecture-generic specification for everything from installation to libraries and commands. The psABI defines processor specific features such as file formats for binaries and objects. Four psABI's for UNIX System V.4 include the following trademarked names:

1 Intel
2 Motorola
3 Mips
4 Sparc

The Black Book defines extensions to both the gABI and psABI for applications support. For example, the Mips ABI Black Book 1.2 added support for asynchronous[‡] input and output required by several database application vendors. It is always desirable to have Black Book features migrate to the psABI; then, psABI features should migrate to the gABI. This will then provide common interfaces and standards across architectures.

---

[*]The generic Application Binary Interface.

[†]The processor-specific Application Binary Interface.

[‡]Disk operations whereby reads and writes do not wait for a synchronous event.

X*, Motif[†], NFS[‡], TCP[*] and other NON-SVID-related technologies are not covered by SVVS4; however, tests for these products will be covered later. Also, it is worth noting that system commands are also not covered by SVVS4; however, these tests will be discussed later.

9.11 SVVS4 (Dependency Issues)

SVVS4 includes special functions for both BA and KE tests in the **src/ tools** directory. These files contain functions, **z_execv.c** for example, that are called directly by each test instead of those that call the **libc** function directly. The **z_execv** function in turn calls the libc **execv** function. This provides a front end so that failures from any **z_function** can be reported by SVVS4. For example, all functions are re-mapped from **Zxyzfunction** to **xyzfunction**.

One problem during testing is that functions (for example **printf**) must be assumed to be working properly prior to testing another function so that results can be reported. This problem in testing is common and can only be eliminated when canned ancillary routines are provided in a step level integration process until every required function has been verified before it is used to test the next. This is opposed to the traditional big bang method of integration, where everything is thrown together to see if it all works. Test plans and matrices provide an excellent means of organizing unit tests and test assertions by isolating prerequisites and dependencies.

9.12 Verification Suite X/Open (VSX)

The Verification Suite XPG (X/Open Portability Guide), VSX, is available from Unisoft Corporation. X/Open consists of several international hardware systems, software vendors and users that create specifications. The X/Open limited group however is not a *standards body* such as the IEEE or ANSI are for technology such as Graphical User Interface, Networking, Commands, Operating Systems, Inter-Process Communication (IPC) and others. X/Open is considered more of a *specifications* body that deals with several standards. They often integrate several standards together into a single specification, for example the X/Open Portability Guide 4. Finally, branding is critical once a published standard is available to determine if a piece of software or hardware is compliant with the standard.

---

[*] The X Window System is a registered trademark of The X Consortium Company.

[†] Motif is a registered trademark of the Open Software Foundation.

[‡] NFS is a registered trademark of Sun Microsystems.

[*] TCP is the Transmission Control Protocol used for networking of heterogenous systems.

9.13 XPG Branding

The VSX test suite must be successfully executed on a system before the X/Open brand can be used for marketing and sales purposes. Several companies in Europe and Japan require the X/Open brand prior to purchase as a checklist item. X/Open provides a yearly XTRA program that surveys both users and system/software vendors. X/Open provides a great deal of support for software and hardware vendors that complete the branding program, such as marketing material for trade shows and signs, etc. The cost for branding can be obtained by contacting X/Open directly; however, successful completion of the VSX test is required before any attempt of branding is made. The X/Open test suites are the key to branding.

9.14 X/Open Test Suites

The latest VSX4 test suite is based on the X/Open Portability Guide 4 (XPG/4). XPG/3 testing using VSX3 ceased in 1994 according to X/Open. VSX3 contains operating system and header file tests for the following standards (remember that this is a specification comprised of several standards):

- POSIX
- ANSI
- XPG3
- XPG2
- Data management/ISAM
- C language

The last maintenance release available for VSX XPG3 was version 3.204, as of this writing. It is important to note that there are waivers for several tests from various systems vendors. These waivers are only granted by X/Open and require detailed documentation describing the purpose and reason for a waiver. An ANSI-C compiler is required for the successful build and execution of VSX3 tests. Installation and execution of VSX can be complex, therefore the enclosed information is provided.

9.15 Setup and Administration of VSX

Configuration file setup is also critical to success. As with SVVS, VSX requires superuser or root access[*] and a spare disk drive. Two serial ports are also required for POSIX testing. Where the system hardware does not support two serial ports, pseudo ttys (ptys) may be used. VSX3 also requires approximately

110mb of hard disk storage for installation. VSX3 contains approximately 4698 test assertions, not including the ANSI-C language section.

It is important to note that some of the VSX tests may fail because of timing-related problems. See X/Open or Unisoft for support if this happens; however, most often only a waiver will be granted. Timing problems can also cause failures with the gABI (generic Application Binary Interface) test suite. The **vsxparams** file contains system-dependent information that must be changed whenever VSX is executed on a new platform.

The UNIX **ranlib** command is no longer necessary with SVR4. However, it is provided in **/usr/ucb** for BSD compatibility. The tester can simply supply the UNIX **echo** command as an assignment in the **vsxparms** file for the **ranlib** command. The **ranlib** command is not necessary because dynamic shared objects or shared libraries are now supported with SVR4. There is no longer a need to build a table of contents using **ranlib** for static archives.

VSX is one of the most complicated conformance test suites available. The primary key to success with VSX, as is the case with SVVS4, is to provide proper parameters in the configuration file. The conformance test engineer must carefully review all documentation provided with VSX for more details.

Branding Details

The XPG4 branding program operates by applicants entering into a Trademark License Agreement with X/Open Company Limited and registering products under the XPG4 branding program. Registered products must meet X/Open's established conformance criteria, which are based where possible on passing stringent verification tests as already described by VSX. Note that the burden is on the licensee, and that the X/Open branding documentation stresses that passing the test suite should be seen merely as an indicator of compliance.

The full set of XPG4 interface specifications is divided into a number of sub-sets, known as components, covering specific topic areas (basic operating system, data management, high-level languages, etc.), just as with SVVS. These can all be branded separately or collectively in a profile (according to X/Open).

XPG4 has 22 components compared to 15 in XPG3. A profile is a collection of components. For XPG3, X/Open had two profiles: BASE and PLUS. The BASE profile is the minimum set of software components required to create a Common Application Environment (CAE) as defined in XPG4. This can essentially be seen as a super-set of XPG3. The main changes have been in alignment with ISO/IEC 9945-1 (POSIX.1-1990), the POSIX.2 and parts of the draft ISO multi-byte support extensions. POSIX.2 contains the definition for shells and commands for the

---

*This usually is the system administrator's account, where all permission and ownership security is overridden.

UNIX operating system. Multi-byte support extensions provide support for foreign languages such as Japanese, and other languages where mega-characters are provided (more than can be represented by an 8-bit character).

A licensee warrants that products registered with X/Open Limited for XPG4 branding comply with the specifications in the X/Open Portability Guide, issue 4. XPG4 is based on a number of national and international standards. Where a conflict exists between a national and international standard, and the XPG4, XPG4 defers to that standard. If any conflicts occur between these standards and XPG4, a permanent waiver will be granted by X/Open.

The standards that XPG4 defers to includes:

- ISO/IEC 9945-1 (IEEE POSIX 1003.1-1990)
- ISO/IEC DIS 9945-2:1992 (IEEE POSIX 1003.2)
- ISO/IEC 9899:1990 (ISO C)
- ISO 1989:1985 for Cobol (and ISO 1989/Amendment 1)
- ISO 1539:1980 for FORTRAN
- ISO 8652:1987 for Ada
- ISO 7185:1983 for Pascal
- ISO/IEC ISP 10607, ISO/IEC 8571 for BSFT

New coverage for VSX4 is included in Appendix B. The main new features of VSX4 include the following:

- Test Environment Tool-kit test harness (TET)
- Built-in support of pseudo tty loopback
- Ability to test ISO POSIX.1-1990, as well as XPG
- Support for alternate privilege paradigms, such as UNIX SVR4.1ES

For more information on VSX, contact X/Open Company Limited. The gABI standards conformance test suite is a by-product of VSX; however, the emphasis of gABI is on the ABI itself, not API testing.

9.16 generic Application Binary Interface (gABI)

The generic Applications Binary Interface (gABI) test suite is available from Unisoft Corporation. This test suite is based on the VSX3 test suite. However, the purpose of gABI is to provide generic binary interface testing based upon the System V Release 4 generic ABI specification. This test suite covers issues such as packaging, C library system calls tests and commands testing. gABI version 2.1 is available for Intel, Mips and Sparc based processors running UNIX System V Release 4.

gABI 2.1 will be based on VSX4 and consists of three main areas of test emphasis:

1 ICTS (Implementation Conformance Test Suites)
2 ACTS (Application Conformance Test Suites)
3 CETS (Compiler Environment Test Suites)

ICTS will provide compliance and conformance tests for system vendors to the gABI, psABI and Black Book standards. ACTS will provide tests for application vendors to make sure that they have not violated the ABI rules. CETS will allow system vendors that provide ABI development or Software Generation System (SGS) products to assure that they are compliant with the ABI standard. As is the case with VSX, gABI is complicated to properly configure and execute. The next section will discuss setup, administration and release information for gABI.

gABI Setup, Administration, and Releases

The gABI test suite is difficult to configure and execute due to the breadth of coverage and complexity of function. Each parameter must be set properly prior to any attempt to execute the gABI suite. At the time of this writing, only a couple of problems were known to exist with the 1.1 release. As expected, the gABI 1.3 test suite does not cover machine-specific or processor-specific features of the System V.4 ABI standard [ATT90]. File archive and object file formats are also not covered. Other items not covered include:

• X Window system
• Motif (OSF Graphical User Interface window manager for X)
• RPC/XDR (Remote Procedure Call/eXternal Data Representation)

The following were to be included in gABI 2.1:

• XNFS (X/Open Network File System test suite)
• **xtest** (with touch tests for X11R5 covered in later chapters)
• Application Conformance Test Tools (ACTS)

The ACT tool tests application binaries for violations to the gABI, psABI and Black Book. gABI 2.1 is also reported to include new tests for **Remote Procedure Calls (RPC)** and **eXternal Data Representation** (XDR). This provides network communication in heterogenous environments. XDR provides the data translation necessary for differences in processor architecture for machine-independent communications (i.e., little endian and Big Endian).[*]

gABI Results Analysis

Begin with native results from VSX first. Then, obtain native gABI results prior to attempting to analyze gABI results from a foreign system. The Mips ABI group uses a Reference Platform (RP) model. With this approach, one system (Silicon Graphics, Inc. or SGI) is used as the development system. All other execution platforms then link object files and execute binaries or both created on the reference platform after correct results are available from the RP. Waivers for gABI tests are also available from Unisoft and must be used during analysis of either VSX or gABI results. Problem reports may be sent via electronic **mail** to Unisoft.

Another approach would be to have more than a single development environment system. Multiple baseline results must then be compared, as opposed to a single reference platform where there is always one tie breaker system when in doubt. The concept of a reference platform, baseline or, golden tree is often used during results analysis. The purpose of using a RP will now be provided.

Reference Platform

A RP provides a reference implementation for standards technologies and is often required with standards documentation. If an ambiguity arises during testing, a tie breaker implementation is required. The system and application vendor, therefore, must have a way to support products on multiple systems without any confusion. Other technologies provided for ABI testing can be obtained from 88Open, PowerOpen, ApTest, and Sparc International.

9.17 ApTest

ApTest is a company created with the advent of 88Open to allow Motorola processor vendors running either UNIX System V.3 or V.4 to share binaries without re-compilation. Many application software vendors such as Frame Technology, Inc. and Oracle Corporation have successfully ported to one Motorola hardware vendor and had their applications work successfully on other compliant systems using the technology provided by 88Open. The technology provided by 88Open for branding, compliance and certification is very well known in the UNIX industry. Unfortunately, the marketing success of the 88000 microprocessor was not as successful. However, the technology for testing binary compatibility has been so successful, Hewlett-Packard's Precision RISC Open (PRO) group purchased all the 88Open technology for binary compatibility testing, at a significant cost.

---

*The term endian came from the use of which end of the egg do you consider first. Big Endian addressing has the most significant byte at the lowest address. Little endian has the least significant byte at the lowest address [KAN87].

ApTest provides several unique tests for gABI, processor-specific and Black Book testing. A Static Binary Checker (SBC), Dynamic Binary Verifier (DBV) and Object Reference Checker (ORC) are provided to perform most of the tasks by evaluating compliance to the various ABI standards for application vendors. This includes evaluating library references, symbol names, section locations and other details as specified in the standards documentation.

9.18 Sparc International (SI)

The Sparc International organization is similar to 88Open Limited, however, the focus for Sparc International is for promotion of the Sparc RISC microprocessor in the UNIX environment. This Sparc Compliance Definition (SCD) is the Black Book or implementation and porting guide supplement to the processor-specific and gABI standards. Sun's Solaris is based on SVR4. Sparc International also provides test suites for both application vendors as well as hardware system vendors to ensure binary compatibility to the published standards.

For application vendors, a binary verifier or checker is provided, as for 88Open. This is called the Sparc Binary Verifier (SBV). This verifier allows application vendors to verify and validate that the binary executable does not initiate calls directly to the operating system without using the proper library interfaces. For example, making a request of the UNIX kernel directly using the **syscall** function would be in violation of the ABI, since this call is unique to each system vendor. Therefore, the SBV would flag this and other violations to the application vendor after the source code has been compiled. System vendors, on the other hand, are responsible for testing that all shared libraries provided are compatible with the standard so that when an application makes a request of a shared library, the syntax and semantics of the library function are consistent across all compliant system platforms.

The primary purpose of a shared library is to hide the machine-specific details from the application, so that library references are fully resolved during run-time via a run-time loader. Unisoft, ApTest, PowerOpen, and Sparc International all provide test technology to help UNIX system and application vendors to provide functional conformance and compatibility testing to published binary standards. If you are a UNIX application software vendor and want to improve quality, do not miss out on the opportunity of providing a single binary for multiple platforms, rather than several different binaries for each system platform of the same processor architecture.

9.19 POSIX Conformance Test Suite (PCTS)

The POSIX (Portable Operating System Interface) is defined by FIPS (Federal Information Processing Standard) publication 151-2. FIPS 151-2 adopts the ISO/IEC 9945-:1990 specification, which defines a C language source interface to an operating environment.

The POSIX Conformance Test Suite is available from the National Technical Institute of Standards (NTIS). It is also available from other companies such as Mindcraft and Unisoft. The purpose of PCTS is conformance testing to the IEEE/ISO POSIX P1003.1 standard. The following sections are included in PCTS:

- DC - Device and Class specific tests
- DEF - Definitions and general requirements
- DIF - Data Interchange Format
- FD - Files and Directories
- IO - Input and Output
- LS - C programming language
- PE - Process Environment
- PP - Process Primitives
- PW - PassWords

PCTS Certification

The following example is provided to demonstrate the PCTS certification process for an accredited lab.

First, the engineer must complete an initial PCTS run that includes installation, PCTS configuration, report generation, and assembly and delivery of test output. The typical cost for this is $10,000. Expect this to take from two to four weeks. Subsequent test runs on the same system usually are $2,500 per run. The cost to do a certification, which includes the above, plus submittal of the results and resolution of deviations to NIST for validation of conformance to the PCTS is about $30,000 if the work is done at the accredited lab's facility. If the work is done at your facility, there are usually additional costs (travel and other expenses, etc.). Expect the validation of certification to take from one to three months to be ready for submittal to NIST. The amount of turn-around time by NIST to issue a certificate is difficult to estimate, but usually one can expect it to be within 30 days. The initial certification (as the rules currently stand) is for a specific system configuration (memory size, disk, ports, etc.). A change in configuration requires an additional certificate. If these certifications are done in sequence, you can usually expect additional configurations to cost $5,000–$15,000 each, depending on the difference in one configuration to the next.

The reader may also want to contact Mindcraft or Unisoft to license the PCTS source code. Experience has shown that the VSX test suite covers the same test assertions as PCTS with many bug fixes. The engineer will probably have much more success with VSX than PCTS as delivered from NTIS. However, NIST has provided some patch updates to licensed customers.

9.20 Conclusions

- Standards conformance testing is one of the more well-established areas for UNIX.
- Standards conformance test suites can be used for either functional or regression/reliability testing. They can leverage the biggest bang for the buck or greatest return on investment. There are well over 10,000 test assertions available from just the few standards-based test suites mentioned in this chapter. (Useful for application and system vendors!)
- Standards conformance test suites are one of the most powerful weapons that engineering and quality managers have at their disposal to combat the continuing threat of software bugs both internally and externally. Unfortunately, standards conformance test suites are expensive to develop and maintain.
- Standards documents alone can take several years to evolve and finalize, not to mention the time required to develop test technology to validate conformance to a standard. This can be resolved by having developers write test assertions prior to product code!
- Test suites can be written using preliminary standards documentation; however, this increases maintenance costs as well as redevelopment and testing if the standard changes prior to approval.
- Create a compatibility lab at your company for your customers to use. Request that they preserve all tests to be used for compatibility (standards) testing.
- As the software industry continues to mature, hopefully more standards conformance test suites will be available for system validation. In the future, it is not unlikely that brands like those used for hardware certification will also be available for software; for example, UL and FCC.
- Users and customers also need standards to help manage rapid technical changes that are starting to move faster than ever before. As standards are combined with different components from various sources into integrated computing system standards, conformance will be critical to marketing both products and services world-wide.
- Leverage your existing standards conformance tests to increase functional, structural, reliability, and regression tests results!

CHAPTER 10 ▶

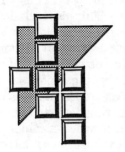

Validation Test Suites

Validation test suites can partially overlap with standards conformance test suites. However, software engineers must always desire to better understand missing source code statements using call tree and call graph entry/exit, statement and decision or branch structural test coverage metrics. This chapter will discuss the following:

- The purpose and need for validation test suites
- The UNIX System V.3 Validation Suite (UVS3)
- The UNIX System V.4 Validation Suite (UVS4)
- The BSD UNIX 4.3 Validation Suite (UVSE)
- The ARTUS Buster test suite
- The X Window System test suite (**xtest**)
- The NFS test suite (Connectathon)

10.1   Introduction Validation Test Suites

The goal must always be to extend coverage using existing test suites and programs using the most cost-effective approach possible. When most computer vendors are asked if they purchase test suites, they usually say they purchase all test suites. This is primarily because it is always less expensive to purchase than to develop tests from scratch. Also, the maintenance cost for test suites will be much more when supported internally than by a third party. This also includes the development of new functions and features. This is because the cost for test suite support and enhancement by the vendor will be sponsored by several customers, therefore reducing the cost to each individual test suite customer or end user. Remember that test suites are often considered an unrewarding expense or necessary evil. Unfortunately, without them, product rework after shipment is often the result, which is an even greater evil. Software engineering departments need to better understand what value is being added by each test to better understand the value added by a complete test suite as a result of the expense or cost incurred.

10.2   Decision Coverage and Validation Test Suites

Several decision coverage tools are available to help in mapping code coverage to test suite execution. When a Berkeley Software Distribution (BSD) UNIX command suite was tested against the Berkeley UNIX commands available with UNIX System V.4 it was quite alarming to discover that approximately 10% of all possible source code statements were executed. Only 10% may look very low, however, this is not very far from the industry average for functional and validation tests.

Most validation tests are usually touch tests that often only scratch the surface of the available functionality. They usually will not provide the same detailed or depth of coverage that is provided by standards conformance test suites (in some areas, not all).

After using company-developed and acquired functional test suites, most company survey results show that few ever achieve greater than 30% statement coverage without the assistance of dynamic structural test coverage and static structural analysis tools. This is because the emphasis is on basic block or statement coverage as a subset of decision or branch coverage. This means that if just one part of a statement branch is exercised, the coverage increases; however, other branches in control flow for that statement may never be executed. Usually, code coverage (decision/branch) can be increased to about 80% or 90% using dynamic structural test coverage tools; however, data flow tools are often required to push coverage higher. Some of the tools available for test coverage will be discussed in the chapter dealing with test tools.

Several of the validation suites covered in this chapter will overlap the purpose of other test suites already discussed. However, SVVS, PCTS and VSX also overlap with each other. So, redundant test cases are not something new and specific to validation test suites alone. However, constant analysis by development and quality engineers will be required to better understand how tests can be optimized for shorter test cycles. ViSTA and MCcov both provide coverage partitioning as one solution to the problem of test suite overlap and redundancy. Using test metrics and structural test tools that provide coverage statistics assists test developers in the comprehension of what value is or is not being added by a particular test case or suite.

10.3   The Need for Validation Test Suites

The primary purpose of validation test suites is to validate that a product has a specific level of functionality, usually measurable only toward the end of the development cycle (when executable binary files are available). Normally, external functional specifications or user documentation is used to validate software products. The following validation suites are based on published UNIX operating system software documentation:

- On-line or hard copy **man** pages from UNIX System V.3, V.4 and BSD 4.3
- System V Interface Definition (SVID)
- X/Open Portability Guide (XPG)
- POSIX 1003.1

As a refresher, validation is different from verification. Verification technology is used to determine if the results of each development phase fulfill the requirements or conditions imposed by the current phase. Validation technology is used to evaluate a product during or at the end of the development process to determine whether it satisfies user requirements.

Test matrices based on validation test suites can be built to identify and validate conditions for each operation of a function under test. Requirements questionnaires and surveys can also be prepared to grasp the complexity of a function prior to design, code and test. Some of many potential questions that could be used to determine the complexity of a function would include:

- What type and quantity of inputs will be provided?
- How many other functions will interface to the function?
- What type and quantity of output will be provided?
- How many data transactions and transformations will occur?

10.4   UNIX Validation Suite 5.3 (UVS3)

UVS3 is the UNIX validation test suite for the UNIX System from Perennial, Inc. Approximately 4.6mb of disk space is required for the UVS3 test suite. Fortunately, as each test is conducted, it is first compiled to an **a.out** binary executable file, then executed. Therefore, the amount of disk space required is greatly reduced over that of SVVS, PCTS and VSX, because only one binary is created, executed and then overwritten by the next test after compilation. A simple modification can be made to the **driver** program to create executable binaries using the source program name rather than the default name of **a.out**. It is always preferable to have validation tests re-compiled each time before use, unless binary compatibility is also a requirement of the validation tests. Compilation ensures that the software generation system (compiler tools, libraries, etc.) is adequately tested, as well as the program under test.

The first step involved with the UVS3 test suite is to build the **driver** program that controls execution of all tests. The **driver** program comes with several run-time options, or it can be executed in an automated fashion by using the **-S** option and **redirecting**[*] input from a file with the first test to start. A **testlist** file with test programs can be tailored to remove or add tests as desired. Approximately 1555 tests accompany the UVS3 suite, which is divided into three main areas:

1 libraries
2 commands
3 system calls

One nice feature that must be considered is to write a **scramble** function to reorder the tests in the **testlist** file in a random[†] fashion to eliminate any potential failures as a result of test execution order. Then, you must rerun the test suite several times and compare baseline results against expected golden results.

An important file with the Perennial Validation test suite is the include file **testhead.h** used for machine-specific or node-dependent information. It is included in the **scaffold** directory with the **another.c** file. The engineer must edit **testhead.h** to reflect your system's maximum number of open files, pipe buffer maximum and node name. Failures, by default, will be left in the **Results** directory for the **libsuite**, **syscallsuites** and **utilitysuite** sections. Files with the test name followed by a **.co** name extension are for standard error compilation failures and **.ex** file extensions are for standard error execution failures. The **.log** files con-

---

[*] File redirection from the UNIX shell allows input to be read from a file or output to be sent to a file, rather than the standard devices (i.e., keyboard for input and screen for output).

[†] Use of the UNIX **rand** or **srand** function will help to reorder the tests.

tain errors that are recognized by the test program, while the **report_file** contains results for all tests and can grow very large. It can be very useful to use the UNIX **grep** command to search the report file for failures and compare actual with expected failures, if any. This is also known as testing with an oracle, or rule set. The UNIX **sdiff** command can also be used to provide a side-by-side comparison between baseline execution results. Illustration 10.1 shows the command syntax:

```
#1> cd Results
#2> grep FAIL report.mymachine > my.fails
#3> grep FAIL report.baseline > bl.fails
#4> diff my.fails bl.fails
```

Illustration 10.1

It is critical that baseline results are clean prior to comparison and that the **testlist** file (list of tests to compile and execute) is identifiable to the baseline golden results.

The UNIX Validation Suite for System 5.3 is also available from Perennial, Inc. The next validation test suite is also provided by Perennial, however, for a more recent version of the UNIX operating system called System V Release 4 (SVR4).

10.5   UNIX Validation Suite 5.4 (UVS4)

The UNIX Validation Suite for System V Release 4 (SVR4) follows a similar structure to the other operating system validation suites (UVS3 and UVSE); however, the **testsources** directory is called **TestSources**. Also, tests have been categorized according to the appropriate section of the SVID, or System V Interface Definition specification. For example, the following sections can be found in the UVS4 rather than the traditional commands, system calls and library sections that, in previous versions were numbered sections 1, 2 and 3 respectively:

- AU_CMD
- BA_ENV
- KE_OS

This organization allows the tester to quickly reference the SVID based on a failure under a specific section. Tests that are not included in the SVID are located in the **NON_SVID** directory. The **NON_SVID** directory contains extensive coverage for POSIX.1 and XPG4 tests. Another portion of UVS4 (**Bsd-Sources**), provides test coverage of BSD 4.3 compatibility features, including sockets.

The UVS4 suite requires approximately 13mb of hard disk space. The engineer will also need to have UNIX superuser or root access, as with all the other Perennial validation suites. The time required to run the suite can vary from approximately a half-hour and beyond, depending upon system load and performance. UVS4 contains approximately 4,900 tests, all written in the C programming language. Tests can also be compiled and executed using the ANSI-C standard definition. If the compiler supports either strict or casual ANSI-C, consider building the tests first using the casual mode flag. If this is successful, consider using the strict flag for construction. The UVS4 validation test suite product is easily portable and provides a very easy interface to build and debug failures.

As with all Perennial tests, test programs are segmented into blocks for better debugging and maintenance. These blocks are also facilitated through the use of a provided library or object module that must be linked with all tests (**another.o** or **libd**). Test *coverage partitioning* can also be improved when large C test files are blocked into individual unit or assertion-based tests. Coverage partitioning allows only select areas of a program to be instrumented for structural test coverage. See the section on ViSTA in the test tools chapter for more details.

It may help to measure compilation and execution time for standards, language, validation and other test suites and compare these times against a baseline value. The time value, along with failure results, can provide a critical measurement for both reliability and stability. If, for example, all functional tests are able to complete, but require two times the length of time required for compilation, execution or both, this result must be considered a functional failure since it involves significant degradation of performance.

10.6   UNIX Validation Suite BSD (UVSE)

UVSE provides the same structure as UVS3 with the **testsources** directory containing library, system call and command tests. UVSE has approximately 2318 tests. It is suggested that the test or development engineer have at least 5mb of hard disk storage prior to installing and running UVSE.

The UNIX Validation Suite for 4.3, BSD[*], is also available from Perennial, Inc. with most of the same terms and conditions as other test suites. This product provides tests specifically for Berkeley-based UNIX operating systems. The test

---

[*]BSD stands for Berkeley Software Distribution.

suite has also been used successfully with the Mach operating system from CMU. Mach, however, provides multiprocessing features by way of threads[*], which aren't necessarily tested by UVSE. See the chapter on load and stress testing for more information on multiprocessor testing.

The UVSE validation test suite for BSD UNIX also contains exercisers for memory management and disk resources. The program **page1** creates a number of processes that each attempt to request a block of memory, write entries into an array and then verify the contents. A **page1** test causes many page faults. The **page2** program is similar to **page1**, with the exception of how data are written to an array. The **page1** or **page2** programs can be used when memory management changes have been made to the UNIX kernel and a basic sanity test of heavy memory references by programs is needed. **inode1** creates several directories and files and then verifies the directory and file tree structure. This program is an excellent test for the kernel hard disk device driver as it creates and removes several inodes within a short period of time. **inode2** is similar to **inode1**; however, it provides the engineer with many options. **inode3** is identical to **inode1**, however, all directory paths are sorted prior to verification.

It might be useful to purchase the UVSE test suite for testing BSD commands, library and system calls for UNIX SVR4 (System V Release 4). The SVR4 operating system provides several of the BSD operating system functions and the UVSE test suite can be very helpful in testing functions where SVVS and other suites already have coverage. Commands, for example, are not tested by SVVS or PCTS. The purpose of validation suites is to provide at least call tree or call graph test coverage tests for functionality. This means that the function exists and provides a reasonable, proper or sane return code upon execution. A good validation test suite must at least cover all functions, or provide 100% functional coverage as a minimum. From this, the depth of the test suite can be expanded using structural testing tools.

10.7   ARTUS Buster

UNIX Systems Labs (now Novell) has developed a fairly well-known secret, the Automated Regression Test for UNIX Systems (ARTUS). ARTUS is a proprietary product and is not commercially available. However, ARTUS or Buster, as it is also known, is provided by Novell for reference implementations. For example, the MIPS System V.4 reference implementation consisted of a SONY NEWS 3200 laptop computer and the Pyramid SVR4 implementation of the UNIX SVR4 release. For this release of SVR4 to be considered complete, Novell required

---

[*]Threads provide the ability for a single process (task) to be divided among various processing resources.

several ARTUS Buster tests to pass. Therefore, several tests were provided for networking, printing, the kernel, libraries and several commands not included in SWS.

10.8   X Window System Test Suite (xtest)

The X Window System test suite (**xtest**) is available from Unisoft Corporation. The purpose of **xtest** is to test the Xlib interface and the X protocol. The X server is responsible for handling all client requests. For example:

- **xterm**
- **xclock**
- Other widgets[*] or programs

Client testing is not provided specifically by the **xtest** test suite. The primary purpose of **xtest** is to provide validation testing of the X Server and Xlib library. **xtest** was designed to be portable to UNIX 4.2BSD, System 5.3 and 5.4 (or other POSIX-compliant systems). **xtest** uses the Testsuite Environment Toolkit (TET). See the chapter on test harnesses for more information on TET. The xtest suite requires approximately 25mb of disk space and approximately 50-80mb to build and execute tests. This will change based on the compilation environment (shared vs. static archives) and the machine architecture.

The **tetexec.cfg** configuration file contains flags and definitions that must be reviewed. For example, XT_DISPLAY must be set to a new value if the engineer is running the test suite on a display that is not local to the system running the suite. XT_ALT_SCREEN and XT_SCREEN_COUNT must be updated when the display has more than one screen. Most values are self-explanatory and well-documented. The **xtest** test suite has 246 tests covering X library testing of everything from **XAllPlanes** to the **XUniqueContext** library, as well as functional tests for the X server. A report file contains details for each test regarding the number of PASS, FAIL or in some cases, UNTESTED.

A window manager[†] cannot be running during the execution of many of the tests contained in **xtest**. For instance, Tom's Window Manager (**twm**) which is part of the standard MIT distribution or the Motif Window Manager (**mwm**) from OSF cannot be running during execution of the xtest suite. If run concurrently, the window manager may die or hang during the course of testing (this must not

---

[*] Widgets are another term for GUI-based program. The term comes from the X Window System widget library.

[†] The window manager is responsible for providing the look and feel of the Graphical User Interface (GUI).

occur, the test must just fail). The mouse buttons can be programmed using a run control, or specifically, **.mwmrc** file.

The **xtest** suite has also been used successfully for binary compatibility testing. In this case, when various X libraries are provided as dynamic shared objects, test cases are required to verify that the binaries that reference X Window System libraries are in fact portable between system platforms. Ideally, several sample client programs and tools must also be built based on the ABI standard for client testing, along with the server and library testing as provided by **xtest**. Some of many possible client programs may consist of:

- **xv**
- **xcmap**
- **xlogo**
- **xdpyinfo**

10.9   NFS Test Suite (connectathon)

Connectathon is an annual event sponsored by Sun Microsystems. The purpose of Connectathon is to allow vendors to test NFS interoperability or network communication between competitors. This is primarily a technical event that does not allow any one company to monopolize the show with press announcements. The primary purpose is to facilitate testing of the NFS protocol across any class of machines available, including:

- Apple Macintosh
- IBM PC and compatibles
- Workstations
- Mainframes
- All others

The connectathon programs are available using anonymous **ftp**. Four sections are available:

- BillBoard
- MAC-tests
- PCNFS-tests
- UNIX-tests

BillBoard provides a Remote Procedure Call (RPC) program to maintain information about test suite completion. RPCs allow communication in a heterogenous environment. BillBoard is most useful at events like Connectathon because it uses a client-server approach, where one host acts as the BB_SERVER and the other as a client. The **xbillboard** tests also act as if you are testing X Window System over NFS.

MAC-tests and **PCNFS-tests** are directories for testing NFS from PCs and Macintoshes to UNIX servers. The total space required for UNIX-tests is approximately 1-2mb. All tests are written in the C language and are classified as either basic, general or special.

Basic tests are provided for file and directory read, write, create, delete, etc. General tests consist of a small and large compile and **nroff** and **tbl** command execution on an NFS file system (specified by NFSTESTDIR).

Tests check for the following operations over a NFS mounted file system:

- **open/unlink** - open a file and remove an inode
- **open/chmod** - open a file and change the permission modes
- exclusive **create**
- negative **seek** - position in the file backwards
- **rename**

Other operations are also performed from the NFSTESTDIR file system. The test engineer will need to set the NFSTESTDIR environment variable for a remote NFS-mounted file system, then execute **runtests** to start testing. The engineer can specify the following options to run tests:

-a	"basic general"
-b	"basic"
-g	"general"
-s	"special"

The basic tests consist of tests for the following:

- File and directory creation test **created** 6 files, 6 directories, 2 levels deep
- File and directory removal test **removed** 6 files, 6 directories, 2 levels deep
- **lookups** across mount point 2 **getwd** and **stat** calls
- **setattr, getattr**, and **lookup** 20 **chmod**s and **stats** on 10 files
- **read** and **write** a 1048576-byte file 1 time, **read a** 1048576 byte file 1 time
- **readdir** 202 entries and **read** 200 files
- **link** and **rename** 20 times and perform **links** on 10 files
- **symlink** and **readlink** with 20 **symlinks** and **readlinks** on 10 files
- statfs

10.10 Conclusions

- Validation test suites provide quick test results for API and ABI specifications.
- It is always less expensive to purchase tests than to develop them from scratch.
- Use validation suites to supplement standards conformance test suites.
- The purpose of validation test suites are to validate (measure) product functionality with customer requirements.
- Careful analysis of test coverage using statement and decision coverage tools must be used to eliminate redundant validation tests that do not add specific value or identify new tests that need to be written.
- Validation test suites increase call tree and call graph coverage using test functions that currently do not have tests. These tests (touch tests) can be expanded further to improve statement, decision or branch and minimum path[*] coverage, if necessary, as defined by structural test metrics.
- Block coverage is the same as line coverage where each decision point in a program, function or module is analyzed.
- Decision or branch coverage will provide coverage information for each change in control flow. In other words, compound predicates (statements with multiple decision points) are evaluated, as is not true with block coverage. An example would be the following condition with two predicates:

  if ((A || B) && (C || D))

- Token[†] coverage collects information about even more details that are associated with a program.
- Validation tests need to be properly integrated with standards conformance tests using test harness technology such as TET.

---

[*] Minimum path coverage is the same as complete decision coverage. It does not take into account all path combinations.

[†] Tokens are commonly described as identifiers, keywords, constants, string literals, operators and other separators [KER88]

CHAPTER 11 ▶

Language Validation
Test Suites

Language validation test suites are similar to operating system standards conformance tests. However, they are specific to high-level language standards and not directly connected to operating system standards testing. As with standards conformance tests, validation tests in general are expensive to develop and always are less expensive to purchase than to design from scratch. This is especially true for high-level language products, as well as for system and application software. However, the price of these and other test programs or suites are not inexpensive. Language test suite licenses can start at $10,000 and increase very easily and quickly (development costs). This chapter will discuss the following:

- The ANSI/ISO C Validation Suite (ACVS)
- The FORTRAN Conformance Test Suite (FCVS)
- The ADA Validation Suite
- The Pascal Validation Suite (PVS)
- The Plum Hall Validation Suites
- The Validation Suite For C

11.1   Introduction to Language Validation Test Suites

As is the case with operating system standards, language standards are critical to both the application and end user, not just the language and system software provider. A standard baseline is the only way to properly measure and obtain a strong quality foundation upon which to build products and customer faith.

11.2   The ANSI/ISO C Validation Suite (ACVS)

The ANSI/ISO C Validation Suite is available from Perennial, Inc.

This test suite is use to validate a compiler's conformance to the ANSI/ISO C Standard (ISO/IEC 9899:1990) for X/Open XPG4 component branding. ACVS is used by the National Institute for Standards and Technology (NIST) for certifying compiler conformance to the Federal Information Processing Standard (FIPS) for the C language.

ACVS contains approximately 2,041 test programs with 9,314 test cases. ACVS provides comprehensive coverage of the ANSI/ISO C Standard. Tests are organized in the same manner as the standard to make it easier to track test coverage and to test isolated features of the C language. ACVS tests that strictly conforming code is properly handled by the compiler. This test suite also exercises the compiler's diagnostic capabilities and ability to handle implementation-defined and undefined-behavior features (positive and negative tests).

Source code configuration control and management for ACVS is directed and managed by NIST. Therefore, strict change control can be expected; however, this is not unreasonable, as the federal government is a primary customer of the ACVS.

11.3   The C Validation Suite (CVSA)

CVSA is a superset of ACVS from Perennial, Inc. It also provides coverage of older style K&R C language as well as tests for the newly adopted addendum to the ISO C Standard. The new addendum defines a new set of library functions for multi-byte character sets. Most C compilers still support the earlier K&R version of the C language and many are moving to include the new the multi-byte character libraries. CVSA consists of over 12,000 tests.

11.4   The C++ Validation Suite (C++VS)

C++VS provides comprehensive coverage of the evolving draft of the C++ language being developed by ISO. As with other Perennial test suites, the structure of C++VS parallels the ISO draft, making it more easy to test specific features of the language, and debug isolated portions of a compiler. C++VS contains over 30,000 tests, and requires more than 20 Mb of hard disk space.

11.5   FORTRAN Conformance Validation Suite (FCVS)

The FORTRAN Conformance Validation Suite is available from the National Technical Institute of Standards (NTIS). It has approximately 70 FORTRAN files for FORTRAN 77 testing, accompanied by five data files.

You might purchase FCVS or any other language validation suite for a number of reasons, such as:

- Development of an F77 (FORTRAN 1977) compiler
- Port of existing compiler technology to a new architecture
- Re-test or acceptance test prior to system acquisition
- Compiler change benchmarking and regression testing

FCVS contains 28 tests and requires approximately 3mb of disk space to install. A FORTRAN 77 compiler is required to build and execute all tests. Approximately one half hour is required to execute all FCVS tests. The build and execution time will vary based on system configuration and processor performance.

Some of the test assertions available with FCVS are listed below:

- Integer variable
- Integer declare variable
- Integer array
- Implicit integer array
- Do initialize integer array
- Real variable
- Extended precision real
- Declared real array
- Real array - name only
- Equivalenced real array
- Real variable - equivalenced integer
- Double precision array
- Dimension double precision array

- Complex variable
- Complex array
- Complex array - equivalence
- Logical variable
- Logical array - equivalence

FCVS, as provided by NIST, does not contain a standard harness, scaffold or driver to compile and execute tests. A shell and an **awk** script are provided as an example of how FCVS tests can be compiled and executed in Appendix C. You are free to use the following shell script with the understanding that this program cannot be sold for profit. Also, the author makes no warranties or guarantees regarding the fitness for use of the program.

The Test suite Environment Toolkit (TET) harness may also be used as a master driver for this script.

11.6   ADA Validation Suites

ADA test suites are also available from NTIS. The version as of this writing is 1.1 for the following:

ADA (Tape/Backup) ADA212551
ADA (Tape/Tar) ADA212437
ADA (Tape ANSI STD) ADA212548
ADA (Disk - MS/DOS) ADA212549

ADA, COBOL and FORTRAN are all included in the Validated Processor List (VPL) are also available from NTIS.

11.7   Pascal Validation Suite (PVS)

The Pascal Validation Suite (PVS) is available from the British Standards Institution (BSI). PVS provides testing of Pascal processors to determine if they conform to federal standards required by Federal Information Resources Management Regulation (FIRMR) 201-8.109.

The PVS contains approximately 870 tests and requires approximately 3.5mb for installation and execution. A Pascal compiler is required for construction and execution of the test suite. No automated test scaffold or driver is available to build and execute the programs. Therefore, it is suggested that a script be built to change directories to each of the following test categories and build and execute each test each every time the PVS test suite is used. It is always better to re-compile test programs prior to execution on new hardware and software systems.

conform - Conformance tests to Pascal standard
deviance - Deviance tests (e.g., nil is a word symbol not identified)
error - Error handling tests (exception conditions)
exten - Extension tests (are extensions supported?)
impdef - Implementation-defined characteristics supported
impdefb - Implementation-defined behavior
impdep - Implementation-dependent tests
level 1 - Level 1 implementation-defined behavior tests
ppg - Pascal Program Generator (not part of validation suite)

The following run shell script in Illustration 11.1 can be used to compile and execute tests for the PVS with the same restrictions as the previous program (FCVS):

```
#!/bin/sh
#PASBIN=pc.ansi      #Define compiler!
#{PASCOM=pc}
rm -f result
touch result
for i do
 ln src/$i ./current.p
 echo ---- Compiling $i ....... >> PVS.'date'
 rm -rf a.out
 rm -rf curent.o
 ${PASCOM} -std current.p >>PVS.'date' 2>&1
 if [ $? != 0 ]
 then
 echo Compilation failed >> result
 else
 echo ------ Excuting $i -------- >> PVS.'date'
 result
 a.out > Results/$i.out
 cat Results/$i.out >> result 2>&1
 echo ------- $i Over ---------- >> PVS.'date'
 fi
done
```

Illustration 11.1

The above script assumes that a list of all Pascal programs to be compiled and executed will be provided as input for the variable i. The programs also reside in the **src** subdirectory. This can be accomplished by redirecting input from a file containing the names of all files for testing.

11.8   Plum Hall Validation Test Suites

Thomas Plum is well-known for his C and C++ language validation suites. Both suites are exhaustive test suites for system and application vendor testing. Plum Hall can be reached at the address located in Appendix D.

Suite++ is the Plum Hall validation suite for the C++ language. This provides compiler testing and bug identification, as well as tracking and evolving requirements of the ANSI-C++ draft standard. Suite++ has been released in two volumes. Volume 1 contains draft sections 2 through 6 of the ANSI-C++ standard and over 190 test cases. Subsequent sections include up to a maximum of 1200 test cases.

11.9   Validation Suite For C

The validation suite for C also has the same two primary purposes as the C++ suite:

1 Compiler testing and defect detection
2 Checking conformance to the ANSI-C standard
3 The C Validation Suite (CVS) provides over 42,000 lines of C source tests with many new sections that have already been added. This suite is an assertion based test suite for validating the proper semantics and syntax of the C compiler to the ANSI standard. The test suite contains the following main sections:

- CONFORM - to test conformance to the C language standard. Three levels are available: K&R (C programming language by Kernighan and Ritchie), Version 7 UNIX and the ANSI standard.
- EXIN - the executive interpreter. When this section is built and it passes a set of tests, it is then used as a basic tool in subsequent sections of the test suite.
- COVER - provides self-checking C programs using the EXIN language processor. It covers all operators and data types.
- LIMITS - compile time limits tests are provided using EXIN scripts; for example, how many **include** files can be provided in a C source file.
- EGEN - tests expression generation for self-checking expression of various complexities.
- STRESS - provides testing of various legal expressions. These can be very complex for stress testing or random under the control of an expression template.

11.10 RoadTest C and C++ Compiler Test Suites

The RoadTest C and C++ compiler test suites include large sets of small individualized compiler test case files, together with complete source code (in C) for a fully automated test driver program. This driver will repeatedly invoke a compiler, interpreter or other similar language processing tool to process each of the individual test cases in the suite(s). RoadTest is provided for both UNIX and DOS platforms. The RoadTest C compiler test suite includes over 400,000 lines of automatically generated test cases. Customized C and C++ compiler test suites that have been automatically generated using TGGS are also available from RG Consulting. See the section on TGGS in the test tools chapter of this book for more details.

11.11 Conclusions

- Language validation suites are critical to the testing environments for either system, application, or language software vendors.
- Many other language validation suites are available, other than those listed in this chapter. The reader is encouraged to research other available technologies. For example, Human Computing Resources of Canada (now owned by the Santa Cruz Operation (SCO)) is another popular vendor that provides C language test suites. UNIX Systems Labs has a C Compiler Suite (**ccs**).
- As is always the case, the best language test suite is the customer's program that must be compiled and executed ahead of the competition.
- The National Institute of Standards and Technology provides a Validated Processor List (VPL), including a Government Open Systems Interface Protocol (GOSIP) registry. This includes programming languages, as well as database language **sql** software and hardware vendors that have successfully completed standards compliance testing for a specific product. A processor is removed from the VPL if one or more of the following conditions are true:

  - The processor is not officially tested within twelve calendar months of the last certification.
  - Testing indicates that the processor contains errors identified during a previous validation.

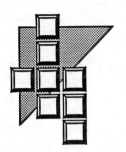

## CHAPTER 12

Stress Tests

Stress tests are probably the least understood among the various test technologies available today. Where do they fit into the software development process? Hardware developers have had the assistance of organizations such as Underwriters Laboratories for years. These individuals could be counted on to saw, burn, drop, hammer, smash, crash, etc. the product under test. Unfortunately, the same has not been available for software.[*] Diabolical thinkers are usually the best individuals to develop and execute stress tests. Unfortunately, most individuals are not made this way. This may be due to the fact that stress and load testing are often *ad hoc* processes or conducted using wild guesses by software and hardware engineers and managers. This chapter will cover some of the many programs available for this mysterious art. See the chapter on load and stress testing for approaches and strategies for stress tests that are covered in this chapter. The following will be discussed in this chapter:

- The X server stress test (**xcrash**)
- Tape and floppy stress tests
- The disk stress test (disk)
- The paranoia stress test
- The UNIX File System stress test suites

---

[*]Some labs have been established for compatibility testing, especially since the advent of the PC clone. However, the author is dealing exclusively with stress testing in this chapter.

12.1   Introduction to Stress Tests

A good stress test will always provide an interface that allows the amount of stress or work to be performed to be tailored or tuned. Building ensembles of stress tests in an organized fashion can help to provide better maintenance and debugging analysis.

It must be noted that test tools unfortunately are often protected and hidden inside engineering departments and rarely are licensed or distributed to the general public. Think about what kind of software might be available today if the best stress tests were available from the best software vendors today. Unfortunately, test programs often provide design information that could give a competitive advantage and therefore often must remain secret. Well, that is usually the official excuse given—or is it that most companies are simply ashamed of their stress tests? I believe that both are true.

Often times engineers will write a function, but will simply forget to perform any type of stress testing using boundary conditions. The failures that result can often be very serious and cause fatal errors such as core dumps, process and system crashes or hangs to occur. If an automated stressor program is available that will provide boundary conditions such as wrong data type, negative and positive value, and others, this program can always be run after compilation, during unit test, to ensure that exception handlers have been written prior to system or integration testing. This can help reduce the amount of time and money required to later isolate and contain problems when more functions and modules are added.

The first stress test tool to be discussed is for the X server. It has been proven to be fairly successful in crashing many implementations of the X Window System.

12.2   X Window Server Stress Test (xcrash)

The **xcrash** program is an X server stress test written by Eric Swildens. **xcrash** has several flags available, with **-nasty** being the worst or most difficult to successfully complete. This stress test program causes color graphics primitives to be drawn way off the screen and results in heavy system swapping as a result of trying to properly clip graphics primitives. The **xcrash** stress test requires approximately 100k of disk and comes with an **imake** file that creates a **Makefile** after execution of the command **xmkmf**.

The **xcrash** stress test is a public domain* program and can be freely used as long as it is not sold for profit as requested by the author. Also, all copyright information must remain intact. If we only had more programs like **xcrash**...

---

*This means that access can usually be obtained over the Internet using anonymous **ftp** without payment to the author. It has been seen on ftp.x.org.

The intent of **xcrash** is to identify memory leaks[*] and crashes in X servers. One test example involves the drawing of dashed lines. The program draws randomized primitives in an **xterm** window looking for problems. The X server is one of the more complex and sophisticated pieces of software available today on UNIX systems. The services provided by the X server are similar to the UNIX kernel. However, instead of process requests to the kernel, client requests are made to the X server using BSD sockets for Inter-Process Communication (IPC). Several companies, such as Pure Software, have found many memory management problems with sophisticated software, such as the X server. By definition, as code size increases, complexity and memory management issues are bound to occur. (Purify from Pure Software will be discussed in the chapter on test tools.)

Included with the **xcrash** stress test is **xcrashmon** which will save all scripts for the reproduction of a server crash. The **xcrashmon** program will execute the UNIX **dbx** command and use the **where** directive to help identify the location of a crash. The engineer or tester must be warned that modifications will usually be needed based on machine architecture and the operating system's version and type. The **dbx** debugger **where** command provides a back trace listing for all subroutine functions in the order of execution. This, in turn allows the engineer to better determine where the failure occurred.

Providing debugging facilities with stress tests is very valuable because the intent of the test is to actually break something (that is a successful stress test). The following command will generate 10,000 to 20,000 random X primitive draw calls to the X server when typed at the shell prompt:

%1> **xcrash -tests 10000**

If the user causes a crash as a result of this test, simply execute the following at the shell prompt:

%2> **xcrash -v -tests 10 > out1**
(**out1** contains a script to play back 10 tests)

Three potential portability problems with **xcrash** as experienced by the author (at the time of this writing) are:

- The math library functions **srandom** or **random** are sometimes only known as **srand** or **rand** (SVR4)
- The **-seed** command line option is requested even if the **time** function is used for randomization
- The code is not ANSI-C compliant

The next program provides stress testing of tape and floppy devices.

---

[*]This is when memory is allocated by a program using the **malloc** call, for example. However, the allocated memory is never returned using the **free** library call.

12.3   Stress Tests (Tape/Floppy)

floppy.c is a C program from the author that provides stress testing as an exerciser for floppy devices and device drivers. The program can be easily modified for tape devices, and other storage device drivers as well. The function of a tape and floppy test is to open different density devices (e.g., QIC[*] 120, 24, and low/high density floppy formats) and then write and read to each device. Blocking factors, record sizes and data patterns are all alternated based on variable array assignments. For example, data patterns could consist of 0x00000000, 0x01010101, 0xFFFFFFFF, etc. Floppy and tape writes using blocking factors, record sizes and data patterns can also be randomized.

The stress test program is best suited for sequential access devices; however, it can be adapted for random access devices as well (add **lseek** function to skip blocks). The reader is free to use the program contained in Appendix A, however, it must not be sold for profit and must include the copyright information as provided. Also, the author makes no guarantees as to the fitness of use of the program exerciser. It is provided as a template from which to build standard reusable (modular) exercisers and stress tests. Many enhancements are possible with the program. For example, it may be desirable to add the ability to pass a device name as an argument if the default device is not appropriate. A rewind function may be written for tape devices that would simply close the device and thereby cause a rewind operation to occur.

A partial sample of output from the **floppy.c** program is included for reference in Illustration 12.1 (when the **-v** option is used):

```
read 0x55555555 rec=1024 fz=2
read 0x55555555 rec=1024 fz=3
write 0x55555555 rec=2048 fz=0
write 0x55555555 rec=2048 fz=1
read 0x55555555 rec=2048 fz=0
read 0x55555555 rec=2048 fz=1
write 0x55555555 rec=2048 fz=0
write 0x55555555 rec=2048 fz=1
write 0x55555555 rec=2048 fz=21
```

Illustration 12.1

Tape and floppy exercisers may be integrated with other device exercisers for ElectoMagnetic Interface (EMI) testing that must be performed on all computer systems prior to FCC certification. In many cases, simple shell scripts can

---

[*] QIC stands for Quarter Inch Cartridge tape devices and media.

be developed using various UNIX commands such as **dd**, **cat** and **cp** to keep devices active for EMI testing. Alternatively, the above floppy exerciser can be modified for non-storage devices such as displays, sound, ethernet, etc. Other devices for which exercisers must often be developed include:

- CD-ROM
- Floppy
- Screen
- Tape
- Disk
- Serial
- Midi
- Sound
- Ethernet
- Printer
- Audio

12.4   Disk Stress Test (disk)

The **disktest** program is public domain software that is available without either a license or fee. This program is excellent for testing either a new or modified device driver or a new hard disk device. You can write, read and compare results using various parameters (block size, pattern, etc.).

Other stress tests can be created for a hard disk device and its drivers. For example, you can create a simple C program to open a file, write large buffers inside a loop as quickly as possible and then close the file. Other test cases can include the variation of parameters similar to the tape/floppy exercisers.

More information on **disktest** is provided in the chapter on benchmarks. **disktest** can be used either for reliability testing or performance comparisons.

12.5   paranoia

paranoia is a public domain program available without license or fee requirements. This program was originally written in Pascal by B.A. Wichmann on Jan 18, 1985. Since then it has been converted to C, however, the engineer will notice that the source code looks very much like it was first written in Pascal and converted to C.

The purpose of **paranoia** is to provide intensive floating point computation. The source code is very portable and requires just a C compiler and math library.

paranoia is an interactive test; however, it is possible to redirect input from a disk file for continuous floating point testing. **paranoia** tests for over/underflow or division by zero errors. Also, it tests the following (at the time of this writing):

- Radix = 1, 2, 4, 8, 10, 16, 100, 256...
- Precision = number of significant digits carried
- U2 = Radix/Radix^Precision = One Ulp
  (OneUlpnit in the Last Place) of 1.000xxx
- U1 = 1/Radix^Precision = One Ulp of numbers a little less than 1.0
- Adequacy of guard digits for multiply, divide and subtract
- Whether arithmetic is chopped, correctly rounded, or something else for multiply, divide, addition/subtraction and square root
- Whether a Sticky Bit is used correctly for rounding
- UnderflowThreshold = an underflow threshold
- E0 and PseudoZero tell whether underflow is abrupt, gradual or fuzzy
- V = an overflow threshold, roughly
- V0 tells, roughly, whether Infinity is represented
- Comparisons are checked for consistency with subtraction and for contamination with pseudo-zeros
- Sqrt is tested, Y^X is not tested
- Extra-precise sub-expressions are revealed but NOT YET tested
- Decimal-Binary conversion is NOT YET tested for accuracy

paranoia.c is approximately 57k and takes only a few minutes to compile and execute.

12.6   UNIX File System Stress Suites

Many possibilities exist for stress testing the UNIX file system. Because there are so many different file systems now available, this makes the task even more important and yet complex. Here are just a few of many possible tests that could comprise a good file system stress test suite:

- **Direct blocks:** contain the numbers of disk blocks that contain real data [BAC86]. Simple test to read, write and check data to all direct blocks.
- **Indirect blocks:** refers to a block that contains a list of direct block numbers (block of pointers) [BAC86]*. Start with same test as direct block, then test first and last second and third indirect blocks.

---

*This is for single indirect, not double or triple indirect. Double indirect contains a list of indirect block numbers and triple indirect contains a list of double indirect block numbers.

- **File fragments testing** can best be described as sprinkling many small files throughout the UNIX file system and then attempting to create one or several large contiguous files.
- **File system testing** activities that create and remove large file and directory trees are excellent file system stress tests. See Perennial validation test suite section.
- **Inodes testing** that creates and deletes empty files and exhausts the number of allocated inodes is one good stress test of the UNIX file system.
- **Pipes testing** using the shell pipe mechanism for sending data using subshells and multiple commands is also a good stress test of the file system.

12.7 Conclusions

- A variety of stress tests must be considered for comprehensive stress testing.
- Stress tests are in great demand, unfortunately most companies do not release this type of software because of potential loss in competitive advantage. More importantly, it is believed that the quality, reliability and maintainability of many of these tests are very poor.
- Stress and load test technology cannot continue to be treated as disposable software. Leverage this work in as many areas as possible.
- Successful hardware and software companies must consider stress and load, as well as other related tests, a critical component in the systematic machinery required to produce quality software.
- Test technology must be at least equal if not of higher quality than the software that is under test. For this to occur, system and software companies must make an investment and expect that this software will be provided on *contribution* tapes along with fully supported products for a minimal charge.
- Validation of bug fixes, as well as performance improvements, can be gained through the use of contribution-packaged test software.
- Identifying and combining the *worst* of customer problems together into a single stress test system can be considered of great value.
- Stress and load tests can also become by-products for customer benchmarks, life-test and manufacturing acceptance testing, to name just a few of many possibilities.

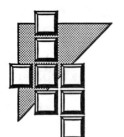 # Benchmarks

Many books have been written on the subject of benchmarking [DOW93], [GRA87]. Few, however, have presented available programs from a test validation and verification viewpoint. This chapter discusses what programs are available and how they may be used as part of an overall verification and validation system and software test system. Benchmarks are often only executed during the last stage of system test. This has often times resulted in products that were delivered late due to re-design or suffered from lack of acceptance by the market. In either case, if performance requirements had been included sooner in the product life-cycle (just as quality requirements must be) these and other problems could have been eliminated. Benchmarking performance and testing software both have one thing in common—measurement. In order for measurement to be useful, both the consumer and supplier must agree on the what, when, where and how (i.e., requirements). Unfortunately, the computer industry is often far to competitive to realize this simple fact. Benchmarking and testing computer software is an important science that must be performed adequately (successfully) to improve the process and product architectures that are developed and used. This chapter will discuss:

- Performance engineering
- Benchmarks for disk input and output testing
- Benchmarks for CPU and floating point processors
- Benchmarks for system testing (networking, graphics, etc.)
- Several commercial and public domain benchmark programs

13.1   Introduction to Benchmarking

Benchmarks can be a valuable technology when used together with either functional-based or reliability-based testing. Regression testing must take into account both functional and reliability tests. For example, with UNIX, this can include disk, tape, memory, CPU, floating point or other devices. It can also include software utilities, such as compilers, linkers, assemblers, searching and sorting, security, installation, etc.

Slow software often is considered a functional failure. There are several potential reasons for slow software:

- Dead code (either not executed, or executed but results not used)
- Needless re-computation
- Unnecessary requests (operating system, window manager, etc.)
- Synchronization delays (parent/child IPC)

Many other reasons are to blame for software slowness. In the chapter on test tools some products are described that isolate performance bottlenecks. The general cycle for performance improvement is contained in Illustration 13.1.

Several of the programs described in this chapter are public domain (**comp.benchmarks** newsgroup) and therefore available for use free of charge. However, the user is responsible for following the instructions regarding copyright and other infringements. Most all of the benchmarks presented were written in the C programming language and were designed for benchmark comparisons of UNIX operating systems and computer hardware. This includes everything from

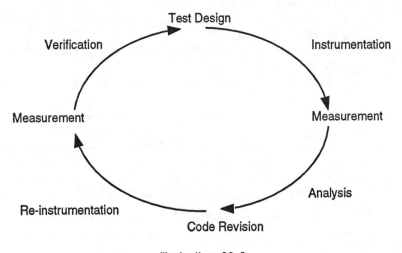

Illustration 13.1

notebook to super computer systems. Many serious benchmarks are also written in FORTRAN (expensive computing resources require serious benchmark tests).

13.2 Performance Engineering

There are four common problems that can contribute to slow software. These four problems include:

- Unused computation (e.g., code that has been replaced, but the old code has not been removed)
- Repetitive computation (e.g., re-executing code to obtain results when the previous results could have been reused, if they were saved)
- Excessive operating system requests (e.g., using **system** function in a shell or **perl** script, when the request can be satisfied using a standard library function). (This forces an unnecessary context switch.)
- Waiting for the completion of a service request (e.g., functions that block further processing after an input or output request). This is often called synchronous vs. asynchronous input and output.

Five common approaches are used to eliminate performance bottlenecks:

- Do not perform the operation (e.g., unnecessary clean-up functions to free data structures when it really is not necessary).
- Perform the operation with less frequency (e.g., reduce the number of requests by first checking if the request must be performed; trying to **open** a file that does not exist).
- Perform the function at a later time (e.g., many unnecessary requests at the beginning of the program).
- Perform the function or operation and save the results so it does not have to be performed again.
- Try to determine a less costly way of performing the same function.

The purpose of performance engineering and code profiling is to understand and identify performance bottlenecks by better understanding the source code under evaluation. This must start by first anticipating potential performance bottlenecks. Next focus on the most critical segments of code that will yield the greatest ROI. Use the model shown in Illustration 13.1 to improve product performance. Quantify is one tool from Pure Software, Inc. that can be used to help instrument and analyze performance bottlenecks.

13.3   AIM Technology

AIM Technology has provided licensed UNIX benchmarks for many years. AIM is well known for the AIM Performance Report or APR service that provides performance information for many UNIX platforms. Many of the AIM benchmarks were a result of the work performed by Gene Dronek. The AIM Suite II is a single-user UNIX benchmark with approximately 41 tests to measure disk, memory, floating point, library/system calls and IPC. Suite II is completely written in C and takes approximately one half-hour to complete. Execution time will vary depending upon system configuration, the processor, operating system and many other factors. It is suggested that the performance and test engineer always average results over several runs, or better yet, compute the *geometric mean.*[*] It is also recommended that the engineer execute this test on a system with a freshly installed operating system that has just been booted to single user mode.

AIM Suite II is a good regression test for kernel changes to verify basic functions that have not degraded by producing, for example, process forks and file locking tests. Because the suite doesn't consume a great deal of time during execution, results can be obtained quickly.

The system call tests in Illustration 13.2 are available with **AIM Suite II** and are measured in both thousands of calls per second or micro/nano seconds per call:.

---

getpid (get process identification)
sbrk (increment more bytes to program data space)
creat-close (how many creat/close operations)
umask (set the process file creation mask)
process forks (how fast can you create a child process)
pipe copy (how fast can data be moved using a pipe)
add LONG, SHORT, FLOAT, DOUBLE (math ops)
array ref short, long (vector operations)
call funct (call functions with mult arguments - int)
ram read (short, long, char arguments)
ram write (short, long, char arguments)
ram copy (short, long, char arguments)
multiply (short, long, float, double arguments)
divide short, long, float, double arguments)
signal (signal operations)
cached disk access
direct disk access

Illustration 13.2

---

[*] The Nth root of the sum of the tests, where N = the number of tests.

13.4   AIM Suite III

AIM Suite III, also from AIM Technologies, is a multi-user benchmark consisting of approximately 31 tests than can be configured to a specific job mix. The following types of tests that are conducted include:

- **tty** - terminal devices
- **tape** - tape devices
- **lp** - line printer devices
- **vm**- virtual memory
- **ram** - random access memory
- **float** - floating point arithmetic
- **pipe** - first in-first out (e.g., output of command becomes input to another command)
- **logic** - CPU instructions
- **disk**
- integer math

Suite III is very similar to **Suite II**, except that each job is *cloned* or propagated to simulate a unique user. For example, certain UNIX commands are selected as a job mix for either a scientific or business user. It is also recommended that **Suite III** be executed in single user mode as is the case with **Suite II**. **Suite III** comes with an exerciser called **vmdrvr** that allocates as much memory as possible without regard for locality of reference. This means that as many pages of memory are touched as possible in a random order to fragment the system memory cache as much as possible.[*]

To execute the benchmark, type the following at the UNIX shell prompt:

%1> **multiuser**

The engineer will then be requested to enter the following information:

- Total number of test iterations
- Starting and ending iterations
- Increment

For instance, the performance and test engineer could start a simulation of 80 users, starting with 10 users in increments of 10, a total of 8 times. To reduce the granularity of adding more users, one can specify a smaller increment, for example 5 or 2. It is also possible to specify a job mix that does not test the following devices to reduce the amount of testing performed:

- tty - terminal device
- tape
- printer

---

[*]In a memory management architecture based on *pages*, the memory management hardware divides physical memory into a set of equal-sized blocks called page [BAC86].

Virtual memory can also be tested. The number of **ram,** floating point, pipe logic, disk and math operations per simulated user can be configured as part of a standard job mix. The example shown in Illustration 13.3 is a typical job mix with the expected results for ten to seventy users:

```
:mysystem TTY OFF, TAPE OFF, LP OFF< VM ON
20 ram 10 float 10 pipe 20 logic 20 disk 20 math

10 512 real 0.1133 jobs/sec/user
20 9984 real 0.00589 jobs/sec/user
30 11474 real 0.03393 jobs/sec/user
40 1969 real 0.0295 jobs/sec/user
500 2464 real 002235 jobs/sec/user
60 2970 real 0.0195 jobs/sec/user
70 3380 real 0.01172 jobs/sec/user

As you can see as the number of users increases
so does the real time required for completion.
The number of jobs that can be completed per
user per second shrinks as well.
```

Illustration 13.3

13.5   AIM Suite V

AIM Suite V is a multi-tasking benchmark consisting of 40 tests for the following types of software application environments:

- Accounting
- Scientific
- Software development
- Spreadsheet
- Database
- Word processing

The **AIM Suite V** benchmark requires only the system name and the total number of processes/users to execute. **Suite V** also consumes only a small amount of disk space after installation. Execution time will vary based on system configuration, processor architecture and the number of tasks to simulate. To build the benchmark, type the following command from the shell prompt.

   %1> **make clean; make**

   The performance and test engineer will probably have to make some minor modifications to the file **st5report** to reflect the system environment under test. The engineer may experience some problems with **Suite V** in the task switching code. Please contact AIM Technologies for more information.[*] This benchmark has been ported and executed on the IBM OS/2 operating system. As is the case with **Suite III**, this Suite can provide the engineer with various job mix options to characterize and test different environments. The following user types can be configured, as provided in Illustration 13.4.

```
memory usage
disk usage
floating point
word processing memory, disk and floating point
scientific processing memory, disk and floating point
database processing memory, disk and floating point

Results will provide data for each user starting
from 1 to however many users were requested.
The amount of real and CPUtime consumed by each
user as well as how many tests were completed
per second, is also provided.

1 49.1140 control 2.604 tests/sec 109.8 real 109.2 cpu
2 50.450 control 2.537 tests/sec 121.7 real 120.9 cpu
3 51.550 control 2.485 tests/sec 53.6 real 52.5 cpu
4 54.030 control 2.369 tests/sec 55.4 real 54.8 cpu
5 53.940 control 2.373 tests/sec 61.3 real 60.7 cpu

<continued to the total number of requested users>
```

Illustration 13.4

---

[*]The code responsible for scheduling execution.

13.6   AIM Milestone

Milestone is another multi-user benchmark that results in an MPH or Milestone Per Hour rating. It is composed mainly of shell scripts to simulate the following:

- Administrative assistant
- Spreadsheet user
- Database user
- Manager
- Scientist
- Software engineer
- Text processing

The sample script contained in Illustration 13.5 can be used to start the benchmark:

```
#!/bin/sh
PATH=:$PATH:/usr/ccs/bin #may need to change
export PATH
cd milestone #suggest creating subdirectory
CLEANUP
echo y | SETUP
echo > input
uname -n >>input
echo 0 >> input
./RUN.milestone < input | tee -a milestone.$$
rm input
echo 'uname -s'""'uname -v'>input
echo 'uname -p'>>input
echo 'uname -m' >> input
MEM='prtconf | grep "Memory size"| awk '{print $3}''
#if you don't have SVR4 use dd if=/dev/mem
echo $DISK "mb" >> input
echo""">>input
echo""">>input
ANALYZE 'uname -n' <input
cp results/report.'uname -n' < input
tail -25 m.out | awk '{print NR,$1,$2,$3,$4,$5,$6, \
$7,$8}' > miilestone.out
rm m.out
cp milestone.out results/report.'uname -n'.'date \
+%m%d'
cd ..
```

Illustration 13.5

The following information is available as output from the Milestone benchmark:

- System configuration data (mostly from **prtconf** (UNIX SVR4 command)
- Benchmark data (average of milestones)
- Benchmark data (details for each user)

The number of miles is the number of simulated user loads. One mile is functionally equivalent to one user load. The load average signifies how well the system handles multiprocessing and input/output device contention. This measurement indicates the expected delay time when more that one user is waiting for a resource. This is usually one of the most critical areas to test from both a functional standpoint, as well as from a performance perspective. The elapsed time for the first milestone indicates the general system speed and can be useful in determining system degradation during regression and system testing.

13.7   LADDIS - NFS Benchmark (SPEC)

LADDIS originated from Legato, Amdahl, Data General, Digital, Intel and Sun Microsystems. The **PRE-LADDIS** version was available to licensed beta sites prior to distribution by the System Performance Evaluation Cooperative (SPEC) (see information below). To build the benchmark, type the following at the UNIX shell prompt:

%1> **make install**

To run the benchmark, execute the shell script by typing the following at the UNIX shell prompt:

%2> **prelad_mgr**

This is a multi-client benchmark to test multiple clients executing the same benchmark. The engineer can continue to increment the load on a server by adding clients.

The following variables are configured with the **PRE-LADDIS** benchmark:

- Number of NFS calls per second to generate on each client
- Number of sub-processes to generate the NFS call
- Number of seconds to generate load
- Number of seconds to warm up

- Mount points of NFS-mounted file systems used in the test
- The NFS call distribution file name; the Prime-Client will propagate a copy to all other clients in the test
- Percent of writes that append rather than overwrite the number of KB in a block, up to 8 KB
- Block transfer sizes file name; The Prime-Client will propagate a copy to all other clients in the test
- Number of directories to use for directory operations
- Number of files to use for read and write operations
- Number of symbolic links to use for **symlink** operations
- Raw data points displayed at end (option)

Three levels are required to execute **prelad**:

1 (batch)
2 (verbose)
3 (interactive)

The engineer will also need to specify an NFS-mounted file system to successfully complete and conduct testing. This benchmark will check NFS operations on specified file systems. It creates and changes directories and executes the following operations in a similar, but more advanced method than Connectathon:

- Mounts file system
- Executes the null operation
- Creates regular files
- Creates directories
- Creates hard links
- Creates symbolic links
- Checks content of each symbolic link
- Performs **fsstat** on all files/directories/links/symbolic links, and checks attributes.
- Execute lookup, **getattrs** and **setattrs** for each created file, directory, link and symbolic links and checks attributes
- Writes blocks and checks against original attributes
- Reads and compares against block checksum and check file attributes
- Executes sequence of **readdir** operations on directories in previously created files/directories/links/symbolic links and verifies
- Renames directories
- Removes and deletes files, links and symbolic links; deletion, makes sure directory entry is removed
- **rmdir**s to delete each directory and verifies that each directory is missing

It is important to note that **SFS 1.0** is a server-oriented networking benchmark for UNIX systems. Therefore, client side activity is not considered directly during performance and functional test analysis. In the future, it is hoped that a client side-specific test may be combined with **SFS. SPEC SFS 1.0** (previously known as **LADDIS**). **PRE-LADDIS** requires approximately 2.7mb of disk space for installation.

13.8   SPEC

The System Performance Evaluation Cooperative (**SPEC**) was founded in the fall of 1988 as a non-profit organization. Its first public unveiling was at Uniforum 1989 with the first product release ten months later. Release 1.2 was available 15 months later. SPEC92 replaced SPEC89 with more tests and the removal of **matrix300. matrix300** was often the cause of inflated **SPEC** numbers, especially for RISC processors.[*] This is mainly because super-pipeline RISC processors could take a 300 by 300 matrix multiply operation and stage the operation, thus defeating the original purpose of the benchmark test. A similar analogy to **matrix300** was when one microprocessor company took one of the major operations of the **dhrystone** benchmark and created a special processor instruction specifically for the benchmark.

Membership in SPEC is available for a one-time and annual fee. At the time of this writing, 21 companies were members. You can purchase **SPEC89**, **SPEC92** or **SDM** without membership. Membership, however, gives you voting and early access to the benchmarks under evaluation prior to release to the general public, if approved by SPEC members.

SPEC89 contains ten tests for floating point and integer CPU computation. It has been ported to VMS and other operating systems and does not require an ANSI-C compiler; however, FORTRAN and C compilers are required to build each test. The tester must make sure not to provide any results without carefully reviewing all documentation. A single **SPEC mark** (the 10th root of the product of the **SPEC** ratios) must no longer be used; instead, **SPECfp** and **SPECint** values must be computed for floating point and integer type tests, respectively. The **SPECratio** is the quotient derived by dividing **SPEC** reference time (DEC VAX 780) by system run-time.

This rule must be applied to testing in general. Often times a single score or value may not communicate the message very well because one single component test can upset every other test. For example, integer and floating point tests are separated to help provide a more clear message regarding results reporting. The same method can be used for functional testing.

---

[*]The term SPECmark was previously used to combine the SPECint and SPECfp values. This has now been abolished and only SPECint and SPECfp numbers are provided.

SPEC89 SPECint is the geometric mean of the following tests:

- **008.espresso**
- **022.li**
- **023.eqntott**

SPECfp is the geometric mean of the following tests:

- **013.spice2g6**
- **015.doduc**
- **020.nasa7**
- **030-matrix300**
- **042.fpppp**
- **047.tomcatv**

13.9   SPEC (SDM)

The SPEC Software Development Multi-tasking (**SDM**) is a multi-user benchmark based on Software Development Environment Tests (**SDET**) from Steven Gaede, and **KENBUS** from Ken McDonell's Benchmark UNIX Systems (**MUSBUS** Monash University Benchmark UNIX Systems 5.2). **SDM** tests CPU, memory, disk input/output and operating system services (system calls). It also simulates software development environments. Each **SDET** script executes about 150 commands, including:

- **spell** - spelling checker
- **nroff** - text formatter for display and line printer devices
- **diff** - compare two files
- **make** - maintain, update and regenerate related programs
- **find** - find files by name or other characteristics

Each **KENBUS1** script executes about 18 UNIX commands, including:

- **cc** - C compiler
- **cat** - concatenate and print files
- **grep** - search for a string
- **mkdir** - make a directory
- **rm** - remove a file

The metric produced for both **SDET** and **KENBUS1** is the maximum number of scripts that can be executed per hour. It is important to read the documentation carefully prior to execution, as system limits may provide degradation or reduce the maximum possible system load. For example, the number of system processes and open files usually must be increased from the system default. To execute **SDM**, type the following at the shell prompt:

%1> **runsdm**

The engineer will be asked to provide the following information:

- **hostname** - network name for the system
- Number of iterations
- Vendor name
- Test run name

To build the benchmark, you must edit or create your **M.vendor** file and then type the following at the shell prompt:

%1> **make -f M.vendor**

See the **RUNRULES** file for more information. The total space required for **SDM** approximately 10mb. **SPEC92** is the updated version of the original **SPEC** benchmark for CPU testing, as opposed to the **SDM** benchmark for multi-user simulation.

13.10 SPEC92

SPEC92 is organized into two trees, **SPECfp** and **SPECint**, making the combination of integer and floating point values very difficult. The following tests are included in **SPECfp** (showing that sample applications provide the best tests and benchmarks):

- **013.spice2g6** is the same as above (**SPEC89**).
- **015.doduc** is the same as above (**SPEC89**).
- **034.mdljdp2** is a molecular dynamics program.
- **039.wave5** is a FORTRAN electromagnetic particle-in-cell used to study plasma phenomena.
- **047.tomcatv** is the same as above (**SPEC89**).
- **048.ora** traces optical rays through spherical plane surfaces.
- **052.alvinn** is an autonomous land vehicle in a neural network.
- **056.ear** simulates propagation of sound in human cochlea (inner ear) and computes a picture of sound - cochleagram.
- **077.mdljsp2** models motion for 500; for example, liquid Argon.
- **078.swm256** is a shallow-water model with a 256x256 grid.
- **089.su2cor** is the Quark-Gluon theory to compute the framework of masses of particles.

- **090.hydro2d** uses astrophysics to compute galactical jets.
- **093.nasa7** is the same as **SPEC89**.
- **094.fpppp** is the same as **SPEC89**.

The following tests are included in **SPECint**:
- **008.espresso** is the same as **SPEC89**.
- **022.li** is the same as **SPEC89**.
- **023.eqntott** is the same as **SPEC89**.
- **026.compress** provides a file compression algorithm from IEEE.
- **072.sc** is a spreadsheet calculator.
- **085.gcc** is the same as **SPEC89**.

SPEC provides a quarterly newsletter with results from several different system vendors, including most of the top computer manufacturers. For more information on **SPEC,** contact NCGA.

13.11 bonnie

bonnie is a public domain file system benchmark for the study of system bottlenecks. It creates and uses a 100mb disk file, by default, to measure both disk transfer bytes per second and CPU time/usage. The original intent of using a 100mb file was that it would not fit in data cache (now very easy with most systems). The purpose of **bonnie** is not to measure just data cache, but system input/output.[*] The benchmark also measures, per character, sequential output (buffered) using the UNIX **putc** library function. The code that performs the writes must fit in instruction cache. Block sequential output is also performed using the **write** system call. A **rewrite** test is available to measure the performance of the file system cache.

Sequential input tests using **getc** and **read** library functions are also used for per-character and block measurement. Finally, random seeks using approximately 4000 **lseek** calls are evaluated for performance, functionality and reliability.[†] Again, the engineer will need to identify the appropriate **random, rand**, or **srand** library calls, dependent upon the particular operating system under test to randomize the read/write access locations.

bonnie consists of a single C program file that is relatively easy to compile and execute. The time required to compile and execute depends upon your system,

---

[*]Cache memory is high-speed memory that is usually on-board the CPU.

[†]The **lseek** function call will request the position in an array of elements to be positioned to either the end or an offset.

however, experience has shown that testing can complete within 15 to 30 minutes. The performance and test engineer will need to make sure that the UNIX file size limit is greater than 100mb before starting execution. Use the following command from the UNIX **ksh** (UNIX System V.4-only Korn shell or Bourne shell) to set the file size limit to unlimited, otherwise use the **csh** (C shell) **limit** command:

%1> **ulimit -f unlimited**

It is important to note that this will only set the file size limit as high as the kernel hard limit for UNIX System V.4. Therefore, unless the user sets the kernel hard file size limit to **-1,** unlimited will only be as large as the value contained in the UNIX kernel. With the original default kernel provided by USL/Novell for System V.4, this was approximately 32mb.

Also, it is recommend to only run this benchmark test in single-user for more consistent results. Illustration 13.6 shows expected results that can be used for comparison purposes. If these strings don't match, there is a fairly good chance that something went wrong during regression testing.

File './bonnie.17051', size: 104857600
Writing with putc()...done
Rewriting...done
Writing intelligently...done
Reading with getc()...done
Reading intelligently...done

Illustration 13.6

Sample results include the number of hard disk megabytes that were used during testing.[*] Also, the number (in thousands) of bytes that were read/written per second are given as results. The amount of CPU time per second is also provided.

The next benchmark, from BYTE magazine, considers many aspects of UNIX performance, not just disk testing and performance. It provides a corner test condition for disk reads and writes that may uncover a fairly important functional failure. Most UNIX applications, after all, can create and utilize a 100mb disk file fairly easily, especially CAD applications for integrated circuit design. **bonnie** was created by Tim Bray in 1990 at Waterloo University.

---

[*] One million bytes or characters (8 bits usually per character) of storage.

13.12 byte

This benchmark is one of the more well-known benchmarks that was provided by BYTE magazine for testing new computer systems using the UNIX operating system. The benchmark also provides a test of several UNIX system functions. The BYTE magazine benchmark, Version 3.4 contains the following tests that can aid in the quest for increased functional testing in the UNIX environment:

- Arithmetic overhead
- Register arithmetic
- Short arithmetic
- Int arithmetic (integer)
- Long arithmetic
- Float arithmetic
- Double arithmetic
- System call overhead
- Pipe throughput
- Pipe context switch
- Process creation
- **Execl** call
- Execute a file
- File system throughput
- Compile and link
- Calculations with **dc**
- Tower of Hanoi
- **dhrystone 2**
- **dhrystone 2** without registers
- **dhrystone 2** with registers
- DataBase Management System client/server
- DataBase Management System engine
- Load system with concurrent shell scripts

All tests are written in the C programming language and are portable to both the BSD and System V operating systems. To build the benchmark, type the following at the UNIX shell prompt:

%1> **make clean; make**

This will start the build process. Once everything has been successfully built, to execute the benchmark simply type the following at the UNIX shell prompt:

%2> **Run**

The user must be logged in as the root or superuser before starting the build and execution process, otherwise several errors may occur. It is also suggested that if performance comparisons are to be made, the test must be run in single-user mode only.

Because the **byte** benchmark tests several areas and provides a complete report, integration into an existing regression test system can be fairly simple. The test engineer may also want to consider instrumentation with the **byte** benchmark to identify new functions or call tree and call graph coverage.

13.13 dhrystone

The **dhrystone** benchmark is from the University of California Berkeley. It was originally coded in Ada by R. Weicker in 1984. Reinhold Weicker has stopped developing **dhyrstone** 1 and 2 and now actively discourages use of **dhyrstone1**.

This is a small synthetic benchmark and an allegory to the **whetstone** benchmark (note the pun in the spelling). It consists of string moves, function calls and assignments. It does not provide floating point computation. That is covered by the **whetstone** benchmark discussed later in this chapter.

The **dhrystone** benchmark is most sensitive to cache memory, compiler code optimization, main memory speed and character and string operations.

The **dhrystone** program is a very controversial benchmark today. Many people feel that it does not provide proper results for system-to-system comparisons like **SPEC**. Compiler optimizations and several processors now have instructions specific enough to make results almost meaningless. Version 2.1 of **dhrystone** provides many changes, mostly for optimizing compilers that move code out of the measurement loop. The **dhrystone** benchmark can be compiled and executed for both register or non-register storage class applications. Register-level operations will be much faster than memory references because faster and shorter locality of reference. In other words, we do not have to go all the way across the system bus to access memory because it will be local to the microprocessor.

The **dhrystone** and **whetstone** benchmarks both provide quick tests for memory references, computation and other basic functions. They are often considered checklist-level benchmarks that most system vendors usually run. It makes sense to provide these benchmarks as tests that can also be used during regression testing because they can be integrated fairly easily. Moving from integer performance functional testing to input and output performance analysis, the **iobench** program provides specific added value in measuring and testing new disk drives and device drivers.

13.14   disktest (Disk Input and Output Testing)

Consider providing input to **disktest** via an input file using file redirection. Then, integrate the program into the regression test system to monitor the system using user and wall clock time. See the chapter on test harnesses for test program integration options.

Here are some example C shell commands that could be used:

%1> time disktest < inputfile | tee outputfile

The program **disktest** is a generalized diagnostic program for random and sequential access devices running under UNIX. It was written in October 1985 by Bill Allen of the Naval Postgraduate School and provides several command line options and/or interactive directives.

The **disktest** benchmark test is written in the C programming language and is very portable. After compilation, simply execute the following at the UNIX shell prompt:

%1> disktest hard_disk_device

The parameter **hard_disk_device** is usually the name of a raw or block device. Make sure that the device can be used as a scratch area before starting the test.[*] If a block hard disk device is used, the UNIX file system will be tested as well and the engineer must expect a somewhat slower response time than if the raw device (direct physical access) disk were used.

A carriage return or **d** will display the following settings, most of which can be modified:

- Block size: 1
- Low block number: 0
- High block number: 0
- Offset blocks: 0
- Repeat factor: 1
- Sequential access
- Output normal
- Abort on error
- No data compare on read
- Program interactive
- Pattern: default set

To obtain help with **disktest**, type?. Several possible commands include:

---

[*]Using the raw device will prevent the file system overhead associated with file input/output.

a abort on error
b set buffer size (blocks)
c data compare on read
d display
f fork on next test
g go: write/read tests
h set high block number
l set low block number
o output normal/errors only
p set pattern
q quit
r read pass
s sequential/random
t set repeat count
w write pass
B name - set badblock file name
O off - offset for R/W in sectors (Gould only)

You may need to change **BSIZE** inside the source to **disktest.c** from 1024 to 512 if you are running on a UNIX System V based operating system. The first two things that will probably have to change are the repeat count and the high block number with **t100** and **h1000**, for example. Then, type **g** to start testing. This will write to the disk various data patterns and verify all data with read operations. Using the **Control** and \ keys together will abort the test and create a **core** file by sending a quit signal, unless this signal has been redefined using the UNIX **stty** command. The engineer may also want to increase the block size from the default of 1 to a larger value for more thorough testing.

13.15 iobench

The **iobench** program is provided at no charge originally from Prime Computer Inc., Natick, MA 01701. There are two versions with the only difference being in how the benchmark is driven. The programs **073.iobenchp** and **084.iobenchpf** contain a fixed *workload* variant. The **iobench** program comes as a UNIX **shar** file (shell archive). See the UNIX **man** page for **shar** for more details. This command allows you to package multiple files for transportation (usually over email using the Internet). The code is fairly portable and has been ported to a variety of UNIX machines.

The total size for both **073.iobenchp** and **084.iobenchpf** is approximately 1mb. To build the benchmark, change directories and type the following at the UNIX shell prompt:

%1> **make -f M.xxx**

Where **xxx** is usually the local system architecture. The test or development engineer will probably want to execute the following command before setting the environment variables covered next:

%2> **make test**

The following environment variable NUMUSERS must also be set at the shell prompt to specify the number of users for four execution runs:

%3> **set NUMUSERS="25 50 100 200"**

This will specify runs with 25, 50, 100 and 200 users. Results with the command **make test** for the program **073.iobenchp** include the number of users and the record size used for input and output transfers. For example, Illustration 13.7 shows typical results for four and eight users.

```
Running test1,  4 users,  100 record
Running test2,  4 users,  4096 record
Running test3,  4 users,  8192 record
Running test4,  8 users,  100 record
Running test5,  8 users,  4096 record
```

Illustration 13.7

Other information that is provided includes the following:

- Number of users
- Record length
- Cycles
- Megabytes used for testing
- Amount of user and system time

These data can be used to compare results; however, the amount of external system activity may impact results as always.

The engineer will probably get error messages from the UNIX command **diff** complaining that **./result.test/test.log** is missing, unless you set the appropriate variables inside the file **Makefile**.

Multiple disks for striping or mirroring file systems can also be used for comparison purposes if available with the operating system under test. Striping provides interleaved access for both read and write operations between multiple disks to improve performance. It allows one disk to prepare for the next operation while the other disk is busy with an existing request. Mirroring provides a similar feature whereby two or more disks work in parallel; however, the purpose of mirroring is for backup and recovery, i.e., when one disk fails, the other may be used as a substitute.

The execution of **make test** for **084.iobenchpf** will be lengthy. Partial sample results are included in Illustration 13.8:

```
Fri Aug 28 08:15:40 PDT 1992 : Running test1, 16 users, 100 record
Fri Aug 28 08:29:30 PDT 1992 : Running test2, 32 users, 100 record
Fri Aug 28 08:42:10 PDT 1992 : Running test3, 48 users, 100 record
Fri Aug 28 08:54:43 PDT 1992 : Running test4, 64 users, 100 record
Fri Aug 28 09:08:26 PDT 1992 : Running test5, 80 users, 100 record
Fri Aug 28 09:23:21 PDT 1992 : Running test6, 16 users, 4096 record
Fri Aug 28 09:35:29 PDT 1992 : Running test7, 32 users, 4096 record
<test aborted at this point>
```

Illustration 13.8

Because the UNIX operating system is so heavily dependent upon disk resource management, several engineers have written programs to test and analyze bottlenecks in the disk subsystem. The **iostone** program is another benchmark similar to **iobench** to help evaluate disk performance.

13.16 iostone

The **iostone** program consists of one C file. If the engineer is building the program on a UNIX System V Release 4 operating system machine, one will probably need to add **libucb.a** (static archive library) to the compile line to create **iostone**. To execute the benchmark, the user can type the following after successful compilation at the UNIX shell prompt:

%1> **iostone**

The size of the source for **iostone** is approximately 10k. When it has finished, the engineer will see something similar to the following:

Total elapsed time is 17 seconds and 390 milliseconds
This machine benchmarks at 115009 iostones/second

The **iostone** program was written by Arvin Park and Jeff Becker while at the University of California at Davis. Jeff Becker now works at NASA and Arvin

Park is now reported to be a lawyer (at the time of this writing). It is suggested that the user also run this benchmark in single-user mode. Also, you must provide 5mb of disk space prior to execution. This benchmark is for testing and analysis of file input/output and buffer cache performance. This is accomplished by creating **NSETS (4)** of **SET_SIZE (99)** files. The **iostone** program then performs random read and write operations on each file in each set.

The program **iostone**, along with **bonnie**, and **iozone** along with other input and output disk-related benchmarks, can be very helpful and useful for testing and qualifying new hard disk drive devices from both a performance, as well as reliability standpoint.

13.17 iozone

The program **iozone** is from Bill Norcott. The **iozone** test writes a 1mb sequential file consisting of 2k records that are each 512 bytes in length. It then reads the file and prints the bytes per second rate for reads and writes. Some sample output is included in Illustration 13.9:

Writing the 1 Megabyte file, 'iozone.tmp'...1.260000 seconds Reading the file...0.440000 seconds

---

Illustration 13.9

IOZONE performance measurements yield on my system:

832203 bytes/second for writing the file
2383127 bytes/second for reading the file

In this case, **iozone** tells you that a 1mb file is not a good test because it does not write a large enough file to properly measure system performance. A suggestion is made by the program to then increase the file size to 11mb. To re-run the benchmark with a 20mb file, type the following at the UNIX c shell prompt:

%1> **iozone 20**

- A good benchmark and test strategy must include tests that are broad enough to include computation, input and output, multi-user and multi-tasking operations.

13.18 linpack

The **linpack** program is a floating point benchmark that was developed by Jack Dongarra at Los Alamos National Laboratories in 1979. The benchmark consists of a series of FORTRAN kernels representing common liner algebra matrix operations on 100x100, 300x300 and 1000x1000 matrices. The results are in Millions of Floating Point Operations per Second (MFLOPS). The program **linpack** is also available from netlib@ornl.gov. You can send email with the following text to obtain an index:

send index from benchmark

This benchmark requires a FORTRAN compiler and is often another checklist-type benchmark that will normally need to run prior to product release. It is useful, therefore, to include this benchmark, as well as part of the regression test suite, for matrix multiplication and floating point computation.

13.19 musbus

The **musbus** benchmark was developed at Monash University in Melbourne, Australia. **musbus** simulates typical and heavy loads on UNIX machines. The benchmark measures process throughput and disk input/output bandwidth and is useful for kernel and configuration tuning. The current version as of this writing is 5.2 and it has been repackaged as the **KENBUS1** benchmark in the **SPEC SDM** suite. For more information, refer to the **SDM** section of **SPEC**. Ken McDonell (the author of **musbus**) is no longer at Monash University and is now reported to work for Pyramid Technology (at the time of this writing). The point of **musbus** and KENBUS is that you use his system as a terminal emulator (RTE). One should not blindly use the **musbus** developed workload. You must always understand your needs and then customize any benchmark or test to reflect the proper workload (needs) for testing. Blind use of any benchmark or test suite is hazardous and must always be prevented.

The test engineer must log in as root or superuser and set the following limits to unlimited prior to execution of this benchmark:

- File size
- Data size
- Stack size
- Virtual memory
- Number of files

musbus has been famous for finding problems when a system is pushed to its limits. For example, the pipe test does no context switching; however, writes and reads a 512-byte buffer 2048 times in a loop. These kinds of corner cases are usually fairly good at uncovering kernel regression test failures.

13.20 nhfsstone

The **nhfsstone** benchmark measures Network File System (NFS) performance. The benchmark was originally developed and maintained by Legato Systems for testing of the Presto Serve product.[*] The only danger with this operation; however, was that if the remote server system went down in the middle of the operation the write would never complete successfully and the client would believe that everything was successful. This is because the write operation occurred asynchronously, or without waiting. The **nhfsstone** benchmark tests NFS operations, even when additional hardware, such as that provided by Legato, is used for battery backed memory. The **nhfsstone** program measures server response time and server load (calls per second). This benchmark, however, contains Sun-specific code and is not easily portable. Several Sun-specific kernel data structures for networking drivers are expected. **LADDIS** or **SFS** from SPEC are better choices due to porting and execution problems. See **SPEC SFS** for more information on benchmarks and testing NFS. The spelling of **nhfsstone** was a pun similar to the **whetstone** and **dhrystone** benchmarks. **nhfsstone** was the original program, prior to the creation of **LADDIS** and then **SPEC SFS**.

13.21 slalom

slalom is a public domain program for measuring system performance; however, it uses scientific calculations rather than NFS operations. The folks with **slalom** now discourage its use and now have a new project called HINT. **slalom** is a small C program that is easy to compile and only requires the UNIX math library **libm**. The **slalom** program stands for Scalable Language-independent Ames Laboratory One-minute Measurement. The benchmark solves optical radiosity on the interior of a box within a fixed amount of time. It is recommended that 60 seconds of time elapse to successfully complete the benchmark test. Therefore, the test engineer must interpolate input values until the benchmark properly

---

[*]This allowed network operations such as writes to be performed asynchronously so the user performing the write operation would not have to wait for completion.

solves the problem in exactly 60 seconds.

It resembles **LINPACK** in that it provides backsolving a dense matrix, however, it is based on a fixed time rather than a fixed problem. Computers must only be compared using the problem size or MFLOPS, never by the ratio of execution times.

It is very challenging to identify the proper number of intervals to successfully execute all operations within 60 seconds (the recommended amount of time to use). If you overshoot, **slalom** will attempt to decrement your suggested interval until the elapsed time is as close as possible to 60 seconds. Sample results are provided in Illustration 13.10.

```
New interval: [410,411]410 patches:
  Task  Seconds        Operations      MFLOPS    % of Time
Reader   0.010              258      0.025800      0.0 %
Region   0.001              964      0.964000      0.0 %
SetUp1   7.100          7777314      1.095396     11.9 %
SetUp2  13.840         20283720      1.465587     23.1 %
SetUp3   0.120           142624      1.188533      0.2 %
Solver  38.400         62883750      1.637598     64.1 %
Storer   0.400            19680      0.049200      0.7 %
TOTALS  59.870         91108310      1.521769    100.0 %

Machine:  NEWS 3250          Processor:  MIPS
Memory:   16 MB              # of procs: 1
Cache:    128 KB             # used:     1
NMAX:     512                Clock:      25 MHz
Disk:     1.2GB+406MB SCSI   Node name:  rn31
OS:       NEWSOS 5.0.1(BL27) Timer:      Wall,
gettimeofday()
Language: C                  Alone:      yes
Compiler: cc                 Run by:     R. Wilson
Options:  -O                 Date:       28 Aug 1992
M ops:    91.1083            Time:       59.870 seconds
n:        410                MFLOPS:     1.5218
Approximate data memory use: 1394800 bytes.
```

Illustration 13.10

Most of the above data can be modified in **slalom.c** in the **What** function that contains strings for your system configuration, etc.

13.22 Stanford Integer Suite Benchmark

The Stanford Integer Suite (**sis**) comes in the Ada, C or Pascal languages. The benchmark is short in both size and execution time (seconds). It does not require any input and prints the execution time for each program using the current CPU time. The programs were originally gathered by John Hennessy and later modified by Peter Nye. The following tests are included in **sis**:

- **Perm** - Compute permutations of 7 elements 5 times
- **Towers** - Solve Towers of Hanoi
- **Queen** - Solve the eight queens problem 50 times
- **Intmm** - Multiply two 40x40 integer matrices
- **Puzzle** - Solve the Soma Cube problem
- **Quick** - Perform quick sort of 5000 elements
- **Bubble** - Perform bubble sort of 500 elements
- **Tree** - Perform binary tree sort of 5000 elements

An example of output from **sis** is included in Illustration 13.11.

```
     Perm   Towers  Queens   Intmm  Mm  Puzzle   Quick  Bubble  Tree
     140     140       80       60       70      410      60    80
     Nonfloating point composite is           169
     Floating point composite is         247
```

Illustration 13.11

13.23 ttcp (now tsock)

The Test TCP **ttcp** (now **tsock**) is a network-performance tester with many options. **tsock** is a public domain socket test written by Terry Slattery and Mike Muuss at BRL. **ttcp** makes a connection on Remote Procedure Control (RPC) port 5001 and transfers fabricated buffers or data copied from standard input (stdin). It has been ported to both BSD and System V. In some cases, with some UNIX System V.4 systems, the SO_DEBUG option may not be supported since BSD sockets are only emulated using the Transport Layer Interface (TLI) library streams protocol. Therefore, the **-d** option cannot be used with the benchmark.

The benchmark contains a single C program and can be compiled quickly. Illustration 13.12 depicts a list of execution options once you have generated a **ttcp** binary.

To execute the benchmark, the engineer must first start the receiver and then the transmitter. The following example will test the local loop back port/connection with plain TCP testing:

%1> ttcp -L -r -p9001 &
%2> ttcp -L -t -p9001 -D rodney &

This benchmark provides a good sanity test of UNIX IPC semaphores and sockets over both Transmission Control Protocol (TCP) and User Datagram Protocol (UDP).[*] Some work needs to be done to convert the program as delivered to use SVR4 semantics for semaphores. The program has also been used successfully for ABI compatibility testing.

whetstone, like its sister benchmark, **dhrystone**, is often a critical checklist benchmark program. It moves our discussion of benchmark programs from network testing back to CPU calculation of floating point numeric operations.

```
Transmitter:
 ttcp -t [-options] host [ <in ]

-l## Length of bufs written to network (default 8192)
-s Don't source a pattern to network, use stdin
-n## Number of source bufs written to network (default 2048)
-p## Port number to send to (default 5001)
-u Use UDP instead of TCP
-D Don't buffer TCP writes (sets TCP_NODELAY socket opt)

Receiver:
ttcp -r [-options >out]

-l## Length of network read buf (default 8192)
-s Don't sink (discard): prints all data from network to stdout
-p## Port number to listen at (default 5001)
-B Only output full blocks, as specified in -l## (for TAR)
-u Use UDP instead of TCP
-L Local connection (host to host)
-d Set SO_DEBUG socket option
```

Illustration 13.12

---

[*]"Datagrams do not guarantee sequenced, reliable, or unduplicated delivery, but they are less expensive than virtual circuits because they do not require expensive setup operation" [BAC86]. TCP is a virtual circuit service and UDP is a datagram service.

13.24 whetstone

The **whetstone** benchmark is from the National Programming Labs, Whetstone, UK. It consists of small looping modules that feature integer and floating point arithmetic, floating point array computation and floating point function calls. It is small enough to fit inside most system cache (both instruction and data caches). The primary purpose of the benchmark is to measure floating point computation speed. It also measures the efficiency of cache memory, math co-processors and math library functions like **sin**, **cos**, and **tan**. If any changes are made to the math library, it is always a safe bet to run **whetstone** and verify results.

13.25 WPI Benchmark

WPI stands for the Worcester Polytechnic Institute, which is the Mach Research Group, Worcester MA. Version 1.1 of the **WPI** benchmark suite is available from anonymous **ftp** to CMU either as a single compressed **tar** file or as a **lharc** file.* The benchmark suite consists of the following:

- **scomp** - Synthetic compilation benchmark
- **sdbase** - Synthetic database benchmark
- **sdump** - Synthetic dump benchmark
- **sftp** - Synthetic FTP benchmark
- **sxipc** - Synthetic X IPC benchmark
- **jigsaw** - **WPI** jigsaw puzzle program

The program **scomp** has been successfully built and executed on a UNIX SVR4 system. It contains a **make** file and to execute the benchmark, simply type the following at the UNIX shell prompt:

%1> **scomp**

Remember, the engineer must run this in single-user mode as superuser The benchmark simulates the **make** program when it compiles **gcc**, very similar to the **SPEC** benchmark for integer testing. It was written by Brad Nichols of the Mach Research Group at **WPI**. Several timing options are available and can be specified during compilation:

---

*In other words, you can use the **ftp** command from a machine connected to the Internet and **login** to the system at CMU as **anonymous** and use a password with your full Internet mail address.

- **gettimeofday** - Get the time
- **getrusage** - Get information about resource utilization
- **ftime** - Get time from start of UNIX
- **time** - Same as **ftime** (different structure)
- **times** - Get process times
- **clock** - Report CPU time used

The program **sdbase** is a database benchmark, consisting of a database server and a multi-threaded client process. This benchmark was developed based on the design philosophy of the **byte** database benchmark. It uses a job mix based on **byte**'s analysis. The client server-based database benchmark uses TCP/IP sockets to communicate between the client and server.

To build the benchmark, first create the **db.dat** database with the command **makedbms**. Next, run the **makefile** and execute the following at the shell prompt to start the server:

%1> **server db.dat**

The engineer must execute the following command at the shell prompt to start client testing:

%2> **client x**

Where **x** must equal the number of client processes to start. See the **README** file provided with the benchmark for more information. It is strongly suggested that unless multiprocessor provisions are available with the system under test, as is the case with the Mach operating system, the engineer not focus on these tests, as that is the primary purpose of **WPI**. (Expected failures will occur if run on a single processor platform.)

13.26 x11perf

The **x11perf** is provided the X Consortium, Inc. The program contains copyright notices from Digital Equipment Corporation. The C source is approximately 23k and is very portable and can be built rather quickly. It comes with an **Imakefile** that can be converted using the command **xmkmf**. The benchmark measures the amount of time to complete several different types of X Window System operations. The performance and test engineer can also use the program **x11perfcomp** to compare results.

The **x11perf** program can be very useful for testing a new X server, or for regression testing in general. Many operations are performed; however, do not expect to continue to use your display once testing has started, unless a virtual server like the X11 Virtual Display System from Software Research is used.

The next program is also a benchmark for the X Window System and can also be useful in increasing the breadth of functional testing of the UNIX operating system and X Window System. The benchmark has been used successfully for binary compatibility testing in the UNIX environment.

13.27 xbench

The program **xbench** was written by Claus Gittinger, a consultant at Siemens Munich. Users are granted permission to freely copy and distribute **xbench** on a non-profit basis.

The benchmark comes in four parts as **shar** files. To build **xbench** type the following at the shell prompt:

```
%1> sh Part01
%2> sh Part02
%3> sh Part03
%4> sh Part04
```

To execute the benchmark after either using the command **xmkmf** or copying the file **mkfile** to **Makefile**, type the following commands at the shell prompt:

```
%5> make
%6> xbench -ask -nruns 1 -timegoal 5
```

See the documentation and **README** file for more information regarding construction of **xbench**. Also, the engineer can get an **xstone** rating by typing the following command:

```
%6> make summary.ms detail.ms
```

13.28 Conclusions

- Benchmarks offer one method of performing functional, reliability and regression testing.
- Benchmarks must be considered a critical test during and prior to customer acceptance and beta test.

- There are a variety of public domain benchmarks available for the UNIX environment and the database continues to grow. (More user involvement in SPEC and other related groups is needed, however.)
- It is critical that an automatic report generation and comparison facility be included with any collection of benchmarks programs.
- Each test in the test library must always strive to be as multi-purpose as possible. In other words, strive to prioritize benchmarks and tests by making multi-purpose tests high priority.
- Using functional tests for just measuring compliance or conformance to specifications is being short-sighted. The cost of test development is not free; therefore, functional tests must be as highly leveraged as possible (i.e., also used for performance analysis).
- Using functional tests for performance analysis as well verification and validation will help to reduce the total of testing (product development).
- Two other common ways are used to reduce the cost of testing. One is to provide defect-free software that is based on a rigorous process (currently only a dream of the future). Alternatively, test automation and integration with the software development environment is another approach to reducing the cost of testing.

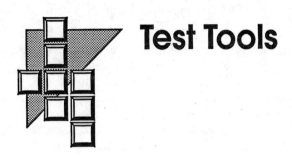

CHAPTER 14 ▶

Test Tools

A good software QA and engineering strategy will always use automated technology whenever possible for the greatest possible return on investment. Because of the lack of automated function, system and regression test tools often result in *ad-hoc* manual processes that, in turn, result in significant customer dissatisfaction (poor quality) and product rework. Therefore, a carefully planned approach is required to facilitate a smooth transition of development and test methods, processes and technologies from a manual to automated process.

Changing company culture from an *ad-hoc* to formal or standardized development process is a significant and difficult task. It is often equally difficult to introduce new tools when *ad-hoc* processes and methods are used. However, an adoption curve model has been proposed by Conner and Patterson [CON82] to describe the typical process associated with introducing new tools into existing processes. When most users encounter a new method or technology, their awareness and skill usually increase in parallel with their maturity and knowledge associated with the tool. If the tool is interesting, a more detailed analysis will be performed as part of the adoption process. Pilot programs often become the basis for promoting new technologies within an organization. In the end, processes that become more consistent (supported by advanced technologies), and that are part of the developer's standard practice, become best practices for change throughout the entire organization.

14.1   Introduction to Test Tools

This chapter will discuss the following product technologies (in alphabetical order by product name):

- Functional test tools for boundary value analysis, equivalence partitioning and cause-effect mapping; also, requirements traceability
- Structural static analysis tools for complexity measurement
- Structural dynamic test analysis tools for code coverage, memory analysis, simulation and interface testing, as well as error seeding
- Computer-Aided Software Test tools for automated regression testing
- Testability and reliability tools for fault/failure identification
- Problem management and tracking tools
- Planning and estimation tools

The following pages discuss several tools available at the time of this writing for planning, design, development and execution of software verification and validation testing. Appendix D contains company contact information for each product, including both pubic domain (free) tools and licensed commercial products.

I'm reminded of the following statement made by a fellow engineering manager as we proceed: "it is a poor craftsman that blames his tools for mistakes." Unfortunately, the state-of-practice in software engineering is often still an art rather than a science and the statement must still hold true; we cannot continue to blame our tools alone for poor-quality products (tools without a process).

Unfortunately, the test tools that engineers are often forced to use are not very easy to learn and often contain hundreds of pages of instructions. Many times, the test tools that are used for software verification and validation are also plagued with defects. Sometimes test tools contain even more defects than the product they test. Test tools and programs must be of better or equal (test tool vendors better use their own tools!) quality (contain fewer defects) than the products they are used to test.

Several issues are important to the analysis and acquisition of test tools (e.g., the platform used for execution is often critical to the successful use of the tool). Few tools in the past have existed for the X Window System and UNIX environments to perform graphical testing using playback and record techniques (now there are dozens). Therefore, planning, combined with a detailed knowledge of available test technology, is paramount to a successful functional, structural, reliability and regression testing strategy (development process model that includes integrated testing methods).

Every effort has been made to provide the most current information in this text; however, changes will and are expected to occur. For example, at the time of this writing CenterLine Sofware has recently acquired ViSTA products from VER-

ITAS Software, Inc. Also, Pure Software, Inc. and Qualtrak Corporation have merged. Changes with test tools and technology providers will continue to occur. However, many of the methods and tools that are included in this text are expected to provide the technology for improvement over the next several years (they must!).

14.2   Other Testing and Tool Resources

The city of San Jose has taken the matter of software testing so seriously that even they helped fund the "Center for Software Development". This self-service organization provides both software and hardware resources for software developers.

The following other resources are also available for the study of software test technology see Appendix D for more information on any of the following resources:

- CAST Report
- Testing Tools Reference Guide - Order R201
- Software Technology Support Center (STSC)
- *comp.software.testing* (Internet newsgroup)
- Guide to GUI Software Test Automation (Revision Labs)
- Software Management News

14.3   Assertion Definition Language (ADL)

Engineers from Sun Microsystems Laboratories, Inc. have an approach to assertion-based testing using an Assertion Definition Language (ADL) and Test Data Description (TDD) language. Their results show that because of the systematic nature of developing the specifications and test-data descriptions they were able to uncover anomalies that normally would not have been detected [SANKAR & HAYES]. They have also reported success with generating English language specifications from ADL.

This is still a fairly advanced method of product development; however, the generation of tests from a specification is one of the best approaches to formal test design and development. Experience has shown that some formal language specifications can be modified-for and interpreted-by these types of tools in a matter of hours. This tool requires a very mature software development organization.

14.4   ATAC (Data and Control-Based Test Coverage for C Programs)

ATAC is a C language structural test coverage analysis tool developed at Bellcore by Bob Horgan and Saul London. ATAC measures how thoroughly a program is tested by a set of tests using data flow coverage techniques. Some of these techniques include the following:

- C-uses (computational uses) or pairs of blocks for which the first block contains an assignment to a variable and the second block contains a use of that variable in a computation.
- Decisions or pairs of blocks for which the first block ends at a control flow branch and the second block is a target of one of these branches.
- Function entry coverage is reported such as when the function is entered at least once.
- P-uses (predicate uses) or triples of blocks for which the first block contains an assignment to a variable, the second block ends at a control flow branch based on a predicate containing that variable and the third block is a target of one of these branches.
- All-uses is the sum of P-uses and C-uses.

ATAC also identifies areas that are not well-tested and areas where overlap exists among tests. Finally, this tool will find minimal covering test sets. ATAC has been used at Bellcore research and development and at several universities for both education and research. ATAC has been ported to many UNIX platforms including **linux** and the following trade-marked systems: BSD, System V release 3, SunOS 4.1, Solaris, Pyramid OSx, ULTRIX V4.2, HP-UX 9.0, AIX 3.2, and UTS. ATAC's source code browser is based on **termcap** or **terminfo**.

To obtain a free copy of ATAC, use the **ftp** command as follows (log in as **anonymous** and use your email address as a password):

%1 **ftp flash.bellcore.com**
%2 **cd atac**
%3 **get README** (and read the instructions for building and using ATAC).

For more information on ATAC, send mail to: *atac@bellcore.com*. A more advanced version of this product is used internally at Bellcore. Data flow structural testing should be evaluated after control flow (i.e., branch coverage).

14.5   Cantata

Cantata is used for unit and integration testing of C and C++ code. It can be used for dynamic and static structural test coverage. It has been used to integrate both static and dynamic test metrics. Cantata is supported on the following platforms: DOS, OS/2, Windows, UNIX and VMS. It also supports many commonly used C and C++ compilers. For more information on Cantata, contact Quality Checked Software, Ltd.

14.6   CAPBAK/NI and CAPBAK/X

CAPBAK/X is provided by Software Research, Inc. CAPBK/X provides capture and replay of interactive tests for X Window System based computer systems. CAPBAK/X is part of Software Research's Software Test Works (STW). STW consists of CAPBAK, along with EXDIFF, SMARTS and TDGEN. EXDIFF and SMARTS help compare baseline results. All of these products are covered in other sections of this chapter. Extraneous or irrelevant differences can be discarded using these tools. The engineer can also edit scripts for conditional execution for regression testing.

CAPBAK/NI is the non-invasive (un-intrusive) version of CAPBAK. A simulation board is inserted into the System Under Test (SUT). This boards is an external box that concentrates all utilized connectors and a host computer. The simulator captures keystrokes, mouse movements and screen images during recording. During playback recorded inputs are reproduced on the SUT. The environment is sometimes known as Remote Job Entry or Emulation (RJE).

Several benchmarks have been provided for this technique of testing and benchmarking. For example, Neal Nelson and Associates have provided a benchmark for evaluating input and output performance for UNIX systems using an RJE or Remote Terminal Emulation (RTE)-based benchmark. As is the case with all CAST tools, verification of results is the most difficult aspect of test design, development and execution. This process often requires that the test designer include control logic in the test script that waits for events. If a specific event does not occur, the control logic produces an error message and aborts the test. For more information on CAPBAK/X, contact Software Research, Inc. as they are reported to now have an object-oriented version of CAPBAK/X.

14.7   CodePlan

CodePlan is from Azor, Inc. and it assists both management and engineering to better determine software schedules based on the COCOMO [BOE81] development model. Although CodePlan is not a test tool, it provides critical data that can be used in the planning and analysis phases of the software development cycle (including testing). This product determines project staffing and schedule needs from estimated lines of code, or *function points*[*]. CodePlan lets the user view and print graphic and numeric requirements estimates.

A supplemental program, called the *bugometer* is also provided, that estimates the potential cost of an undiscovered bug in the delivered code. Another tool lets the user compare the test schedule estimated by CodePlan to figures drawn from past experience using baselines from previous projects. Input factors considered include the following:

Size of code (K lines or function points):

New or Adapted (percent needing design and code change)
- Relative integration effort of new and added code
- Converted (percent needing design and code change)
- Relative integration effort for converted code and design

Development team (rate from low to high, degree of structure).

Risk factors (levels from low to high):

Product (reliability goal, database size, complexity)
- Computer (execution time, storage, volatility, turnaround time)

Personnel:
- Analyst capability
- Application experience
- Programmer capability
- Platform experience
- Language experience

Project:

Use of modern programming practices
- Use of software tools
- Development schedule tolerance

---

[*]Function point complexity consists of evaluating the number of user inputs, outputs, inquiries, number of lines and external interfaces [PRE92].

A results summary is available that includes effort, productivity and schedule or average staffing requirements. Specific functional areas can be viewed in terms of staffing or activity effort.

By default, CodePlan requires a PC or compatible, running MS Windows 3.1 or above. However, the author has used SoftWindows from Insignia Solutions, Inc. to use CodePlan on a SUN SPARCstation IPX with SunOS 4.1.3. Approximately 1mb of hard disk space is required for PC-based systems. For more information on CodePlan, contact Azor, Inc.

14.8   DDTs (Distributed Defect Tracking system)

DDTs is from Qualtrak Corporation. It is a distributed defect tracking and management system that provides the ability to automatically find the appropriate developer's machine and login name so that the appropriate individual will address the problem. Although DDTs is not a test tool, problem tracking database systems must be integrated with the functional, structural, reliability and regression test framework. A subscription feature of DDTs allows other users to obtain local copies of project bug reports. This system is integrated with RCS, SCCS, PVCS, ClearCase, and Aide-de-Camp. This is an important feature that enables source code changes to be associated with bugs in the DDTs system. It also complies with existing standards for problem tracking systems (IEEE, ISO 9000 and DOD-2167). DDTs comes already packaged with 40 management reports and quality metrics that can be used for both process and product improvement. Qualtrak also has provided Xtester for GUI automated testing and test generation, and Xsimul•test for multiple GUI testing. For more information, contact Qualtrak Corporation. This tool has been integrated with a test management system (TestExpert) to provide

14.9   Data Generation Language (DGL)

DGL is a automated test generation tool from Peter Maurer of the University of South Florida. DGL was designed to create functional tests for VLSI designs; however, this tool can also be used for general function and system testing. The language (**dgl**) was designed to help in the construction of data generators that select items at random from a set of items described by a "probabilistic context free grammar". This is a public-domain tool that is available from pangolin.usf.edu (131.247.1.30) and is located in **/pub/faculty/maurer/dgl-source** directory. Also, see TGGS from RG Consulting and AOL from Sun Microsystems.

14.10 Evaluator

Evaluator is a hardware-assisted software testing system involving a host and target system. It is provided by Eastern Systems, Inc. It is a non-intrusive system that allows the host and target to communicate over a high-speed interface. Evaluator provides complete operating system independence, as is also the case with TestRunner and FERRET. Evaluator provides a **learn** facility that captures keystrokes and allows them to be resent to the SUT. It also has a complete programming environment that is based on TCL or the Toolkit Command Language. Again, verification of test results is the most challenging aspect of CAST test design, development and execution.

For example, when an ASIC (Application-Specific Integrated Circuit) router program optimizes the length of a route between two blocks, comparing graphics geometries is not a valid verification technique. Instead, a value-based comparison method must be used where the results of database properties are used, instead of the output (graphical) results. In this case, a human being must eventually be present to confirm that the database values are accurate with what is displayed on the user's screen. This is a common problem for all CAST test technology. For more information on TCL, see the section on Expect TCL in this chapter. For more information on Evaluator, contact Easter Systems, Inc.

14.11 EXDIFF and Spiff

EXDIFF is the EXtended file DIFFerencing system from Software Research, Inc. that extends commonly available file comparison utilities for both the UNIX and DOS operating systems. EXDIFF is part of the Software Test Works (STW/Regression) suite of tools to automate and manage the capture and playback of both text and window-based applications. This program not only compares file differences between expected and actual results of interactive regression test suites, but it can also mask user-defined areas within a recorded session. This prevents false alarms; for example, it checks fields or data that are expected to change, such as date and time values, during the playback of pre-recorded events. The following types of regions can be masked:

- Byte offsets (individual characters)
- Line offsets in line-oriented files
- Matched patterns (a sequence of characters)
- Regions in saved images (for example, a rectangular area)

Another system that provides differences between expected and actual test results is a public domain or "freeware" program called Spiff. Spiff compares the contents of file1 and file2 on UNIX systems and prints a description of the important differences between the files. White space is ignored except to separate objects contained in the file. Spiff maintains tolerances below which differences between two floating point numbers are ignored, which is especially useful for comparing scientific notation using different machine architectures. User specified delimited strings (e.g., comments) can also be ignored by the Spiff tool. Operations can be altered via command line options provided from the shell. This program has been reported to have been seen on **bellcore:/pub/spiff.Z** and is also available on other *comp.sources.unix* archive sites.

14.12 expect TCL

expect/TCL (Toolkit Command Language) provides a programmable approach for testing of interactive programs. For example, the following UNIX commands:

- **uucp**
- **vi**
- **sh**
- **mail**
- **ftp**
- **news**
- **telnet**
- **cu**

Each of these UNIX utilities requires input from the user, however, using expect and TCL user input is not required. The name expect came from the idea of using **send/expect** sequences that are used by many communications protocols. Here are just two examples of what expect can do:

- It can cause the computer to dial back, so the user can use the UNIX **login** command to obtain access to a remote system without having to pay for the call.
- It can start a program and, if the optimal configuration or results don't appear, then restart it until a match is found.

TCL was originally developed for UNIX system administrators who needed to develop scripts for interactive programs. These batch programs would be executed in the middle of the night via UNIX **cron** jobs.[*] One example that has

---

[*] **cron** executes commands at specified dates and times according to the instructions in the **crontab** file.

already been created includes a program to collect CompuServe bulletin board posting information on a nightly basis and download all new articles to a UNIX server for review by engineers the following day using UNIX **news.**

Since expect and TCL are both public domain "freeware" programs, the following discussion will explain how to get started with these tools. The build process for expect TCL consists of first building the TCL (Toolkit Command Language) library. TCL was created by John Ousterhout of the University of California at Berkeley (now reported to be at Sun). The first step in the build process is to execute the **config** program. This shell script pokes around in your system to see if you have *standard* UNIX header or **include** files, libraries, etc. On my system, the only complaint that I had was that my **libc.a** was located in **/usr/ccs/lib/libc.a** not **/usr/lib/libc.a.**

Several example test scripts are located in the test subdirectory; however, many of these scripts have trouble executing for various reasons. For example, some commands and games were not installed on my system. Illustration 14.1 is an example script that was created to simply execute the UNIX **ls** command and expect the first file returned would be **Makefile**. It then executes the UNIX command **whoami** and expects the result to be **rodney.**

```
##
# simple test for ls
#
spawn ls
expect Makefile
spawn whoami
expect rodney
```

Illustration 14.1

There are many other features of the expect tool. Only one problem was experienced during my testing of an early version of expect/TCL. This problem resulted in improper handling of modem control signals when expect scripts were used to connect to various on-line bulletin board systems. These problems where resolved, however, using proper escape sequences. There are several good papers available via anonymous **ftp**. The expect program was created by Don Libes of the National Institute of Standards and Technology (NIST).

14.13   FERRET (Automated Software Testing System)

FERRET is an automated software testing system similar in function to XRunner from Mercury Interactive and QAPartner from Segue Software. FERRET is, however completely *non-intrusive* by connecting to the keyboard, pointing device (mouse) and graphics cables of the system under test. Because FERRET is non-intrusive, it is really much more like TestRunner product (no longer supported). For more information on FERRET, contact Azor, Inc.

14.14   FlightRecorder

FlightRecorder is a tool similar to a video camera recorder. It is used for managing and dispatching bug tracking information. This information is useful for technical support as well as usability analysis and testing. This tool is currently in the alpha stage of production at Mercury Interactive (at the time of this writing). FlightRecorder allows the user to capture GUI-based application defects and email the actions as part of a bug report. The best part about this method is that proprietary data and third-party application products do not have to be released to demonstrate a failure. The user can record all application events that demonstrate the failure and then email a single file that contains both a text description as well as a replay file for the defect. The application or software under test and test data used to create the failure are not required since the X Window System events will display the user's actions to reproduce the failure. The downside to this method is that debugging support will be limited since the actual application text and data are not provided. However, this is an excellent method that can be used to better determine customer use models during alpha and beta testing. This is a big advantage to both the user and vendor in cases where proprietary data cannot be released to reproduce a product failure. Performance Awareness has a similar product called Xaminer. The ideal tool would mirror user actions over the Internet so that the software vendor technical support can view problems in real time.

14.15   Generic Coverage Tool (gct)

gct is a freeware or public domain tool that measures structural test coverage for C programs. See Chapter 3 for details regarding structural testing using white-box test coverage techniques. The author of gct is Brian Marick. This tool provides the following features:

- Branch coverage including **case** statements in a **switch** directive
- Multiple logical conditions (i.e. if ((X || Y) && (Z || X) then...)
- Loop iteration (0, 1 or more times)
- Boundaries of relational operators
- Call coverage
- Multiple threads of execution (race conditions)
- Weak mutation coverage (see Glossary for definition)

gct is available via anonymous **ftp** from **cs.uiuc.edu.** As of this writing, the current version is located in the **pub/testing/gct.files** directory. To retrieve **GCT** use anonymous **ftp** and **get** the file **GCT.README.** The current version of **GCT** is in the directory **pub/testing/gct.files.** To retrieve **GCT,** change directories to **gct.files** and use the **ftp** command **get** to retrieve **ftp.ps** (a postscript file) or **ftp.txt** (formatted to be read on-line). Follow the instructions in either file to retrieve, build, install and execute **GCT.**

Gct@cs.uiuc.edu is a mailing list for GCT users. It is used to distribute bug reports, bug fixes, troubleshooting hints, proposed major and minor revisions, documentation errata, and anything else of interest to GCT users. Send mail to **Gct-Request@cs.uiuc.edu** to get added to the email distribution list.

14.16 GNU Bug-Tracking System (GNATS)

GNATS is a bug tracking system where a central site is used as a repository for the maintenance and administration of problem report management. It is critical to integrate problem report information with functional structural, reliability and regression testing systems. Problem Reports (PRs) are assigned an incremental unique number often known as a *serial key.* There is a program, **gen-index,** that will create an index file for an existing GNATS database. Also, the program **rmcat** will remove a category, for example: compilers, networking, operating systems, etc. The command **file-pr** allows a user to submit a problem report. Several features are available with the commands **file-pr** and **pr-addr:**

- Will look to the **Reply-To:** header before the **From:** header when sending acknowledgment of a problem report.
- Will send mail to everyone that must be notified about a submitter and category when a reply to a PR came in. It will only send them to the person responsible for the submitter, and the person responsible for the category.
- Will put response times in terms of *business hours* in any mail it sends.

For information on how to order GNU software on tape, floppy or CD-ROM, check the file **etc/ORDERS** in the GNU Emacs distribution, ftp the file /pub/gnu/GNUinfo/ORDERS, or e-mail a request to gnu@prep.ai.mit.edu. As with all free software, you must always consider if product support will be available.

14.17 Insight++

Insight++ is provided by ParaSoft Corporation. This product falls into the same category as Purify from Pure Software as a memory management and debugging tool.

Insight++ is based on a source code instrumentation methodology. This method is reported to be more accurate than object code insertion methods. The following classes of errors are reported to be detected by Insight++:

- Memory corruption errors in all memory segments (i.e., heap (free store), stack and static). Errors in the static memory area (i.e., memory over-write and corruption) are reported.
- Using uninitialized memory
- Memory leaks are identified down to the source code statement (i.e., memory that has not been freed after allocation)
- Dynamic memory errors are also reported (i.e., using memory after free-ing and freeing memory more than once)

Insure++ is often used to pinpoint errors in calling sequences to standard libraries, as well as erroneous format specifiers in the UNIX **printf** and **sprintf** family of library printing functions. During run-time execution it can be used to locate and identify the following problems:

- Memory reference errors (e.g., array out-of-bounds)
- Invalid arguments to standard libraries
- Arbitrary user-specified parameters
- Return code violations
- Algorithm analysis

For algorithms, errors in access patterns to arrays and anomalies in values of arrays or scalar variables are identified. Tools like Insight and Purify must be used early in the implementation phase prior to system integration and throughout the product development life-cycle. QASE, Inc. also provides a similar product called MCmem for memory debugging. Purify and MCmem currently perform dynamic memory analysis. However, Parasoft has announced support for static memory analysis with Insight++. This is important because **performance is** often a big issue with the execution of most test tools.

Memory analysis and debugging tools will ensure that hard-to-diagnosis integration and system failures will be reduced by proper unit and integration testing. This type of testing includes memory reference access violations and other errors. UNIX utilities such as **lint** can be useful during unit testing to help identify errors that may have been missed during code inspections, code swaps, peer reviews and design reviews. For more information on Insight++, contact ParaSoft Corporation.

14.18 Interactive Development Environments (IDE) - StP/T

IDE, Inc. provides an automated test development technology called T. According to IDE, most companies spend between 30% and 60% of their software budget on testing and produce anywhere from 30 to 300 test cases per staff month.

The input to T is a file called a Software Description File. The SDF can be generated with graphical software development tools such as IDE's Software through Pictures (StP) or with text editors. If StP is applied, the user draws diagrams such as object, state transition, or data flow models. The user can then instruct StP to produce the Software Description File (SDF) using the **extract** command. If a text editor is applied, the user must write the file, which is a requirements specification. This specification must be in the Semantic Transfer Language format from IEEE Standard 1175 1991— a real challenge.

Output from T consists of test cases that can be used for automatic test execution by capture/playback tools such as XRunner and others. T's test cases for domain testing include boundary value analysis, equivalence partitioning, cause/ effect relationships, event-driven analysis and state-driven analysis, all derived from the software model.

The diagrams from several different methodologies provide the design documentation or classes for automatic generation of tests. StP/T supports Yourdon's "Structured System Analysis", Hatley's "Strategies for Real-Time System Specifications", Rumbaugh's "Object Modeling Technique (OMT)", Booch's "Object-Oriented Analysis and Design" and Jocobson's "Use Case Driven Object-Oriented System Analysis".

Requirements-based testing is critical to the development of functional tests. VERITAS and QASE also provide tools to help in the development of functional tests from requirements and other specification documents. However, these tools are useful more for tracking the relationships between requirements and

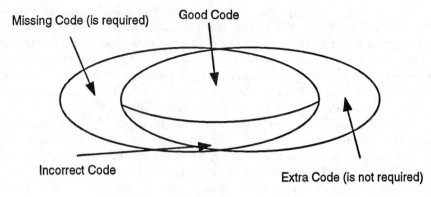

Illustration 14.2

tests, not automatically generating tests from object models. However, using requirements tracking tools is a good stepping stone to automatic test generation. The tests that are generated by T can also be provided to XRunner for automatic execution (capture/replay). IDE's T tool provides an important aspect to testing, that is testing from requirements as opposed to testing from just the source code. Illustration 14.2 shows the relationship between testing from the code using structural testing tools and testing from the requirements using tools like T.

The goal must always be to have one circle containing only required and correct code. Therefore, it is critical to eliminate the bottom half (incorrect code segment) of the center circle through functional, structural, reliability and regression testing processes. To eliminate extra code, use structured reviews, structural analysis and testing. To identify missing code, use functional requirements-based testing. Another useful technique for functional testing is called guided synthesis testing from IDE. See Illustration 14.3 for details.

In Illustration 14.3 a reference value is first assigned where the screening and debugging vectors intersect (e.g., the value 1). Next, a screening vector is defined based on low and high values from the reference point. These values are usually restricted to values inside the "valid" data space as defined by the functional design requirements. For example, screen vectors could include the values 2 and 3 (assuming valid values are in the range from 1 to 7). Next, a debugging vector can be constructed on top of the existing screening vector's data elements. This process starts by using a low and high value on top of the existing screening vector's data elements. For example, if the screen vector had values 1 and 3, the debugging vector would start with 4 and 5 (low and high values). Next, values that are above the low and below the high values are added to the debugging vector. Finally, above the high and the out-of-type values are used to complete values in the debugging vector. Out-of-type values would consist of all values that are not included in the specified equivalence class.

Visualizing guided synthesis as applied to numerical values is simple and straight forward. However, visualizing the same approach applied to non-numerical data items and data structures requires a little more thought. Text data items can be expressed as an enumerated list of values and as ranges of values. In the list of values: "red, blue, green, black, white", red is the first item and is called the low-boundary. Of course the last item, white, is called the high-boundary and green, the middle item is called the reference item. The items in the list and next to the boundaries are called the low-adjacent (i.e., blue) and the high adjacent (i.e., black) values. Since there are no values just outside the boundaries, those sample values are excluded. One invalid value is included for the enumerated list, that value is called the invalid out-of-type value and is assigned a value of "not-in-list."

When text data items are defined as ranges of values they are defined with regular expressions. For example, a last name would be defined with the regular expression "[A-Z][a-z]1,36". This definition has two components illustrated by the square brackets. The first component is defined as A-Z. This definition means to take a character from the set of letters, capital A through capital Z. The second component is defined as a-z 1,36 and it means to take as few as one or as many as thirty-six characters from the set of characters beginning with a lower case "a" and ending with a lower case "z". The low boundary value for this data item would be "Aa". The high-boundary would be "Zabcdefghijklmnopqrstuvwxyzabcdefghij".

The guided synthesis method applies a similar set of rules for data structures. For example, the high boundary for an array is the full array while the low boundary is the empty array. By standardizing on a specific set of samples and then developing rules for choosing samples for each data type, the guided synthesis methodology simplifies data sampling, while building on the history from which data values have frequently discovered failures (i.e., extended finite state machines). This tool is also for advanced/mature software development organizations.

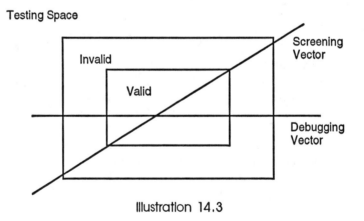

Illustration 14.3

14.19 IPS

IPS is an interactive, trace-driven performance measurement system for parallel and distributed programs. Data are presented and organized in a hierarchical fashion from the whole program down to particular procedures inside the application.* Many metrics are presented, including:

- CPU time
- Synchronization blocking time (messages and busy waiting)
- Input and output rates
- Procedure calls
- Message rates

Profile data are also provided that include critical path information. A master part includes the X Window System-based user interface and a slave analyst runs on the same machine as the application under test. Evaluating metrics vs. time using histograms can be presented in graphical representation. Also, profile tables can be displayed, as well as critical path tables. The critical path function provides a feature whereby sections of code in a parallel program that cause the program to run slowly are identified and located. This can include interactions between programs for message passing and locking operations. A directed acyclic graph of dependencies is developed for path analysis. The thickness of a line is determined between two points based on the amount of CPU time consumed during program execution. For more information on IPS, send email to ips@cs.wisc.edu. IPS was created by Jeff Hollingsworth, Bruce Irvin, and Barton P. Miller of the University of Wisconsin-Madison.

14.20 METRIC

METRIC is another tool provided by Software Research, Inc. as part of the Software Tools Works (STW/Advisor) series of products. It is used for software metrics processing and generation. Seventeen complexity metrics are provided along with Halstead's Software Science, which includes the following information:

- Total unique operators and operands
- Length and predicted length
- Purity code ratio
- Volume
- Effort

---

*The UNIX file system has a structure that starts with **/** or **root** and expands outward.

Some of the many features of METRIC include the following:

- Language support for Ada, C, C++ and FORTRAN
  Various complexity metrics (Software Science and Cyclomatic Complexity)
- Complexity reports
- Summary reports
- Exception report for modules that exceed complexity ratings
- Kiviat diagram for functions that exceed complexity standards (see the section on ViSTA for an example of a Kiviat diagram)

14.21 news, notes and MOSAIC

Another much less formal approach to bug tracking that can be used is the UNIX **news** utility. This utility can be used to provide a fairly open forum for either internal or external communications. One of the biggest problems most companies have is determining the Return On Investment (ROI) for new defect containment and defect detection methods. This is true unless a system is in place to help identify the reduction in problems discovered by engineering. Often-times the customer bug management system does not include problem reports from engineers. Instead, if an engineer discovers a problem, it is usually simply fixed and checked into the source code control system. Using **news** facilities, an article can be opened quickly regarding a problem and submitted by an engineer for all other project members for review. All the engineer needs to do is type in text using the editor of choice and exit the editor to post the note.

Another useful utility that is similar to UNIX **news** is **notes**. When a problem is fixed and verified, it can be marked as a *director* note by using the **d** command inside **notes**. Priorities can also be assigned directly in the title, making searching and sorting by title fairly simple. It is strongly recommended that the QA group monitor and manage the contents of the **notes** database. Some organizations ask that the individual who opens a problem be responsible for closing it. Other groups rely on the independent verification of the QA group to close all problem reports.

Open problems can provide excellent input to the regression and functional test systems. Also, new tools, such as stress test systems for boundary conditions can be better analyzed for ROI when integrated with the defect tracking system. For example, if the cost of a serious defect after product release is $10,000 and it is discovered by a stress test tool, before release, the ROI of the test development and execution cost can be better determined. This is obviously not the best problem tracking system available, however, it does serve the basic purpose and more importantly, provides an open communication channel. A "thread" of communication can be built for each problem report by providing a series of comments that are all linked together.

MOSAIC is another alternative to **news** that provides a GUI to the Internet as an information browser and World-Wide-Web (WWW). MOSAIC has also been ported to Microsoft Windows, as well as to the Macintosh. MOSAIC is from the National Center for Supercomputing Applications at the University of Illinois, Urbana—Champaign. NetScape is another option. Use these tools to better organize and browse requirements documents.

14.22 ParaSET

This tool is provided by Software Emancipation to help engineers and quality functions to better understand software products by linking the requirements specification to source code. It uses a hyper-linked-based approach for navigation from the requirements specification documentation to the product source code. If, for example, you change the requirement specification to state that: "The color of the box will now be blue instead of red...." the hypertext links will allow you to quickly identify relevant source code that must be changed. This tool is more for software development and change control management than a test tool, however, it is critical to the functional aspects of testing. ParaSET provides support for the **emacs** and **vi** editors, as well as **gdb** and **dbx** debuggers. Frame documents that contain specifications are also supported. ParaSET provides two important features:

1 *Impact analysis* which is the ability to perform what-if analysis of proposed source code changes
2 *Intelligent change propagation* which is used after impact analysis to quickly and accurately make system-wide changes that are automatically reflected in product text, diagrams and documentation.

14.23 preVue-X

Performance Awareness provides a product called preVue-X for non-intrusive automatic capture/playback and performance analysis. The approach that Performance Awareness uses is to capture the X Window System protocol between the client application and the X server. This method is non-intrusive since it does not require the application program to link with any special libraries or object modules. All that is required is to capture the X protocol between the server and client application.

One method that Performance Awareness uses for script playback when the application changes location is to base all replay events on text field locations. Therefore, if a regression test script was created with the application in a different screen location, it does not matter since the reference is by text rather than screen location. As long as a text field can be identified and associated with a GUI object, the application can be retested without difficulty. However, if a GUI object (e.g., button or window) does not have any text associated with it, playback must be by location or geometry. If some anchor text is located away from a button, you can include a delta offset for playback. In general, non-intrusive testing is always better than changing the application under test. However, if the text for an object changes, the test engineer will have to be able to read the X protocol to find the old name and replace it with the new name for proper playback—not an easy task.

14.24 PiSCES

Reliable Software Technologies (RST) provides a product called PiSCES Software Analysis Toolkit that provides a suite of software testing and analysis tools. These tools provide testability analysis, automated test case generation, mutation testing, and software safety analysis. The toolkit comes with a GUI for UNIX and X Window System-based systems. The tools currently operate on C source code; versions for C++, Ada and FORTRAN are reported to be available from RST the third quarter of 1995.

The PiSCES Software Analysis Tool kit automates the process of performing dynamic software *testability*. Testability predicts the likelihood that software faults will be found during unit and system testing. Three different dynamic analysis checks are combined to calculate a testability score:

1. Execution analysis
2. Infection analysis
3. Propagation analysis

These analyses estimate the three conditions necessary for a software fault to cause program failure: the fault must be reached (*execution*), it must change the state of the machine (*infection*), and this change must impact the output (*propagation*). By estimating these three conditions within software source code locations, predictions can be made as to how likely real faults in the code are to be revealed as program failures.

Testability results provide predictive measurements as to the ability to properly test all program statements and variables. The engineer can direct

PiSCES where to target testability analysis. Some of the primary benefits of testability include:

- Better understanding of code complexity and a better indications of where testing resources and effort must be focused (functional, structural, reliability, and regression testing)
- Dynamic analysis using test cases to identify existing faults
- Schedule completion criteria based on test completion criteria
- Identification of where code inspections and walk-throughs will have the greatest impact
- Identification of source code decisions and statements that need additional testing

Testability within PiSCES can be performed without a functional requirements specification. This is because PiSCES is only interested in the difference between simulated faults and the actual code, instead of correctness (which is the job of testing).

Testability metrics are said to aid in the ability to better determine regression testing criteria based on source code CM change control information. If a bug fix or modification request is made, one can determine the relative risk involved by first evaluating the testability of the module. If the module has a high testability rating, the risk can be considered less than if the module has a low testability score (is difficult to test).

PiSCES must be able to compile programs that are contained in project files. Therefore, the user must provide all command line options, including file locations and names, preprocessor options and other data to a compilation dialog box. It would be even nicer if the user could retain the standard **makefile** environment during instrumentation for testability, instead of being required to use the PiSCES compilation windows. This problem is expected to be resolved in a future release.

The PiSCES Mutation Testing Tool can automatically generate unit test cases that satisfy both weak and strong mutation adequacy. Mutation testing is a fault-based testing technique that has been shown to reveal more faults than coverage-based testing techniques (according to RST). PiSCES will automatically generate test cases for unit testing according to mutation adequacy. RST has plans in place to incorporate new methods to improve mutant selection adequacy (probably one of the most complex aspects of testability analysis). These new methods will reduce the number of redundant live mutants reported by PiSCES.

The PiSCES Automated Test Case Generator automatically generates unit test cases for both statement and branch coverage criteria. Future plans include support for the following: condition, condition/decision and multiple condition. Condition coverage requires tests that evoke all outcomes of each condition in a decision. Condition/decision coverage requires tests for all outcomes for all conditions and decisions at least once. Multiple condition coverage requires test requirements for all possible combinations of conditions in each decision evoked at least once. This is the most difficult coverage-based testing technique to achieve with automatic test generation.

      With an automated test case generator, the user must specify what variables will be used as inputs and the minimum and maximum values that can be used. Also, either a continuous or discrete distribution must be specified to compute the selection criteria of inputs from the range that has been specified (equilikely is commonly recommended). Having to manually select variables for automatic test generation is probably the most difficult aspect of using the automated test generator. This is one of the best methods known to generate tests from the source code; however, it is always better to generate tests from the specification first.

      The PiSCES Safety Analysis Tool performs dynamic safety analysis on software. PiSCES can simulate both software faults and hardware failures coming into software. The purpose of safety analysis is to help determine the likelihood that hardware and software can cause catastrophic failure of a system. This is a fairly new tool for RST that the author has not used. Contact RST for details.

14.25 PureCoverage

      PureCoverage is a structural test coverage tool from Pure Software, Inc. used to identify blocks of source code that have not been executed during functional test execution. PureCoverage uses the same object code insertion technique that is used by the Purify product. PureCoverage provides a GUI-based interface for casual users, as well as integrators, that need to perform the following:

- Expose blocks (currently not segments) of your application that were not executed during unit, integration and system testing
- Accumulate and calculate coverage data over the course of multiple test runs
- Merge data from different programs that all share common source code (i.e., libraries, object files, etc.)
- Work with Purify to detect run-time errors
- Generate many different structural testing and analysis reports
- Allow the user access to structural test coverage data, to write custom reports

      Since only basic block coverage is supplied, Pure recommends that multi-decision statements be separated on individual lines. The UNIX **indent** command can be used to perform this task (separation of compound or multi-predicate statements). This process will often increase the number of lines of source code. Support from software developers may also be difficult, even though writing code with each predicate located on a unique line is believed to be the best practice according to Pure Software.

14.26 Purify

Purify is a memory debugging product provided by Pure Software, Inc. When many programmers are asked what test tool they absolutely cannot live without, it is often a memory management debugger/analysis tool like Purify. Purify is a product to detect memory access violations in C programs during execution. Purify detects dynamic memory errors where memory is allocated but can no longer be accessed because there are no pointers to it. This is often called a *memory leak*. The product will also flag memory access violations that can force a UNIX system memory core dump. This will immediately halt program execution. Core dumps are typically considered critical since loss of data or functionality could occur.

The following types of errors can be detected by Purify:

- Having memory leaks (no pointers to allocated memory)
- Reading or writing beyond the bounds of an array
- Reading or writing freed memory
- Freeing memory multiple times
- Reading and using un-initialized memory
- Reading or writing through null pointers
- Overflowing the stack by deeply recursive function calls

Purify inserts probes into the object code prior to the link edit phase (aka. object code insertion). Then, before each memory operation occurs, Purify is able to determine before statement execution if an error will occur, such as an access violation to memory that has already been freed.

To use Purify, the user simply first compiles the program with the standard C compiler, and includes the command **purify** in front of the compilation command line. The process usually begins by first compiling a program using the standard compiler. If this process is successful, the **purify** command will instrument the program for memory analysis. Finally, the output from the program during execution will generate memory management analysis results. (The same process is used for Pure coverage.)

The following list of vendors all provide general-purpose memory debuggers available for UNIX systems:

- Purify from Pure Software, Inc.
- MCmem from Quality Assured Software Engineering
- Sentinel from AIB Software
- Insight++ and Insure from ParaSoft Corporation
- TestCenter from CenterLine Software

14.27 QA Partner

QA Partner is an automatic record and playback tool for UNIX-based systems that use the X Window System protocol. QA Partner additionally has support for MS Windows and Apple Macintosh.

QA Partner uses a *context-free* approach to the record and playback of GUI events. This means that the application under test can change either contents or location without problems during playback of pre-recorded tests. If specific or physical screen locations were used during recording, any minor changes made to the application prior to playback would cause all events to fail. *Object-oriented* or context free recording provides the ability to map events to generic or logical objects so that playback can occur even if screen locations change or the application under tests adds, deletes or changes functionality. Even though QA Partner provides the ability for automatic record and playback of events, having a "scripting" feature is where the true power of CAST still resides.

Scripts can be modified to enhance the test. They can also be changed to reflect new product functionality. It is important to note that true object oriented facilities are not provided by most capture/playback tools. This is because the standard object-oriented facilities of polymorphism[*] and data abstraction[†] are not provided. The QA Partner approach or strategy is that ultimately, scripts are easier and faster to maintain. However, starting the test development process using a GUI-oriented record mechanism is best; however, ultimately it is the script files that will be maintained and controlled through the CM system, along with the product source code.

Integrating the facilities of a test harness for establishing the test environment and building and executing the tests along with automated capture/playback is a good approach. Using the facilities of scripting the regression testing process can be accomplished much easier. QA Partner is provided by Segue Software, Inc.

---

[*] A way of giving different meaning to the same message, depending on the type of data being processed.

[†] A named collection of data that describes a data object [PRE92].

14.28 QASE

Quality Assurance Software Engineering, Inc. was founded by the chief architect of ViSTA from VERITAS Software. QASE provides a range a products including the following:

- MCman (for functional coverage analysis)
- MCtst (automated test driver)
- MCcov (code coverage analysis and instrumentation)
- MCsim (interface simulator)
- MCmem (dynamic memory analysis)
- MCkrn (kernel extension for coverage analysis)
- MCasm (assembly code extension)
- MCprt (enhancement to C profiler)
- MClint (enhancement to **lint** interface)
- MCobj (object code extension)
- MCrev (code review and analysis)

These products from QASE offer very similar functionality to the ViSTA products from VERITAS, however, all commands names are different. QASE's chief architect reports that the Meta-C++ coverage analyzer uses a lexical based engine, rather than the ViSTA products, which are all grammar-based using the UNIX **yacc** facilities. QASE also support's Fortran programs using assembly language coverage analysis (MCasm) and maps reverse engineering assembly language code back to the original FORTRAN source.

MCman provides the capability for R&D engineers to place delimiters between functional requirements during specification creation for automatic traceability between unit, integration and system tests and functional requirements. Either Framemaker or **troff** source code (**man** pages) can be used to create requirements with automated traceability. Once each individual functional requirement has been properly identified using delimiters and a checklist and test stub or empty file for each functional test is complete, a shell-script or XRunner TSL script is used to replace the stub file with a real test case. Next, the test harness MCtst or XRunner (for example) is used for test execution and results reporting. At this point, the R&D engineer can then determine the ratio of functional test cases to functional requirements (functional coverage) to improve project tracking and release estimation methods. For example, if the product only has 10% functional test coverage and you need to ship the product very soon, either you will slip the release date or, with a great amount of risk, use a well-defined recovery plan. After functional coverage has been identified, MCcov is useful in determining structural test coverage provided by each functional test (how many decisions, statements or function calls have been exercised).

Interface simulation using the MCsim tool is often beneficial for increasing test coverage for error conditions that are often difficult to produce (e.g., out of memory conditions). MCmem is used to provide dynamic memory analysis information as a result of functional test execution. Many people also use Purify from Pure Software, Inc. for memory management analysis and debugging. It is important to note that all of the above tools are dependent upon the execution of functional tests, to provide any dynamic coverage metrics information.

14.29 QualityTEAM

Scopus Technology provides QualityTEAM, a software defect tracking and quality management system. This is a critical tool for test and development automation as defects often become future product requirements. Problem reports often become requirements for automated regression tests. The product allows software quality departments to report, track and control bugs and change requests. It handles duplicate bugs, cross-referencing, data validation and notification.

QualityTEAM is available for OpenLook, Motif, MS Windows and Macintosh window environments. QualityTEAM has been integrated with other ProTEAM modules for software CM integration. This capability provides the functionality to cross-reference and map problem reports with engineering change requests and vice versa. This is a critical requirement that is often lacking in many software bug tracking systems available today.

Often times the contents of the bug management database must become the primary source of requirements for the next major customer release, especially if the customer's requirements were not accurately or completely captured in the product requirements specification that was used to originally develop and test the product. The spiral software development life-cycle model provides the basis for constant update of requirements and design specifications during the implementation and test phases [PRE92]. Using the bug management database and CM system is one step in this critical direction.

For more information on QualityTEAM and ProTEAM products, contact Scopus Technology.

14.30 Quantify

Quantify is another product from Pure Software, Inc. It is used for the evaluation of system performance bottlenecks, including both system as well as application library calls. Quantify shows function call relationships between functions and graphical call chart displays for the amount of time spent in each function. The product creates wider lines for paths between functions that often require more accumulated time for execution. Therefore, performance bottlenecks between functions can be better identified.

Functions with a high degree of usage must be optimized. Code that is continually used by only a small number of functions must be considered for consolidation, or *inlined* into the function making the request. The process of *inlining* is when a function is moved to the main section of code from an external or internal function. This is somewhat analogous to the difference between automatic vs. internal and external variables. Because automatic variables come and go with function invocation, they do not retain their values from one call to the next, and must be explicitly set upon each entry. As an alternative to automatic variable, it is possible to define variables that are *external* to all functions, that is, variables that can be accessed by name by any function. Internal static variables are local to a particular function just as automatic variables are, but unlike automatics, they remain in existence rather than coming and going each time the function is activated (data segment vs. stack) [KER88]. This process also can improve performance when the overhead cost of making the function call request outweighs the benefits of reuse (context switch penalty). See the section on Performance Engineering in Chapter 13 for more details of how to use Quantify.

Quantify also provides performance characteristics per each non-commented source code statement. For more information on the vendor of Quantify, see the section on Purify.

14.31 Remedy Corporation's Action Request (AR) System

The Action Request System from Remedy Corporation is one of many very good problem management and tracking systems for the UNIX and X Window System environment. The graphical interface for the AR system allows the user to customize reports and inquiries with fairly little effort. Remedy's products can be used for the following applications:

- Internal help desk
- System and network management
- Customer support help desk
- Defect tracking

One of several features available with the AR system is the ability to personalize views and defaults. This means that the user can tailor the forms for both entering as well as analyzing problem report data. This is one of the biggest problems most engineers have when the subject of defect tracking and problem management software is analyzed and evaluated or discussed. The author knows from experience that there always seems to be at least one engineer that will not like the user interface for a given problem reporting system. Any new system is often discounted as either too cumbersome or different from the existing obsolete home-grown system that is currently in use. Remedy solves this problem by allowing the user or engineer to customize the interface fairly easily. For more information, contact Remedy Corporation.

14.32 ReplayXt

ReplayXt is a capture/playback tool for UNIX platforms that support X Window System and TCL (Testsuite Command Language). Capture/playback tools are most useful for automated regression verification and validation testing. ReplayXt uses the TCL (pronounced tickle) language for testing the X Window System Intrinsic library applications using either Motif or Athena-based widgets. It is a freeware or public domain product that is provided by Jan Newmarch. See Appendix D for more details.

14.33 SMARTS

SMARTS is a Software Maintenance And Regression Test System from Software Research, Inc. that is used as part of the language-independent Software Test Works (STW/Regression) suite of tools. SMARTS provides a user-defined test description file to determine what actions to perform for each test or suite of tests for test case management and execution. The description file uses a format similar to the C language called the Automated Test Script (ATS) language. The ATS language test commands and analysis can be performed for automated regression testing. This system can utilize the CAPBAK program to perform automated interactive regression testing for record and playback functions. SMARTS then acts as the test manager for baseline comparisons when CAPBAK is used to playback pre-recorded events.

14.34 SoftTest

SoftTest is a functional test case design tool from Bender and Associates, Inc. This tool constructs test cases from cause-and-effect diagrams. This is a technique where boolean diagrams are created from the functional specification. It can, therefore aid in debugging requirements specifications. SoftTest is used for validating requirements by specifying test cases from the requirements specification. Dick Bender, in a presentation entitled *Writing Testable Requirements,* stated that 56% of all defects were attributed to requirements failures in the functional design [Software Testing Analysis and Review, 1993]. For more information on SoftTest, contact Bender and Associates.

14.35 S-TCAT

S-TCAT is a System Test Coverage Analysis Tool from Software Research, Inc. that is included as part of the Software Test Works (STW) suite of products. Once module and function branch coverage is complete (C1), system interface (call entry/exit) coverage can be analyzed as part of system coverage (S0 and S1). Call graphs are provided by S-TCAT for static coverage information. Dynamic analysis is also possible using test cases. The primary purpose of S-TCAT is to ensure that all functions have been tested during the system and integration testing process. S-TCAT provides the following benefits:

- Unexercised program function call entry points
- Frequently hit function calls
- Redundant test cases
- Dead or unused code
- Support for code in C, C++, Ada, Fortran and Pascal

The GUI-based use model can be cumbersome at times to use with this product. For example, the path to a source code file will not be retained during many operations and result in fatal errors during compilation and instrumentation. The next described tool is also from Software Research, Inc. It provides test coverage analysis of source code paths under test that would normally only be used during unit and function testing.

14.36 TCAT

TCAT is a Test Coverage Analysis Tool from Software Research, Inc. for engineers and QA. It is part of the Software Test Works (STW) suite of products. TCAT supports C, C++, Ada, COBOL, F77 and Pascal. Directed graphs or *digraphs* provide strongly connected pictures for branch coverage using an *anno-*

tation feature. Source annotation shows the branches and statements that have been executed in bold print. This feature allows the user to pinpoint statements with high-complexity (i.e., high potential for failure). Clicking on any node in a digraph, the user can see the source code for the specific switching node. Coverage reports include:

- Unexercised or executed program branches
- Frequently executed branches
- Bottlenecks
- Redundant test cases
- Dead or unused code

It must be noted, however, that graphical representation of complex code using digraphs can often be very difficult to read and interpret. Therefore, the use and benefit from graphical code representation must be carefully analyzed based on the product under test. A command like the UNIX **csh**, or a complex device driver with several thousand lines of code may end up looking like spaghetti with a digraph. Therefore, it is very important to target your approach to structural testing (especially when it is used during the integration and system testing phases).

14.37 TCAT-PATH

TCAT-PATH is a path test coverage analysis tool from Software Research, Inc. and it is also part of the Software Test Works (STW) suite of products. The primary purpose of TCAT-PATH is to help analyze path coverage for the application software under test. A *path* is defined as a sequence of logical branches (decision points) in the program under test. Each grouping of branches for each function contained in the software under test is evaluated and can be later analyzed for test coverage. By definition, when each unique branch has been exercised, many unique paths will have been exercised as well (however, not each and every path combination). Full path coverage is when all unique paths or combinations of branches have been exercised. This is usually such a large number of independent paths that it has only academic value. However, TCAT-PATH provides the following selected path metrics:

- Basis paths (the set of all non-iterative paths-no loops)
- Essential edges (each edge on only one of the original set of paths)
- Unconstrained paths (edges that imply execution of other edges in the program)
- Essential paths (paths with one essential edge or an edge on no other path)

The essential edges and unconstrained path methods are currently not implemented. The author was also unable to complete the essential paths analysis using the demo as provided. (A problem report was submitted.)

14.38 tcov and Hindsight

tcov is the BSD UNIX command available on Sun-3 and Sun-4 systems. The command is used for test coverage analysis and statement-by-statement analysis and information on C programs. This program is also used by other commercial products. For example, Hindsight from ASA (Advanced Software Automation) uses the **tcov** facilities for program profiling and statement coverage analysis. Hindsight provides call graphs based on information collected by **tcov**, as well as other critical information not available with **tcov**. This is very similar to the function of digraphs provided by TCAT from Software Research, Inc. For more information on Hindsight, contact Advanced Software Automation.

Illustration 14.4 provides examples for compilation and execution analysis for the program **hello.c**.

```
%1> cc -a -o hello hello.c
%2> ./hello
hello world
%3> ls hello*
hello hello.c hello.d hello.tcov
%4> more hello.d
2 1
%5> more hello.tcov
 main()
 1 -> {
printf("hello world\n");
}


Top 10 Blocks

Line Count

2 1


1 Basic blocks in this file
1 Basic blocks executed
100.00 Percent of the file executed

1 Total basic block executions
1.00 Average executions per basic block
```

Illustration 14.4

The results show that we have executed 100% of the file. It is important to note that **tcov** provides block or statement coverage only. Therefore, for compound or multiple predicate statements where more than one decision is possible, limited information will be presented.[*] The following files are required or provided as output with **tcov**:

- **file.c** - input C program file
- **file.f** - input Fortran program file
- **file.d** - input test coverage data file
- **file.tcov** - output test coverage analysis listing file
- **/usr/lib/bb_link.o** - entry and exit routines for test coverage analysis

tcov, as well as several other commands, can be used for performance analysis. Other commands include **pixie** and **lprof**. [DOW93] states: "**lprof**'s output looks very much like **tcov**'s. **pixie** is a little different from **tcov** and **lprof**. Rather than reporting the number of times each source line was executed, **pixie** reports the number of machine clock cycles devoted to executing each line." Therefore, **pixie** can be considered a performance analysis tool, as well as a code profiler for structural testing.

14.39 Test Generator Generator System (TGGS)

TGGS is comprised of a compiler called Generate Test Generator (GTG) and associated run-time library for the Specification Language (SL). GTG compiles specifications written SL into executable test case generator programs when used in-conjunction with a C or C++ compiler. These test case generator programs can generate large quantities of randomized input test cases or test data for a variety of programs.

The GTG compiler will translate SL specifications into tabular data structures represented as sets of C/C++ statically initialized arrays and structures. Output from GTG is a C or C++ source file. The output of GTG is compiled using a standard C or C++ compiler, and linked to the TGGS run-time library. This forms a test case generator program that can produce large sets of test cases (test data) based on the original user-supplied SL specification file. Both valid (clean/positive) as well as invalid (dirty/negative) test cases can be generated by the TGGS run-time engine from an SL file.

Debugging of a generated test case generator program can be accomplished using the tracing facility provided with the run-time system. For more information on TGGS, contact RG Consulting.

---

[*] The information returned indicates only that the statement was exercised, not which part of the branch or predicate.

14.40 WinRunner and XRunner

XRunner is an X Window System client program that does similar things to TestRunner; however, it does not require a hardware board for Remote Job Emulation (RJE). Mercury Interactive suggests that users adopt XRunner or Win-Runner if either the X Window System or Microsoft Windows environment is available. Otherwise, TestRunner must be used for environments where, for example, proprietary operating systems or an embedded system is used. The cost will be greater using TestRunner in these environments. (Mercury Interactive has now discontinued support of TestRunner.)

XRunner is based on the X-Input Synthesis extension to the X Window System server from Hewlett-Packard. XRunner and capture/playback tools in general have many applications besides just testing (i.e., automated demonstrations, benchmarks, training, as well as many other possibilities).

XRunner runs in native mode* on several computer systems, as does QA Partner and other CAST (now called Automated Software Quality or ASQ) tools. The engineer or tester can also log in remote to a Sun or other XRunner-supported system running the XRunner server daemon. In this instance, the results can be displayed on a local machine. Context-free recording allows the Application Under Test (AUT) to change or move screen positions and still replay previously recorded tests without loss of synchronization.

In analog mode, screen coordinates are used to replay previously recorded tests. This means that if the AUT changes screen coordinate location or buttons change position within the application, the replay of a previously recorded test will fail.

WinRunner and XRunner record keyboard and mouse actions (also capturing screen bitmaps), replay them and verifying them by comparing against expected results (comparing screens).

Sample X-Runner Applications

XRunner comes with several sample applications. One application is called Motif Burger. The **motifbur** application is the command that starts an X Window System-based program that simulates the register at your favorite fast food hamburger restaurant. You can place an order after selecting the size of drink and french fries, as well as hamburger configuration desired. The purpose of this application is to show that the engineer can not only repeat a test script, but also change the application with **newmotif.bur** and still playback recorded events.

Approaches to CAST Testing

As previously mentioned, the analog approach to recording was the original approach used to record tests. For review, this is where screen coordinates are

---

*Other system processors and platforms are also available.

passed to an interpreter for playback at a future time. In the case of XRunner, all commands are based on the Test Script Language (TSL). A critical problem with analog recording is that if the AUT changes location on the display (or root window to be precise) playback, will fail. With object-oriented or context sensitive testing events are sent directly to the window manager. Therefore, relative coordinates rather than absolutes are used to activate events like pushing a mouse button or typing in text. Therefore, the location or contents of the application can change without the need to re-record test cases. This is because a GUI map is created to tag events with objects. The objects can change or move to different screen positions and it will be transparent. If the properties of an object change during replay, the user simply needs to remark the new object and XRunner will continue processing the TSL script.

Test Script Language (TSL)

XRunner uses the Test Script Language (TSL), similar to the use of TCL by expect/TCL and VistaREPLAY. Using TSL, users can design and create test scripts in a C-like programming language. When the engineer creates a record file, test scripts are automatically created by XRunner. These scripts are written in TSL and can be edited or written manually. The **check_screen** function, for example, will capture and compare a complete screen image. Many other functions are provided for verification during replay of a regression test script.

For more information on XRunner, and WinRunner, contact Mercury Interactive.

14.41 ViSTA

ViSTA from VERITAS Software (now CenterLine Software) provides both program and kernel code coverage. VERITAS Software provides many tools for test automation, including structural analysis and functional testing, as well as automatic record and playback facilities. ViSTA is the original product provided by VERITAS Software for structural analysis and testing.

VistaREPLAY

VERITAS has combined the benefits of automated regression testing using capture and playback features with structural testing. This allows the development or test engineer to *witness* increases (hopefully) in code coverage as automated regression tests are replayed.

Before any structural analysis and testing project or program is attempted, it is strongly recommended that a subset of target functions is selected for instrumentation. This can be accomplished using the ViSTA coverage compiler, **covcc**, or other similar tools.

Using the functional, structural, reliability and regression testing framework is one approach, where standards conformance functional tests are first used to identify *fragile,* or error-prone areas. Structural testing or decision coverage must then be used specifically for functions that will end up yielding the greatest ROI (most defects from functional testing). Static complexity or structural analysis can also help target dynamic structural testing efforts of specific functions based on code complexity. The following factors can also be used to target functional and structural testing using dynamic coverage metrics:

- Modification history
- Performance constraints
- Testability analysis
- Critical interface for other functions
- Complexity
- Quantity of critical problem reports

Decision, statement, call, interface and other test metrics are also available. Statement or line test coverage simply provides an account of which source code statements for the program under test have been executed during the test. Call coverage identifies the routines or functions that have been executed during testing. Interface coverage provides insight into each external function reference and identifies output behaviors as well. Many people confuse system and interface testing. Interface testing must be conducted prior to system testing. See the section on unit, integration and system testing at the beginning of Chapter 1 for more details. A critical first step in structural testing is to first evaluate the program under test for complexity. This is also called static structural analysis.

Static Structural Analysis Reports

Several reports are available as part of static structural analysis. McCabe's Cyclomatic complexity counts the number of decisions or branches contained in a program function. If the total number of decisions exceeds 10, the program must be split (if possible) into smaller modules, by default. Also, McCabe suggests that each independent decision must have at least one unique test program or test case. (McCabe also sells tools for testing, not in this version of this book, yet.)

Halstead's Software Science is another static, yet very controversial metric as it relies on psychological studies for program length and testing difficulty estimation. It provides metrics for the following:

- n1 = Unique operators
- n2 = Unique operands

- N1 = Total occurrences of operators
- N2 = Total occurrences of operands
- N = N1 + N2   (Program size)
- n = n1 + n2   (Vocabulary)
- V = N*log2(n) (Volume)
- Difficulty = n1/2*N2/n2
- Effort   = V/((2/n1)*(n2/N2)))
- Bugs   = V / 3000

The number 3000 is based on psychological studies and is recommended to be tailored to the actual development environment and not a fixed value. To provide static structural analysis reports, a map of the source code must be created; however, this does not require source code compilation, just execution of the pre-processor. Instrumentation is normally an intrusive operation that is performed using a coverage compiler that augments source code prior to pre-processing by the compiler software generation system.

Coverage Compilation

The coverage compiler is required for instrumentation of source code under test for any of the following operations:

- Dynamic structural testing
- *Error seeding*[*]
- Simulation
- Selective instrumentation
- Augmented source

Lexical approaches to structural test coverage analysis embed instructions in source code without being true compilers. The term coverage compiler has been used historically, however, the term coverage analyzer is often used now. The following sections are provided to help the reader become familiar with the process using VistaTEST for structural analysis and testing. The methods and commands are similar for most structural testing tools.

In addition to creating a static map file, the ability to view the augmented source code after instrumentation is often helpful during debugging. In the case of ViSTA, the file is called **source.A**, where **source** has the same file name as the original source file.

---

[*]"The process of intentionally adding known faults to those already in a computer program for the purpose of monitoring the rate of detection and removal, and estimating the number of faults remaining in the program" [IEE94] 610.12-1990.

The Structural Testing Process

This type of testing is also sometimes called *testing in the small* [HET88] or white box testing and focuses on the depth of testing. Functional testing is then often considered *testing in the large* [HET88] since it uses a higher-level view of testing (the breadth of test coverage). The structural testing process starts first with source code that must be compiled using a coverage compiler. The ViSTA product provides the command **covcc** for instrumentation. Coverage compilation usually requires linking with a *coverage monitor* using one of the following files so that data can be recorded as function calls, statements, decisions or paths are exercised:

- cov1.o
- cov2.o
- cov3.o

The coverage monitor (**cov3.0**) provides full support including multiple processes, simulation and tabulation, as well as many other features that are common with most structural analysis and testing tools available today. QASE provides one coverage monitor that offers complete support. In any case, the coverage compiler will build a geography file called **map** in the directory containing the source code. This file will consist of the basic structure of the source code that will be used to generate reports. The **map** contains information such as the number of tokens, non-commented source lines and white space for example. Illustration 14.5 shows the events involved in the construction of a **map** file.

Once the **map** files are constructed, the user can then run test suites or individual test cases against the instrumented program under test and obtain reports for what has or has not been tested. This process is also known as *dynamic* structural testing. This will produce results in a **hits** disk file. See Illustration 14.6 for details.

The other approach is to instrument the program using the coverage compiler and then generate a static **map** or geography of the structure of the program and identify the control complexity. Static analysis does not require program execution. Using static analysis, the following complexity metrics can be obtained using the appropriate command line options:

- Halstead's Software Science
- McCabe's Cyclomatic Complexity
- McCabe's Essential Complexity
- Token counts

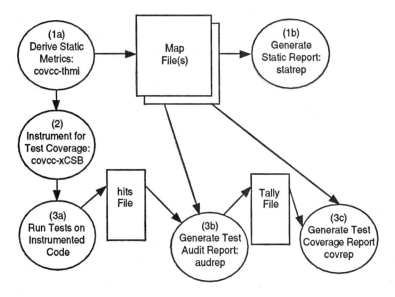

Illustration 14.5

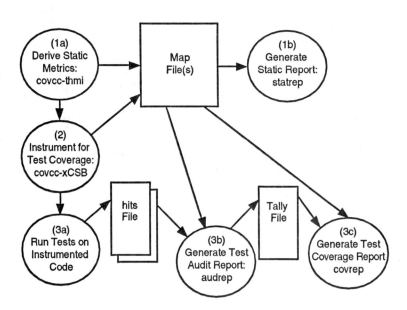

Illustration 14.6

Static Structural Analysis in the Product Life-cycle

It is strongly recommended that static metrics be used during the design of products prior to the development of source code using methods such as design reviews and inspections. The computer industry must change from the attitude that there is no time for detailed design development and review because we must hurry up and test the code.

A remark made years ago by a development manager is still very clear in my mind. He said, "We don't have time for design reviews or detailed requirements documents, unless the president can see my engineers typing on the computer, he does not believe they are really working." Many engineers and managers often say that after they have identified that a module is complex, nothing else can be done. So, in other words, their attitude is: we identified that this piece of code is complicated and that is the only way it can be written. Unfortunately, this statement is missing the entire point of static complexity metrics analysis.

One of the primary purposes of static complexity analysis is to alert engineering and quality departments to the need for more structural and functional test development and execution. Also, the analysis will assist in determining what will be required in terms of resources and time for proper regression and reliability testing, plus support. Finally, a general battle plan that defines risks and contingencies for complex functions can be drawn.

The following results are available from **statrep** using the VERITAS ViSTA command for static report analysis:

Statpnic Metric Report
    Tue Feb 25 13:49:10 1992
    File: "/usr/vista/triangle/main.c"
    Number of Tokens: 172
    Number of Whitespace Tokens: 95
    Number of (Non-Commentary) Source Lines: 22
    File: "/usr/vista/triangle/main.c"
    (n1) Number of Unique Operators: 21
    (n2) Number of Unique Operands: 23
    (N1) Total Occurrences of Operators: 118
    (N2) Total Occurrences of Operands: 54
    (N) Program Size (N1 + N2): 172
    (n) Vocabulary (n1 + n2): 44
    (V) Halstead's Volume (N * log2(n)): 939
    (D) Halstead's Difficulty ((n1/2)*(N2/n2)): 20
    (E) Halstead's Effort (V/((2/n1)*(n2/N2))): 0.01
    (B) Halstead's Error Prediction (V/3000): 0.31
    File: "/usr/vista/triangle/main.c"
    Number of Regions: 6
    Number of Non-Reducible Regions: 3
    McCabe's Cyclomatic Complexity (Ave.): 6
    McCabe's Essential Complexity (Ave.): 3
    File: "/usr/vista/triangle/main.c"
Number of Independent Paths: 8

Dynamic testing is now discussed as the most likely second step in the process of structural-based testing after or during static structural analysis.

Dynamic Structural Testing

Dynamic structural testing is useful for the analysis of software, applications or programs during either automated or manual testing (operator inputs). Results from dynamic structural testing can be obtained using either of the VISTAtest commands, **covrep** or **audrep**. The **audrep** program must be executed before **covrep** to create a **Tally** file containing a collection of execution and hit results (test coverage). QASE products only provide one command, **MCcov**, to determine coverage results. This helps remove confusion when the user is not sure which command must be used to increase test coverage. The **MCcov** command provides an option (not the default case) to identify areas of the code that have not been executed.

One approach that may be useful for a more automated approach to test case generation would be to include comments directly in the code or a pointer to a file that contains help for testing the function. This information could include both boundary conditions and values that would be useful for unit, function, integration, system or acceptance testing. These comments could then be referenced when dynamic structural testing has uncovered serious gaps in test coverage using function, reliability and regression tests. Some products such as T from IDE, for example, automate the test development process for boundary conditions.

The command to create test audit reports will now be discussed as a critical part of the structural testing process.

audrep (Test Audit Report for What Has Been Tested)

Sample output for **audrep** is contained in Illustration 14.7.These results show that all function calls were covered and greater than 90% of all decision points (branches) were executed using the tests. ViSTA calls these decisions *segments*. Each **if** statement that is listed has been executed. In some cases, both the true and false conditions have been executed. The numbers on the far right show that either the second or third predicate in a compound statement has been executed for a given source line number.

The next command provides the reverse functionality of **audrep**. The **covrep** command shows source code coverage based on unit and function test execution, rather than showing what source code *has not* been executed.

covrep (Coverage Report - What Has NOT Been Tested)

Sample output for **covrep** is contained in Illustration 14.8 to show specific **if** statements in the program under test that have not been executed using the tests contained in the test suite.

```
                              Test Audit Report

                          Wed Sep   2 21:24:43 1992


        The following was hit :

                type           id       branch      source line

           File "/1home/tmartin/class/lab1.c"
                Function main                           6
                Basic Block    0                        7
                Basic Block    1                       12
                Basic Block    2                       15
                Basic Block    3                       17
                Basic Block    4                       18
                Basic Block    5                       18
                while          0       T F             12
                while          1       T F             12       (2)
                if             2       T F             14
                if             3       T F             16
                if             4       T F             16       (2)
                if             5         F             16       (3)
                if             6       T F             18

           Call Coverage          : 100.00 %    (1/1)
           Basic Block Coverage   : 100.00 %    (6/6)
           Segment Coverage       :  92.86 %    (13/14)
```

Illustration 14.7

Illustration 14.8

```
                            Test Coverage Report

                          Wed Sep   2 21:26:04 1992


        File : "/1home/tmartin/class/lab1.c"

           Call Coverage          : 100.00 %    (1/1)
           Segment Coverage       :  14.29 %    (2/14)

        The following are statistical data for totals :

           Call Coverage          : 100.00 %    (1/1)
           Segment Coverage       :  14.29 %    (2/14)

        The following was not hit :

                type           id       branch      source line

           File "/1home/tmartin/class/lab1.c"
                while          0       T               12
                while          1         F             12       (2)
                if             2       T F             14
                if             3       T F             16
                if             4       T F             16       (2)
                if             5       T F             16       (3)
                if             6       T F             18
```

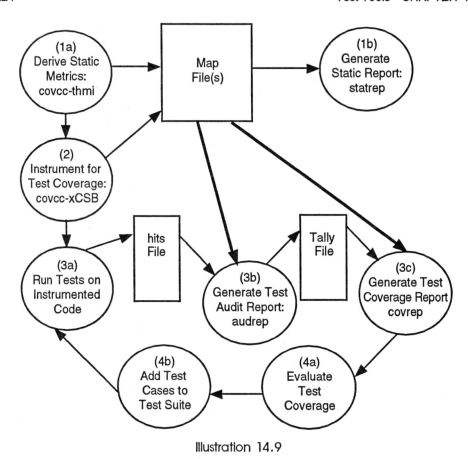

Illustration 14.9

Once **audrep** and **covrep** results are available, the process continues by adding more test cases to increase test coverage. Most engineers use **covrep**. See Illustration 14.9. This Illustration shows how test coverage is increased by locating and understanding source code statements and decisions or branches that have not been executed. The next command will provide an *annotated* source code listing to help better determine what code has or has not been exercised as part of the dynamic structural test process. This command can be used along with **audrep** or **covrep** during dynamic test case analysis.

listgen (Annotated Source Listings)

The **listgen** command provides an annotated C source listing for portions of source code that either have or have not been executed. The code is highlighted and can be viewed using the UNIX commands **nroff** or **troff.** This command is

```
/* VERITAS ViSTA Annotated Source Listing
 *
 * Source File:        /usr/vista/triangle/smalloc.c
 * Coverage:           Basic Block
 * Highlighted:        Hit
 */

#include <"/usr/include/stdlib.h">
# 3 "malloc.c"

main()
{
  char * bp;

  bp=(char *) malloc(64);
  if (bp != 0)
  {
      printf("malloc() returned address %d\n", (int)bp);
      free(bp);
  } else {
      printf("malloc() returned a NULL; errno = ENOMEM\n");
      exit (-1);
      }
}
```

Illustration 14.10

helpful for the programmer or test engineer to better determine what actual code needs further testing or has already been tested. Rather than simply supplying the source line number and the type of statement, an annotated listing will show all code statements and highlight in bold all statements that have been executed.

The example shown for the following C shell prompt highlights statements that have been executed, see Illustration 14.10 for sample output.

%1> listgen -bt tally -- malloc.c

Another command that is useful during dynamic structural testing is *error seeding*. This is where failures or errors are introduced into the program under test to see if the test programs can identify all errors introduced.

Error Seeding

The purpose of *error seeding* is to test the efficacy of the test programs to uncover test program problems, the software under test is injected with *error seeds* and then monitored as to how many injected errors were discovered by the test suite. Another way of looking at this is testing the test suite's effectiveness by re-bugging the product under test (aka. bebugging). For example, the logic for an

if statement may be reversed causing an error in the expected result or outcome by the following statement:

    if (foobar == 1)

If an error seed were injected, the statement would look like the following:

    if (foobar != 1)

Two other approaches are to make all conditions either always true or always false as follows:

    if (1 | | condition) /* always true condition */

    if (0 | | conditions) /* always false condition */

If each decision in the program has enough test cases, as recommended by the McCabe Complexity metric, the error seed must be uncovered; however, this is not guaranteed. The command **seedrep** is used to report on the status of injected error seeds. Error seeding is probably most useful for analyzing the strength of a pre-existing test suite.

The following sample output in Illustration 14.11 is available after the coverage compiler has been requested to inject the default of 64 error seeds per every 1000 lines of source code:

```
Error Seed Report
Mon Jun 15 16:04:43 1992
Statistical Totals

(Ns)  Total Number of Error Seeds : 2
(Nc)  Total Number of Covered Seeds : 2
(ns)  Total Number of Detected Seeds : 2
(ni)  Total Number of Seeds to Inspect : 0

(Yr)  Test Yield (ns/Ns) : 100.00 %
(Ye)  Adjusted Test Yield (ns/Nc) : 100.00 %
```

Illustration 14.11

The next step that is useful during dynamic structural-based testing is to use *coverage partitioning*. This is where the test suite driver is used to tag or categorize tests so that dynamic test execution results can be better linked to individual test case execution.

Coverage Partitioning

This facility provides a method using the **covpart** command to categorize or partition results reported from **audrep** into test case *partitions*. One primary benefit of **covpart** is that the development and test engineer can quickly determine duplicate test cases, as well as test cases that are weak and not providing any added test value. Some engineers may take exception to the statement that a test that does not provide additional statement or decision coverage must be thrown away. I agree, however, the priority of tests that do not increase test coverage must be careful understood and reduced if possible to optimize regression and function test execution time. For example, if Test Case 1 uses different data than Test Case 2, the end result may be a different effect or possibly failure. This could continue to be true even if both execute the same source statements and decision branches. This is because data flow testing and dynamic structural testing are very different. We can execute all statements or decisions successfully and still have program errors. For example, some errors that may result include missing exception handlers for incorrect data input or a boundary value. Products that provide simulation library support, such as MCsim and VistaSIM, as well as PiSCES for testability analysis, also provide basic data flow testing capabilities. Simulation libraries can force specific return values to be provided by a function.

The test case for **equilateral** using the classic triangle program [MYE79] will produce the results provided in Illustration 14.12 after execution of the **audrep** command. The following command is provided prior to execution of the **equilateral** test case for coverage partitioning:

%1> covpart equilateral

```
equilateral
        type id branch source line
        File "/usr/vista/examples/triangle/main.c"
        Function main 10
  if       0            F        16
  if       1        T   F        21
  if       2            F        22
  if       3            F        23
  if       4            T        25
        File "/usr/vista/examples/triangle/triangle.c"
        Function triangle
  if       0            F         4
  if       1            F         6
  if       2            F         8
  if       3            F        10
```

Illustration 14.12

Once adequate unit and functional test coverage is available using dynamic and static structural analysis and tests, simulation may be used to test external interfaces. These external functions may or may not be available for testing. Also, the ability to test each instance of an external interface may be very difficult. Therefore, *simulation* is often used for interface testing of external functions prior to central CM and integration.

Simulation

Simulation is different from emulation in that simulation provides the exact same facilities of the function using stub routines. Emulation however, provides a program that is used as a substitute for the real program, often with limitations. The same is true for data simulation and emulation, just as with program text execution. VistaSIM provides the command **usim** for interface testing using simulation libraries.

One of the greatest difficulties most programmers and test engineers experience is properly testing program functions as they are used by other programs prior to integration testing. For example, using the UNIX **malloc** library function could result in an error condition if insufficient memory is available to satisfy the request. However, providing the required circumstances to test this condition may be very difficult to generate. Therefore, simulation libraries allow the engineer or QA professional to model a specific behavior for external functions to test if the program under test can deal with these various potential failures or anomalies. A simulation library is simply a *stub* around a library routine. For example, the following code fragment could be used for the **malloc** function:

```
char *Cov_malloc(bytes)
if (simulation assertion) {
set errno;
return (simulated error);
}
else
return (malloc(bytes));
```

The definition of a stub or simulation function is simply the service being simulated; for example: **read, open, malloc** and **close**. The simulation behavior of a function is one of many possible output results of calling the function. This result is usually stored in a global variable called **errno** and is contained in a return value from the function. Creating stub files for each and every function could be a very time-consuming process. Therefore, QASE provides the ability to automatically create simulations using QASE's generic simulator. This inserts code into the assembly language code so that when a function returns a single value, it can be directly stored in a machine register, based on the desired simulation loaded in the simulation table. This is a preferred method over the "custom" simulator, which requires the user to create a stub file. The custom simulator is still required for functions that don't return a scalar value, but instead may pass a pointer or a complete structure. These functions cannot be simulated using an assembly language generic simulator. For example, with Sun systems, the following command must be used for the program under test (in this case the program name is **smalloc.c**).

%1> **covcc -XCSthmia -F sun4.1.S -o cov3.o,libsim.a -- -o smalloc smalloc.c**

The following results show the sequence of events once the program under test has encountered a problem using the simulation libraries:

%2> **smalloc**
malloc() returned address 2692227560

The above returned address is actually provided by the operating system and not by the simulation library. Next, add the **malloc** behavior **ENOMEM** to the simulation table to check the results of program execution:

%3> **usim -A malloc ENOMEM**

Now, print the simulation table contents to verify the desired state:

%4> **usim -p**
function behavior flags
malloc ENOMEM

FInally, run the instrumented binary with simulation libraries:

%5> **smalloc**
malloc() returned a NULL pointer; errorno = ENOMEM

The above message from **malloc** is actually provided by the simulation library **malloc** routine and not the operating system function. It is very important to note that the simulation table must always be cleared to avoid confusion in future simulation testing sessions:

%6> **usim**

Charting results once structural testing is complete is extremely useful during the verification and validation development process.

Charting Results

The old saying: "A picture is worth a thousand words" seems to be the best way to explain charting and metrics collection. The old saying holds true even with state-of-the-practice approaches to structural analysis and testing. To create a bar chart using VistaGRAPH, the following command can be used at the UNIX shell prompt (not available with Metal):

%1> **chartgen -dmap,tally -cALL bar.ctl | chartvw -**

This command will create a bar chart using a sample bar chart template and will create a chart description language file as output for the command **chartvw** to use. Other types of charts are also available. The command **chartvw** will allow the user to view the output in the specified format using data collected from test execution and stored in the **hits** file. The **hits** file will be appended to each time the program under test is exercised using a specific test case. Therefore, the user must be careful to monitor the size and location of the hits file. The hits file will normally always be in the directory where the binary was executed for testing; however, an environment variable is also available to change the location to a different directory. Illustration 14.13 serves as an example of one of the many charts available using the commands chartgen and chartvw with coverage results contained in a Tally file. A Tally file can be created using the audrep -T command to consolidate hits file data.

The bar chart shown in Illustration 14.14 shows a graph using data collected from VistaTEST.

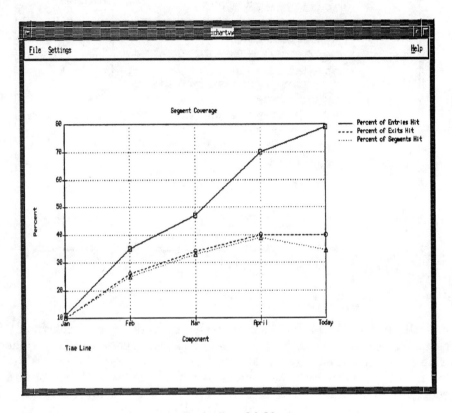

Illustration 14.13

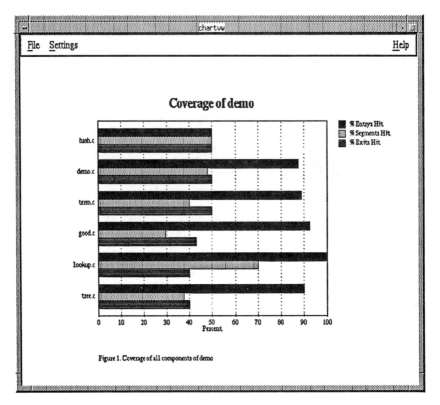

Illustration 14.14

Illustration 14.14 shows a common bar chart that is available from ViSTA for charting structural test coverage results. These reports can be very helpful during management operations reviews. These are the types of charts that are often missing from many software and hardware company's board of directors meetings. Unfortunately, they are often buried in the quality managers desk drawer, if they exist at all. This is also often the difference between satisfied customers and dissatisfied customers that are an enormous expense to support and maintain because of poor-quality products.

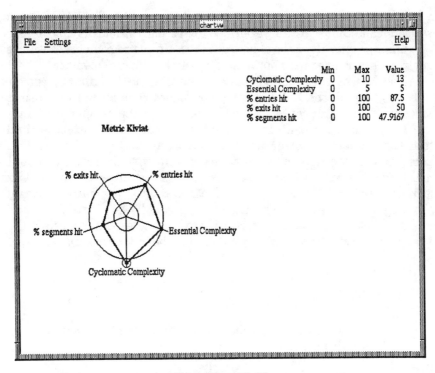

Illustration 14.15

Illustration 14.15 shows a standard Kiviat diagram using coverage information obtained using the coverage compiler and presented using **chartvw**.

ViSTA provides many features that are common to most structural analysis and testing technologies. It is critical that these types of testing functions be used to supplement standard functional testing.

14.42 X11 Virtual Display System

X11 Virtual Display is from Software Research, Inc. This tool provides the ability to simulate multiple user sessions from the same machine for purposes of load generation, performance assessment, and multiple test execution. QA Partner and LoadRunner provide similar facilities. The tool can be used to run tests in parallel when doing so is necessary to speed up execution of a test suite. X11 Virtual has been successfully used to test clients without having a standard X server running. This method of testing can be useful during performance testing. Another benefit is when expensive hardware resources (display monitors or controllers) are not available for use during test execution; tests can be run using the X11 Virtual server. This also means that you can perform GUI testing without having to have an X server running (you will not be able to use the **xvmon** program to see your results). Each virtual session requires approximately 4mb of virtual memory.

The X11 Virtual tool comes with some sample scripts to run multiple **xclock** programs in the X11 virtual environment. The author has also successfully recorded XRunner context-sensitive scripts for the sample **motifbur** application. Three copies of the XRunner scripts were successfully executed in the X11 Virtual environment, however, it is very important that the XRunner TSL script include **aut_connect** as the first statement, otherwise the script will not be able to connect to the application under test in the virtual environment. Software Research's CAPBAK/X and Performance Awareness' preVueX, or Segue Software's QA Partner are all reported to be supported by X11 Virtual.

The following shell script, **motifrun**, can be executed to start three virtual copies of a test (the **xvinit** command must be in your path):

```
#!/bin/sh

XVMONDISPLAY=:0
export XVMONDISPLAY
xvinit -r mymotifrc -- :1 -width 1280 -height 1024 -dpi 91x92 &
xset s off -display :1
sleep 1
xvinit -r mymotifrc -- :2 -width 1280 -height 1024 -dpi 91x92 &
xset s off -display :2
sleep 1
xvinit -r mymotifrc -- :3 -width 1280 -height 1024 -dpi 91x92 &
xset s off -display :3
```

The script **mymotifrc** contains the following three commands:

```
#!/bin/sh
mwm > /tmp/mwm.log 2> /tmp/mwm.log &
xterm -geometry +20+20 -e "Motifbur.Command" &
exec xvmon
```

The application test script **Motifbur.Command** is used to start the application and run the XRunner test script that contains the following:

```
#!/bin/sh
motifbur &
sleep 2
xrun.motif -t /usr/mnt/rodney/motifbur -run &
```

14.43 xtrap

xtrap is provided by the X Consortium, Inc. It was originally developed by Digital Equipment Corporation. **xtrap** was designed for automated control of an X Window System workstation. **xtrap** can be implemented on any sample X server. This program intercepts X events and client-generated protocol requests. It is able to take pre-recorded events stored in a disk file and replay what was recorded. Sample clients include **xtrapin** and **xtrapout**.

To record events for future playback, use the following command from any **xterm** window.

%1> **xtrapout -e -f filename**

To replay all events that were previously recorded in the file called **filename** use the following command also from any **xterm** window:

%2> **xtrapin -f filename**
(where filename is the file that was specified with xtrapout)

It is very apparent during playback using **xtrapin**, that the speed of events will vary greatly and can seem sporadic. Consequently, some events are lost. This means that the playback script will simply hang; however, you can usually kill the script using the UNIX **kill** command or by sending an interrupt signal by holding down the **Control** and **C** keys together. It is recommended that all mouse and arrow key movements be slow and smooth while recording to prevent problems during playback. Several patches have been provided by the X Consortium for these and other problems. Products such as XRunner and QAPartner have commercial support and are recommended over public-domain tools.

14.44 Conclusions

- Automated test tools for regression, combined with products for structural analysis and testing, can provide a complete and rich environment to measure product quality improvements.
- This environment will provide the development and test engineer with a significant amount of useful information regarding the quality of the product that can be used to improve planning and estimation techniques.
- Remember, product development is not complete until all tests have been identified and successfully executed with known results. Another way of stating this is: "If it is not tested, it does not work". Your gambling with your reputation if you deliver products without testing.

- It is important that the QA function provide the training and support required to improve the software development process. This includes training engineers how to use state-of-the-practice tools and techniques for functional, structural, reliability and regression verification and validation testing.
- Many functional, structural, and regression testing tools are available. Most vendors will allow you to evaluate their products. If they don't, forget it.
- Don't forget about tools for reliability and test ability; your customers won't.
- Tools will only be as successful as the people and methods that are employed.

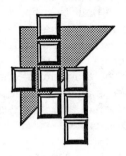

## CHAPTER 15

Test Harnesses

A good software QA strategy will consistently utilize technology based on existing standards when possible. One major area of difficulty for software quality engineers has been the availability of standards-based test technology and processes. Lack of standard technology for configuring, building and executing tests often results in the lack of test reuse, high maintenance costs and poor morale, to name just a few of many problems. This chapter will discuss:

- The definition and purpose of a test harness
- The Testsuite Environment Toolkit (TET) test harness
- Perennial's **driver** test harness
- DejaGnu from the FSF
- MCtst from QASE
- TestExpert from Qualtrak Corporation
- TestDirector from Mercury Interactive Corporation
- Test harness benefits and challenges

15.1   Introduction to Test Harnesses

Test harness technology is often referred to as a test *scaffold* or test *driver*. The term *scaffolding* is often defined as programs and data built to support software development and testing, but not intended to be included in the final product. For example, stub files, test case generators, monitors and emulators [IEE94]. A *test driver* is a software module used to invoke the program under test. It often will provide test inputs and is used to control and monitor program execution. Finally, the driver must report test results. A test harness is another name for a test driver. A test driver is often required to perform interface and unit testing using a bottom-up approach when an entire subsystem or complete system is not available for testing.

Few areas in the study of software development and test can capture the attention of quality management the way that a well thought out test harness methodology and technology can. This is primarily because the computer software development and test industry is still in an adolescent stage of maturity. This is evident by the lack of standards and technologies for sharing and reusing tests between customers and software vendors. This is slowly changing, however. Very few test harnesses are available, however. Hopefully this will change.

15.2   Purpose

The purpose of this chapter is to explore available test harness technologies and tools. Moreover, the chapter discusses how to take available tests and test harnesses and integrate them into a single coordinated software development and test environment. One critical component required for a successful software development process is a central test harness or *glue* from which unit tests can be constructed and executed. Unit and functional tests are often simply lost or left buried somewhere in a developer's directory hierarchy. This means that this *testware* or test software is often lost forever when an employee leaves the company for a better job assignment. This represents a huge waste, since these tests could often be added to a regression test suite using a standard harness and reused when modifications are made to a related function. Most customers would usually love to have installation and configuration tests for new product releases. These software tests could be considered equally important to hardware power-on tests that ensure proper functioning of a computer system prior to booting the operating system.

For engineers to use a more formal approach to software development and delivery using the functional, structural, reliability and regression test framework, more work is often required. [HET88] states: "An effective testing life cycle must be imposed on *top* of the existing work flow before significant testing improvement can be assured. The goal is to bring these two together in such a way that testing flows naturally out of the development work. The trick is to establish the testing techniques without adding a burden to the development cycle!" This chapter is all about how to accomplish these two critical goals through the use of test harness technology.

15.3 Available Test Harnesses

Probably one of the biggest problems associated with modern-day software development environments is the major shortfall of available test harness technology. Most companies have invested great sums of money in the development and maintenance of proprietary test harnesses or drivers. As a result, many engineers have been tasked with the proverbial problem of re-inventing the wheel whenever various types of tests are to be collected. The Testsuite Environment Toolkit (TET) is a product available from X/Open to solve this unusually common problem. Perennial, Inc. provides a program called **driver.** This program is oriented specifically toward the compilation and execution of C test programs for the Perennial operating system validation suites. Computer-Aided Software Test (CAST) products provided by Segue Software (QAPartner) and Mercury Interactive (XRunner) also can be used for both the driving and validating of functional tests. See the chapter on test tools for more information on CAST products. The DejaGnu, MCtst and TestExpert test harnesses and management systems will also be covered in this chapter. Other tools will hopefully be added to a later edition.

15.4 Testsuite Environment Toolkit (TET)

One standard approach for driving both the construction of test programs and their execution is the Testsuite Environment Toolkit (TET). The key program used with TET is the Test Case Controller (**tcc**). The **tcc** program comes with various options which may be used singly or in any combination. All of the other options modify the behavior of the **tcc** program in one or more modes. Unless otherwise specified, journal information and saved intermediate result files are placed below a sequentially- numbered directory under the **results** directory of the test suite selected. The **tcc** command writes the name of the **journal** file to the UNIX standard output device on start-up (usually the display or terminal screen). The following **tcc** options are available for the test case controller mode selection:

- Cleaning
- Building
- Execution

15.5   TCC Operations

The first step with most test suites is to compile or build the tests. This is accomplished using the **tcc -c** option in the TET **scenario** file. Before describing the syntax and process for building and executing tests, we must first describe the demo that is provided with the TET test harness. The demo is located in the **demo** directory and contains **.cfg** files for build, clean and execute operations. To clean the demo program, type the following:

> %1> **tcc -c -s tet_scen demo all**
> You will receive a notice similar to the following:
> journal file name is: /usr1/rodney/TET/demo/results/0004c/journal

The above command will tell the test case controller (**tcc**) to perform a **clean** operation using the **tet_scen** scenario file. The **demo** option defines the name of the test suite and the **all** option requests the "all" version of the **tet_scen** scenario file. The user can have multiple scenarios per individual scenario file (i.e., all, quick, real-quick, etc.).

The command for building a test or test suite is very similar to the **clean** command, however, the **-b** option is used instead of **-c**. Both the **clean** and **build** operations create **journal** files in a subdirectory in the **results** directory under the current test suite directory that is incremented each time an operation is invoked. For example, the first clean operation would be called **0001c**, the second **0002c**, etc. The next build operation journal file must be contained in the results file in the **0003b** subdirectory. If all operations were to be performed via the **-cbe** option, the results would be stored in the **0004bec** subdirectory in the file called **journal.**

To obtain TET free of charge from X/Open, send the following email request to info-server@xopen.co.uk. Be sure to include the following text in your email message:

> Request: tet
> Topic: index
> Request: end

The other option is to use anonymous **ftp** to **xopen.co.uk** and change directories to the **pub** distribution. The distributed version of TET (**dtet**) is located under the **pub** subdirectory, as well as the extended TET (**etet**). The **dtet** version provides execution, cleanup and compilation of test suites on remote systems and parallel operations. The **dtet** version also provides interactive support.

To build TET Release 1.10, enter the following commands:

%2> cd tet1.10/src/posix_c
%3> make clean; make (will build and install **tcc** and **libapi**)
%4> cd tet1.10/src/xpg3sh/api
%5> make (will install the following):

  •**tcm.sh** - Shell Test Case Manager
  •**tetapi.sh** - Shell API support routines.)

To use **tcc,** the following environment variables must be defined and set to match your local environment:
% TET_ROOT=$HOME/..; export TET_ROOT
% TETBASE=$TET_ROOT/test_suite1; export TETBASE
% PATH=$PATH:$TET_ROOT/bin; export PATH
% LD_LIBRARY_PATH=${TETBASE}:$LD_LIBRARY_PATH
% export LD_LIBRARY_PATH
(LD_LIBRARY_PATH is only needed for dynamic linking in shared object environments.)
To clean/build a test suite using a *scenario* file, the following can be used (where **t1** is the **scenario** file for Test Suite 1):

  %6> tcc -c -s scen t1 build 2>&1 | tee -a ./t1.build.out
  %7> tcc -b -s scen t1 build 2>&1 | tee -a ./t1.build.out

The scenario file would look as follows with the following two tags:

```
#
# This scenario is used to build executables.
#
build
/tset/t1_test
#
# This scenario is used to run the executables.
#
exec
/tset/t1_test
# <end scenario file>
```

The **scenario** file assumes a C test suite program. **t1_test.c** in the **tset** directory can be compiled and will generate a binary called **t1_test**. Once everything has been compiled, the following command can be used to execute tests:

%8> **tcc -e -s scen t1 exec 2>&1 | tee ./t1.out**

You may want to consider copying log files with a new name, date or time appended to the name. Three files will be required for each type of scenario (i.e., clean, build and execute):

- tetbuild.cfg
- tetclean.cfg
- tetexec.cfg

Both Unisoft and X/Open own copyrights to all TET source files. The engineer can freely modify the macro definition, such as the build and clean command directives. These are usually invoked by the UNIX **make** command. Other macro definitions usually found in most **makefiles** are also included in each **config** file. For an example, they can be found where the compiler and linker live, as well as in **ranlib, tsort,** and other UNIX command locations.

The **tset** directory contains the **makefile** or **Makefile** with the source code to be compiled and executed as part of the test suite. One of the nicest features of TET is that if you have a problem in the middle of execution or compilation, the whole process can be restarted from the last failure, without the need to start from the beginning. The engineer can execute the following command to restart the process:

%8> **tcc -e -m FAIL,UNRESOLVED**

This will resume execution from the last Individual Component (IC) that gave a FAIL or UNRESOLVED result. Each time **tcc** cleans, builds or executes, a **journal** file is created. An example using the clean option is shown below:

%9> **./bin/tcc -c -s scen t1 build**
journal file name is: /usr1/rodney/TET/tet1.10/t/results/0016c/journal

Illustration 15.1 is the sample output of the journal file from our clean operation.

The next step would be to build the test suite using the **-b** option with the **tcc** command and execute the directives as provided by the **tet_scen** scenario file. Some environment variables are also very important. For example, **TET_OUTPUT_CAPTURE** can be significant so that all normal standard input,

```
0|1.10 10:24:43 19930914|User: rodney (154) TCC Start,
Command Line: tcc -c -s tet_scen
20|/usr1/rodney/TET/tet1.10/demo/tetclean.cfg 2|Config Start
30||TET_VERSION=1.10
30||TET_OUTPUT_CAPTURE=True
30||TET_RESCODES_FILE=tet_code
30||TET_EXEC_IN_PLACE=False
30||TET_CLEAN_TOOL=rm
30||TET_CLEAN_FILE=-f
40||Config End
70||"starting scenario"
300|0 /ts/tc1 10:24:43|Clean Start, scenario ref 4-1
320|0 0 10:24:43|Clean End
300|1 /ts/tc2 10:24:44|Clean Start, scenario ref 5-1
320|1 0 10:24:44|Clean End
300|2 /ts/tc3 10:24:44|Clean Start, scenario ref 6-1
320|2 0 10:24:44|Clean End
70||"done"
900|10:24:44|TCC End
```

Illustration 15.1

output and error files are available for results analysis. The test engineer can look in the **journal** file for the results of build, clean and/or execution operations once this flag has been set.

Several API functions are available with the TET library. In the **tc1** demo example, a call is made to the function **tet_infoline** to display "This is the first test case (tc1)" in the execution journal file. Then, a call is made to **tet_result** with the value of **TET_PASS.** The program **tc1** could have included some conditional logic prior to providing a status of PASS. For instance, if the return code to **tet_infoline** was non-zero, we would not want to call **tet_status** with the input **TET_PASS**, but use **TET_FAIL** instead. The following values are available for the **tet_result** function (Table 15.1).

15.6   Perennial's "driver"

driver is a C program provided by Perennial, Inc. It is used for validation testing of UNIX operating system products. The **driver** program provides the ability to compile or execute tests that are contained in a **testlist** file. The user can

Table 15.1

TET Results	
Output	Input to **tet_result**
"PASS"	"TET_PASS"
"FAIL"	"TET_FAIL"
"UNRESOLVED"	"TET_UNRESOLVED"
"NOTINUSE"	"TET_NOTINUSE"
"UNSUPPORTED"	"TET_UNSUPPORTED"
"UNTESTED"	"TET_UNSUPPORTED"
"UNINITIATED"	"TET_UNINITIATED"
"NORESULT"	"TET_NORESULT"

always modify the contents of the **testlist** file to reflect tests that are to be added or deleted from a test suite.

Individual test programs make function call references to either the **libd** library or **another.o** object file, as either is linked with the test program prior to execution. The functions are considered part of an overall test scaffold from which test suites are often constructed. This includes, for example, functions that display and print information when a new block or section of a test case has been either entered or exited. This can be extremely useful during debugging. In this particular case, the function names **blenter** and **blexit** are used by the Perennial **driver** for block enter and block exit. Many other facilities are available.

15.7   DejaGnu

This product is provided free of charge from the Free Software Foundation (FSF) and Cygnus. DejaGnu is a framework for testing other programs and therefore is considered a test harness. The primary purpose is to provide a single front end for all tests. Beyond this, DejaGnu offers several features:

- Consistency of test construction, execution, and analysis
- A layer of abstraction for portability (front-end/back-end approach)
- Written in Expect, which uses the Testsuite Command Language (TCL) pronounced "tickle". This gives DejaGnu the ability to test interactive programs as well as batch oriented command and shell scripts. Using

TCL gives test suite engineers the responsibility of providing more flexibility and ease of use.

Discussions of bugs in DejaGnu are available at: bug-dejagnu@prep.ai.mit.edu. The Cygnus URL is **http://www.cygnus.com**.

DejaGnu is supported by Cygnus for a fee. The **runtest** demo is packaged with DejaGnu and it is one way to get started. The **calc** test is another demo that can be used. You will need to update the shell **path** environment variable before executing the demo. To execute the **runtest** demo, simply type **make check** at the shell prompt in the **testsuite** sub-directory.

Version 1.3 is expected sometime in the future. To obtain a copy of DejaGnu version 1.2, five **shar** files in the **dejagnu-1.2.tar.gz-split** directory must be obtained. I suggest that you copy the README file first. Use the **gzip** utility to create an uncompressed **tar** archive. The DejaGnu release may also be available from one or more of the following **ftp** sites:

- ftp.uu.net/packages/gnu
- nic.funet.fi/pub/gnu
- gatekeeper.dec.com/pub/GNU
- archie.au/gnu
- src.doc.ic.ac.uk/gnu
- utsun.s.u-tokyo.ac.jp /ftpsync/prep
- Other GNU archive sites
- prep.ai.mit.edu/pub/gnu

15.8   Internal Tools (Test Harnesses)

Internal tools form the basis for the majority of test harnesses that are in use today. In most cases, companies typically use either *super makefiles* or master shell script programs to control and coordinate the construction and execution of individual test cases into test suites. The problem with many of these tools is that support is non-existent usually. Support includes training, maintenance, problem resolution, documentation, etc. Usually, since most engineers have other *more important* customer product responsibilities, test harness tools usually end up with the lowest possible priority. This results in a serious problem since the absence of a test harness usually means that if unit tests are developed (if at all), they end up in the trash after they are executed once, either successfully or non-successfully. This is also known as *disposable testing* and it accounts for serious productivity and financial waste.

Unit tests must be integrated into regression and reliability test suites for future use. Also, because test harness tools are never provided as products to customers, the general quality of internal test tools is usually very poor. Another major problem with internal or proprietary test harness technology is that customers and other vendors are unable to participate in validation. This includes the evolution of the regression, system, integration and other test suite technologies provided by test cases that cooperate with the test harness framework and architecture. Debugging support is often lacking from most "home-grown" test harness tools, making support and maintenance of tests an even bigger problem than product support.

15.9   Test Harnesses and POSIX

Test harnesses are probably the most critical tools for both the engineering and quality groups within any software development organization. Unfortunately, these tools often have not been considered important by management and are often not included in the planning process. Therefore, the quality of software products has reflected the absence of test coverage from unit tests controlled by an automated test harness. However, with the advent of many new standards for the development and production of both system and applications software, a standard for testing has also emerged.

Working Group 1003.3, was developed and chartered with the responsibility for identifying and providing a standard for testing as a result of the work performed by other working groups. For example, the P1003.1 Work Group first identified a standard set of operating system library calls for the UNIX operating system. After the standard was complete, a set of test assertions was developed for each function call. Furthermore, a test harness was required to act as the *glue* for each test assertion.

The Verification Suite for XPG (X/Open Portability Guide), or VSX, was provided by Unisoft Corporation using the TET harness as approved by the P1003.3 Work Group. Therefore, the P1003.1 committee developed the specification and the P1003.3 Work Group developed the test methods for testing the standard. TET is the result of a great amount of work of many companies including X/Open, the Open Software Foundation (OSF) and UNIX International. Unfortunately, support for TET from X/Open has terminated. However, TestExpert from Qualtrak Corporation is a test management system and test harness that is based upon TET and is fully supported.

15.10   MCtst

MCtst is a test harness provided by QASE. This product alone provides the ability to execute commands and compare expected inputs to outcomes. Outcomes include standard output, error and any requested files. The following command calls the MCtst test harness to test the **calc** program and expects the output shown (**stdout**, or file descriptor 2 will be the value "4"). MCtst also expects that no errors will occur and that **stderr**, or file descriptor 2 will be null:

> %1> **MCtst -e 0 -1 "4" -2 "" ./calc 2 + 2**
> MCtst: testinput: calc 2 + 2
> MCtst: action: exec()
> MCtst: passed!!
> MCtst: action: check exit code
> MCtst: expect: 0
> MCtst: passed!!
> MCtst: action: check stdout
> MCtst: expect:
> 4
> MCtst: actual:
> 4
> MCtst: passed!!

This test expects that the exit return code from the **calc** program will be zero as defined by the **-e** option. One of the more attractive features of the MCtst harness is its integration with other products provided by QASE. A **demo.sh** program is provided that first walks the user through the creation of a checklist from a requirements specification. This checklist for analyzing functional test coverage is generated by MCman after macros are inserted in the functional requirements specification. Each macro helps to define the start and end of a functional requirement. This operation is followed by the automatic creation of a test stub file for each functional requirement. A flag of 0 is inserted into each functional test file to indicate that a test is not present currently. The user can then create a test for each stub file or use the MCtgn or MCcap tool to capture command tests. Test procedures and data can then be incorporated into each test stub file. Finally, when the MCtst test harness executes all tests, information regarding functional test coverage can be provided. It is also a good idea to measure structural test coverage once functional test coverage has been analyzed. The MCtst and MCtgn tools are designed for non-GUI based testing.

15.11 TestExpert

TestExpert (previously known as Qtest) is a test management and test harness product. Test management technology often provides similar functions to a test harness. However, a test harness is often used more for unit test design, development and execution. Test management often provides facilities on top of a test harness for better management of test data, including documentation, execution, reporting and defect reporting. TestExpert includes a test execution engine, the ability to create IEEE conforming test plans, a test scheduling module, requirements traceability and a test reporting system. TestExpert includes a sample database of tests (**perl** and shell scripts, C, etc.) and test results.

The system also contains a test reporting system that allows display of test summary information as well as color postscript graphs of test execution results. The **pageview** command can be used to display postscript results, or results can be printed to a postscript printer.

TestExpert is also integrated with Qualtrak's bug tracking system (DDTs). TestExpert also provides the following integrated features:

- Test development environment (template files for shell scripts, **perl** scripts, C programs and others)
- Test Execution (Regression) Engine
- Test repository (probably one of the most important features)
- SQL database of test documentation
- SQL database of test results
- Color Postscript report writer
- Numerous "canned" test metrics
- Integration to CM

CM tools that are integrated with TestExpert include ClearCase, Aide-de-Camp, PVCS, SCCS, RCS and CVS. This means that test and product sources are integrated. For more information on TestExpert, contact Qualtrak Corporation.

15.12 TestDirector

TestDirector is a test management system from Mercury Interactive Corporation. TestDirector provides facilities to perform:

- Information management
- Visual test planning and design
- Central execution and control
- Bug tracking
- Customized test data analysis

TestDirector (at the time of this writing) is only supported on MS-Windows based platforms. UNIX support may be provided in the future. A table is used to identify various attributes about testing. A test tree graph can then be displayed. After test execution, several graphs can be display to help identify test results. For example, tests that have passed, failed or not executed.

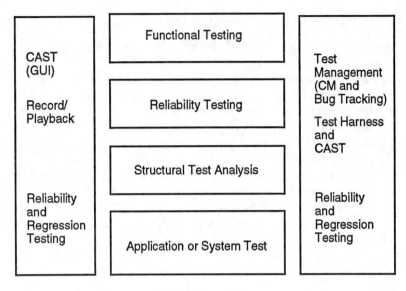

Illustration 15.1

15.13 Test Harness Architecture and Features

One possible architecture for testing with a test harness is to use a Computer-Aided Software Test (CAST) product along with a test harness technology. This provides the ability for the CAST tool to focus on GUI test cases, but also to drive test harness-controlled test cases if needed. XRunner from Mercury Interactive and QA Partner from Segue Software are two of many available CAST tools. Functional testing must be used to drive the development of tests that exercise the application or product under test. Structural testing and analysis is used to evaluate the implementation (source code) coverage provided by functional and reliability tests. Reliability testing is used to evaluate the MTBF, MTBC, testability and probability of failure using functional tests.

Functional tests to requirements traceability must be considered as part of the structural testing layer for the mapping of functional tests to product requirements. Tests that are non-graphic in nature can be driven by a test harness. These types of tests often include batch commands, libraries, raw text and other non-graphical-related testing.[*] Test management features can also be built on top of the test harness. The test harness must be able to use CAST technology as well.

A block level diagram is shown in Illustration 15.1.

---

[*]That is not to say that CAST tools cannot be used for this type of testing, however, often they are more cumbersome to use than tools like TET.

15.14 Benefits Of A Test Harness

Some of the many benefits of a standard test harness include the following:

- Higher confidence and less risk with product release via automation of unit testing and test coverage metrics results.
- Performance characterization using unit tests under the control of a test harness and evaluation using structural analysis and test tools during and after execution.
- As mentioned previously, customers and vendors would like to have and provide tests using a standard test harness technology and methodology for verification and validation testing.
- Binary compatibility testing using various binaries can be integrated using a central test harness for control and management of execution and analysis.
- Documentation, examples and training can be provided by integrating test cases using a single test harness and providing these data to customers.
- Regression testing requires a test harness and provides the ability for groups and divisions within a company to share unit tests for system and integration testing. This can save lots of money and duplicated effort when tests are reused, instead re-written.
- Having a central harness for engineering to check in and run unit tests from will help free up the QA group to focus on more global testing issues, including customer requirements, configuration, integration, system and other types of testing.[*]
- Having a good test harness with sufficient unit and functional level tests will help make employees more interested in participating in such a program. Morale will improve as well.
- Better scheduling, estimation techniques and metrics can be provided once sufficient unit and function tests are available using a standard test harness, including the number of lines of new or re-modeled code or function points based on test code coverage and reliability history. These factors can provide management with a benchmark for time, engineering staff and other required resources.
- The order of execution and construction of tests can be better organized when a test harness is available. Test harnesses such as TET provide facilities to mix and match tests in any desired combination. A scramble function may be useful in avoiding a false sense of success when tests always pass after execution in a consistent manner.

---

[*] Many software vendors may want to consider providing a list of credits for each product that include the following: engineer, QA engineer, documentation and other responsible individuals.

- Another advantage to test harnesses is the ability to order test execution based on prerequisites. Therefore, failures can be determined when dependencies have already been tested.
- Another test management function with significant benefit is the ability to restart tests from the last failure. This can greatly increase productivity for both engineering and QA personnel.
- Having a consistent report function derives many benefits. For example, a common filter program can be written so status and error messages are always written by each test using a standard method. Having a standard location and name for each report file will improve analysis and debugging efficiency.

15.15 Challenges and Problems (Verification)

One of the most significant and complicated problems that can occur during regression testing is dealing with product changes. If a product has changed, then *golden* baseline data that are being compared against may no longer be appropriate. These golden data are often considered to contain the current correct result; however, it is also hoped that the data can be used for future comparisons. The golden data file often contains values that will not be appropriate for comparison. Therefore, one approach that is often used is to mask various data elements from comparison. Another approach is to filter differences based on a set of predetermined rules with a hierarchy of priorities. For example, date and time fields can be considered a class of elements that may be highly volatile and therefore mis-comparisons may be considered to be of low priority. They may even be ignored or not displayed if the appropriate flags are used. Output results, such as termination codes or return values, on the other hand, would probably be considered critical and must always be flagged.

15.16 Methodology, Responsibilities, and Return on Investment

Unit tests must be specified based on a test plan developed in conjunction with a functional specification, which is founded on a customer requirements document. Development of unit tests must be provided by engineering and QA. Quality engineers must audit test plans and cases developed by engineering. If engineering is unable to successfully develop objective and unbiased tests, product code must not be promoted to central CM for integration, system and acceptance testing. The ROI for unit and system tests developed and integrated using a central test harness can be significant, however, and will vary from company to company. Most studies have shown that the cost of repair for a defect caught in the field is 100 times the cost of a defect discovered during requirements, phase, and somewhat less during the design and code phases.

Mips ABI Group Case Study

Member companies of the Mips ABI group have worked together for several years to provide binary-compatible platforms for software vendors. This standard allows software vendors to build programs on one manufacturer's system, but with the option to sell products on other vendor's hardware. The Mips ABI group has successfully integrated several tests for binary compatibly testing using a single test harness, TET. After several years of study, it was concluded that tests could be provided from various companies and integrated together using a single test harness, TET, implemented by engineers from Unisoft Corporation.

Several tests were provided by one vendor for testing the dynamic linking library **libdl**. Various operations and conditions were tested using source code successfully integrated into a suite of tests called the Platform Verification Test Suite (PVTS). PVTS contained a conglomeration of tests from several system vendors. These tests in turn were compiled and executed and then compared with results from a standard *reference platform*. Because TET is available without a license, this facilitated the efficiency of an integrated testing environment much faster than if a proprietary test harness were used.

15.17 Conclusions

- It is important to note that software development is not complete until testing is over and successful. Unfortunately, far too often, many engineers feel that once the code compiles it can be shipped to customers.
- Test harnesses provide the glue for automated integration and system-level testing using unit and function tests.
- Starting the requirements phase with *testing* verification and validation in mind will help provide a superior product closer to schedule.
- Don't allow the schedule to determine test metrics and strategies. Instead, allow quality goals to shape the schedule.
- Having a standard test harness will facilitate a common communications channel for engineering, QA, customers, technical support, marketing, sales and other individuals.
- Each employee must share critical data regarding the product capabilities vs. customer requirements as early in the development process as possible.
- Other test management systems include:
- TeamTest from Software Quality Automation (SQA)

- T-Plan from Software Quality Assurance Ltd.
- Testing Management System (TMS) from Finite Computer Systems
- QA Plan from Direct Technology
- Software test development requires real tools (test management and harness), as is the case with product development.
- Don't allow unit and function tests to simply be thrown away in the bottom drawer somewhere. Use a test harness to preserve and use this important software!

## CHAPTER 16

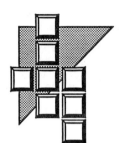 # Final Remarks

Several approaches, strategies, processes, tools and technologies have been presented in this text. It is up to the reader to incorporate the tools and strategies that will work best for the environment that is of the greatest interest. This environment can include new product development, combined new and old product development (as is often the case) or even maintenance and support. In any case, techniques and strategies for defect detection and containment through testing must include a complete framework using tools and approaches identified for functional, structural, reliability and regression testing. Each area provides a unique dimension to verification and validation with some overlap.

Structural testing must not be limited to just dynamic and static analysis, but must also include code inspections, requirements reviews and detailed design reviews and walkthroughs. Reviews and walkthroughs are typically peer group discussion activities that focus on team building as well as product and process improvement. Walkthroughs are generally a training process, and focus on learning about a single document when a top-down approach is used. Reviews focus more on consensus to a particular document or code segment. Inspections are the most formal of all methods, with the primary focus on quality improvement (defect prevention and detection). Few tools other than static analysis checkers are known to provide these critical services that are often very labor intensive. However, they have been shown to uncover even more problems than testing.

Both original development as well as integration environments provide difficult challenges to the development and test engineer. It is critical that a solid foundation of unit testing that leads to functional validation using functional tests based on product specifications be provided for comprehensive defect containment. Several methods are available and presented in this book to help determine a strategy for testing. This must be followed by interface, system and acceptance tests. Using the functional, structural, reliability and regression testing model, several alternatives to the common adhoc approach to verification and validation of software systems are possible.

In order to create cultural change, you must first design or develop a strategy. First identify the key decision makers in the company and select from this set of individuals, those that appear to have the most amount of pain (e.g., customer complaints, late releases, etc.). Next, focus on the highest risk areas with this individual (i.e., defect density, customer satisfaction, code/design complexity, interoperability, etc.). Continue to experiment with small incremental changes and try to be as flexible as possible. Make sure to follow-up on the success of the change and advertise the methods used by the team and/or individuals involved. Move to evolve the team's best-practices into a company-wide defacto standard. All the tools in the world will never replace the process-related activities required to release high-quality software.

16.1   Test Architecture

The following diagrams are provided for reference. The first diagram (Illustration 16.1) shows the importance of mapping tests to product requirements using the format of a test matrix. A variety of input sources to the functional specification must be considered.

Individual test elements contained in the test matrix must be incorporated into the requirements specification for documentation and cross-reference purposes. This test matrix can contain either individual test cases for specific function requirements under specific conditions or test status information after testing has completed for analysis. An inventory of tests must first be determined. Next, link tests together for integration and system level testing.

The second diagram (Illustration 16.2) shows how unit tests become the foundation upon which all other tests for defect containment must be based (interface, system and acceptance). This also means that structural test coverage must increase as unit tests are combined to form functional, subsystem, system and enterprise-wide tests. Structural test tools can be used as filters whereby the contribution of all other tests can be evaluated. Systematic testing approaches using test harnesses and CAST technology must be used once test development is com-

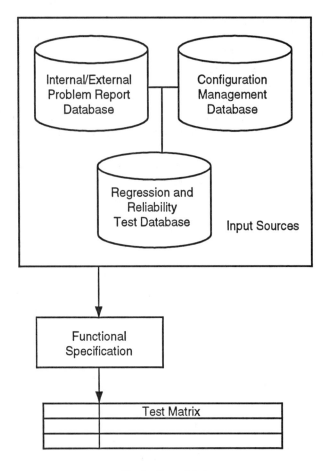

Illustration 16.1

plete and has been analyzed using structural analysis and test tools.   Illustration 16.2 shows the basic building blocks once test requirements and matrices have been developed during the requirements phase of the product development life-cycle. Functional, structural, reliability and regression testing can be combined together into a systematic approach to testing using GUI CAST and non-GUI auto-mated regression testing technologies. Test coverage detail must decrease as test-ing moves from unit to acceptance testing. Unit tests must be evaluated using the most difficult to accomplish goals for structural testing (at least branch level cov-erage). Interface, subsystem- and system-level testing will evaluate call entry/exit coverage. Releasing software products without functional, structural, reliability, and regression testing will mean lower customer satisfaction and more re-work.

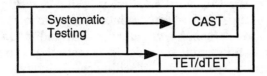

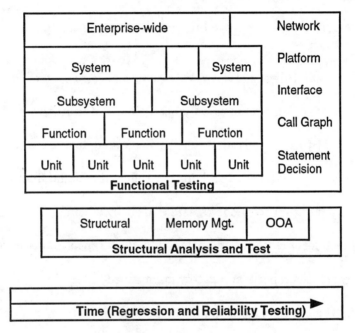

Illustration 16.2

16.2 Quality Assessment Survey

The following questions are provided to help determine areas of improvement in both the development and test of production software. They have been taken from the Software Engineering Institute (SEI) and modified. The SEI maturity questionnaire can be obtained via anonymous **ftp** from 192.58.107.148 and is located under the **/pub** directory. These questions can be used in concert with this book for continuous quality improvement and the definition of best practices.

However, one of the best questions to always ask first is "What one thing would you do to improve the quality of the software you produce today?" Also, it is important to use open questions that don't lead to a yes answer. If an individual continues to provide yes answers, ask for sample documents or tests that can validate their claims. Also, always start any interview by telling the individual that the purpose of the interview is to benefit the individual and to improve his/her efficiency and effectiveness on the job. At the end of the interview, ask the individual "what one issue did you discover during our meeting that will be helpful to you in the future?".

1. Are test procedures approved prior to the start of testing? If so, how and who approves them?

2. Are the test hardware and software acceptable and controlled?

3. Are all tests conducted in compliance with a test procedure?

4. Are all software and test deficiencies discovered during testing recorded?

5. Are all test data recorded and do they reflect the actual findings of the test?

6. Are all software corrections retested? If so, by whom?

7. Is all test documentation maintained to allow repeatability of tests?

8. Are test status reports accurately maintained?

9. Do test reports reflect the requirements of the test?

10. Is design documentation updated to reflect changes made during testing? (This is seldom performed; however, it is very important.)

11. Is there a time when testing is complete, problems are resolved and software is acceptable for the next phase of testing or for delivery?

12. What is the testing philosophy and methodology employed and are alternate test methods considered to achieve acceptance of the software?

13. Who are the personnel required to support the test program, including the number of people and their qualifications in terms of training, organizational affiliation and experience?

14. What computer facilities are required to conduct testing?

15. Is any test software required to support the test programs?

16. Do test schedules, including locations, test configurations and test flow diagrams apply?

17. Is there a correlation between all software and design requirements to individual tests? (This question is a critical!)

18. Is the plan based on performance, interface and test requirements?

19. Is there a test plan for checkout of each software module written, as well as a test plan to verify that the system meets the requirements?

20. Is there a description of all tests to be performed, including inputs, test conduct and expected results? (The expected results must include the measurement tolerances and acceptance criteria.)

21. Are test results obtained in each test?

22. Does the test plan encompass an integrated test cycle from the system level down to the lowest level?

23. Does each test verify at least one requirement and is each requirement verified in a test?

24. Are all tests accomplished with the test software and equipment identified?

25. Are the tests performed in a logical sequence, so that early test results can be used in later tests?

26. Do the tests verify interface compatibility?

27. Are there no areas of over-testing or under-testing? (This is one of my favorites.)

28. Are all supporting resources identified? Does this include beta sites and third parties that will help in the validation process?

29. Are the responsibilities of the test participants identified?

30. Is the description of each test sufficient for correct test conduct?

   30a. Does marketing provide a good feeling for which features are important to the customers and how the product is positioned in the marketplace? (This is another critical question.)

31. Is the criteria for success or failure of each test unambiguously clear?

32. Are the test inputs and outputs identified and listed?

33. Is sufficient consideration given to data storage and data reduction?

34. Is the test schedule compatible with the design cycle?

35. Are the actual results of each test listed and compared with the predicted results?

36. Do the test results meet the acceptance criteria?

   36a. If the software under tests were responsible for a device that activated a rip cord on a parachute, would you test it more?

37. What three attributes best describe the product assurance group?

38. What three attributes best describe the engineering group?

39. How would you best describe the current relationship between the product assurance (QA) and the engineering groups? Why is it a success or failure?

40. What else do you feel is important and relevant about the current situation? What tools, processes and technology are lacking?

41. Please rate the following software quality product factors from 1 (low) to 5 (high):
   a. Correctness
   b. Efficiency
   c. Flexibility
   d. Integrity
   e. Interoperability

   f. Maintainability
   g. Portability
   h. Reliability
   i. Reusability
   j. Testability
   k. Usability

42. Please rate the following people-ware quality factors from 1 (low) to 5 (high):
   a. Correctness (fitness for use)
   b. Efficiency (gets things done)
   c. Flexibility (ability to adapt to change)
   d. Integrity (yes means yes; no means no)
   e. Interoperability (communication skills)
   f. Maintainability (fit, good health, spirit, etc.)
   g. Portability (versatile, multi-functional)
   h. Reliability
   i. Reusability (memory, efficient)
   j. Testability (can locate and isolate problems)
   k. Usability (friendly)

APPENDIX A

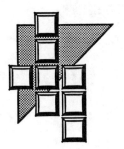

Floppy Exerciser

```
/*
 * floppy.c (can be adopted for other devices as well).
 *
 * Copyright (c) 1993 by Rodney C. Wilson, San Jose, CA USA.
 *
 * Permission to use, copy, modify, distribute, and sell this software and its
 * documentation for any purpose is hereby granted without fee, provided that
 * the above copyright notice appear in all copies and that both that
 * copyright notice and this permission notice appear in supporting
 * documentation, and that the name of Rodney Wilson be used in
 * advertising or publicity pertaining to distribution of the software without
 * specific, written prior permission. Rodney Wilson makes no
 * representations about the suitability of this software for any purpose.
 * It is provided "as is" without express or implied warranty.
 */
#include "sys/types.h"
#include "sys/ioctl.h"
#include "sys/fcntl.h"
#include "sys/stat.h"
#include "sys/file.h"
#define BLK 'b'
#define CHR 'c'
#define NOREW 4
```

```
struct stat statbuf;
extern int errno;

int pattern[] = { 0x55555555, 0x01010101, 0xAAAAAAAA, 0xFFFFFFFF };
int rec_sz[] = { 512, 1024, 2048, 4096, 8192, 10240 };
int f_sz[] = {1,2,3}; /* to save time, change to 1, 10 100 or 1000 */
long buffer[2560];
int verbose;
int rcount;
/*
 * Record size (rec_sz) is the buffer size used for read/write.
 * File size (f_sz) is the number of times buffer is read/written.
 */

struct FLOPPY {
 char *name;
/* int density; */
 char type;
 int tmajor;
 int tminor;
 } floppy[] = {
 { "/dev/rfd0", CHR, 54,2}, /* major and minor numbers */
 { 0 }
 };

#define major(tp) (tp->tmajor)
#define minor(tp) (tp->tminor)

int main(argc, argv)
int argc;
char **argv;

{
 struct FLOPPY *tp;
 int patt,rec,file,fz;
 int unit=0,sz=0;

/* Do we want verbose info? */
 while (argc > 1) {
         char c0 = argv[1][0];
         char c1 = argv[1][1];

 if (c0 == 'v' || c1 == 'v')
         verbose++;
 /* if ('0' <= c0 && c0 <= '3')
  * unit = c0-'0';
```

```
*/
argc--;
argv++;

}
check_devices(unit);

for(patt=0; patt<4; patt++) {
    for (rec=0; rec<6; rec++) {
        for (fz=0; fz<3; fz++) {
            for (tp=floppy; tp->name; tp++) {
                test(tp,pattern[patt],rec_sz[rec],f_sz[fz]);
            }
        }
    }
}
return(0);

}
check_devices(unit)
{

struct FLOPPY *tp;
int bmaj = -1;
int cmaj = -1;
int fd;

for (tp=floppy;tp->name;tp++) {
    tp->name[strlen(tp->name)-1] += unit;
    tp->tminor += unit;
}

for (tp-floppy; tp->name;tp++){
    if (tp->type == BLK) {
        if (stat(tp->name, &statbuf) <0)
            continue;
        if ((statbuf.st_mode &S_IFMT) != S_IFBLK)
            continue;
        bmaj=major(tp);
        if(bmaj < 0) {
            printf("Can't find maj number\n");
            exit (-1);
        }
        break;
    }
}
```

```
for (tp=floppy; tp->name;tp++) {
    if(tp->type == CHR) {
        if (stat(tp->name, &statbuf) < 0)
            continue;
            if ((statbuf.st_mode & S_IFMT) != S_IFCHR)
                continue;
            cmaj=major(tp);
                if (cmaj<0) {
                    printf("Can't find maj number\n");
                    exit(-1);
                }
            break;
    }
}


for(tp=floppy; tp->name; tp++){
        tp->tmajor=(tp->type == BLK) ? bmaj : cmaj;
        if (verbose) {
            printf("Opening %s %c %d, %d\n", tp->name,
            tp->type, tp->tmajor, tp->tminor);
        }
        if ((fd = open(tp->name, O_RDWR)) <0) {
            perror(tp->name);
            exit(-1);
        }
        close(fd);
        if (stat(tp->name, &statbuf) < 0)
            perror(tp->name);
        if(tp->type==BLK && (statbuf.st_mode & S_IFMT)!=S_IFBLK) {
            printf("%s not a block device\n", tp->name);
            exit(-1);
        }
        if(tp->type==CHR && (statbuf.st_mode&S_IFMT)!=S_IFCHR) {
            printf("%s not a char device\n", tp->name);
            exit(-1);
        }
        if(major(tp) != tp->tmajor || minor(tp) != tp->tminor) {
            printf("%s does not have correct maj,min\n", tp->name);
            exit(-1);
        }
}
```

```
for(tp=floppy; tp->name; tp++){
        if(tp->type == CHR) {
            if ((fd = open(tp->name, O_RDWR)) <0) {
                perror(tp->name);
                exit(-1);
            }
            close(fd);
        }
    }
}


test(tp,pattern,rec_sz,f_sz)
{
struct FLOPPY *tp;
int wcount, rcount, fd, i,j;
int buffer[10240];

/* write test */

for(tp=floppy; tp->name; tp++){
        if(tp->type == CHR) {
            if ((fd = open(tp->name, O_RDWR)) <0) {
                perror(tp->name);
                exit(-1);
            }
        /* strcat pattern to buffer */
        for (i=0; i<rec_sz; i++)
            buffer[i] = pattern;

        /* write file size number of times to device */

        for (j=0; j<=f_sz; j++) {

        if (verbose)
            printf("write 0x%X rec=%d fz=%d \n",pattern,rec_sz,j);
        if ((wcount = write(fd,buffer,rec_sz)) < rec_sz) {
            perror("write test");
            printf("errno = %d \n",errno);
            exit(-1);
        }
    }


        /* read test */
```

```
/* read file size number of time from device */

for (j=0; j<=f_sz; j++) {

    if (verbose)
        printf("read 0x%X rec=%d fz=%d\n",pattern,rec_sz,j);
    if ((rcount = read(fd,buffer,rec_sz)) != wcount) {
            perror("read test");
            exit(-1);
            }
        }
    }
    close(fd);
}

return(rcount);
}
```

/* End of Program */

New Features for VSX4

P1003.2 C Bindings:

confstr() - get configurable variables
fnmatch() - match file name or path name
glob() - generate path names matching a pattern
globfree() - same as **glob** but don't return a value
regcomp() - regular expression matching
regerror() - map from error codes returned by **regcomp**
regfree() - free compiled regular expression structure
wordexp() - perform word expressions
wordfree() - reset word expression value
fnmatch.h - file name matching types
glob.h - path name pattern matching types
regex.h - regular expressions
wordexp.h - word expansion types

ISO C

atexit() - add program termination routine
difftime() - compute the difference between two calendar times

div() - compute the quotient and remainder
fgetpos() - reposition a file pointer in a stream
fsetpos() - reposition a file pointer in a stream
labs() - return integer absolute value
ldiv() - compute the quotient and remainder
localeconv() - get numeric formatting information
mblen() - multi-byte character handling
mbstowcs() - multi-byte string functions
mbtowc() - multi-byte character handling
memmove() - memory operations
raise() - send signal to program

ISO MSE (WP interfaces):

fgetwc() - get a wide character code from a stream
fgetws() - get a wide character string from a stream
fputwc() - put wide character code on a stream
fputws() - put wide character string on a stream
getwc() - get wide character from a stream
getwchar() - get wide character from standard in stream
iswalnum() - test for an alphanumeric wide character code
iswalpha() - test for an alphabetic wide character code
iswctype() - test character for specified class
iswcntrl() - test for a control wide character code
iswdigit() - test for a decimal digit wide character code
iswgraph() - test for a visible wide character code
iswlower() - test for a lower-case letter wide character code
iswprint() - test for a printing wide character code
iswpunct() - test for a punctuation wide character code
iswspace() - test for a white space wide character code
iswupper() - test for an upper-case letter wide character code
iswxdigit() - test for a hexadecimal digit wide character code
putwc() - put wide character on a stream
putwchar() - put wide character on **stdout** stream
towlower() - transliterate upper- case wide character code to lower
towupper() - transliterate lower-case wide character code to upper
ungetwc() - push byte back into input stream
wcscat() - concatenate two wide character strings
wcschr() - wide character string scanning operation

wcscmp() - compare two wide character strings
wcscpy() - copy a wide character string
wcscspn() - get length of complementary wide sub-string
wcsftime() - convert date and time to wide character string
wcslen() - get wide character string length
wcsncat() - concatenate part of two character strings
wcsncpy() - copy part of a wide character string
wcspbrk() - scan wide character string for wide character code
wcsrchr() - wide character string scanning operation
wcsspn() - get length of wide sub-string
wcstod() - convert wide character string to double precision number
wcstok() - split wide character string into tokens
wcstol() - convert wide character string to long integer
wcstombs() - convert a wide character string to a character string
wcstoul() - convert wide character string to unsigned long
wcswcs() - find wide sub-string
wcswidth() - number of column positions of a wide character string
wctype() - define character class
wchar.h - wide character types

XPG4 only:

iconv() - code set conversion utility
iconv_close() - code conversion de-allocation function
iconv_open() - code conversion allocation function
strfmon() - convert monetary value to string
strptime() - date and time conversion
iconv.h - code set conversion facility
monetary.h - monetary types

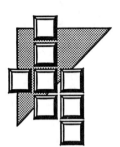

APPENDIX C ▶

FCVS Run Script

Fortran Conformance Validation Suite (FCVS) Shell Script

```
#!/bin/sh
SHELL=/bin/sh
export SHELL
ECHO=/bin/echo
FORT=f77
#SOURCEFILES="500 503 506 509 514 517 520 700 701
710 711 715 718 719 722 800 801 802 803 804 805
806 807 808 809 810 811 812 813 814 815 816 817 818 819
820 821 822 823 824 825 826 827 828 829 830 831 832
833 834 900 901 903 905 906 907 908 909 910 912 914
915 916 917 918 919 920 921 922 923"
#
# Compile the source programs
for cfile in ${SOURCEFILES}
do
        INPUTSRC=/dev/null
        SRCNAME=FM${cfile}.f
        TESTNO=f.${cfile}
```

```
                DATAFILE=FM${cfile}.dat
                case ${cfile} in
                  900|901|903|906|923)
                    INPUTSRC=${DATAFILE};;
                    *)
                    INPUTSRC=/dev/null;;
                esac

        ${ECHO} "compiling file:${SRCNAME}"
        ${FORT} ${SRCNAME} -o ${TESTNO}
        ./${TESTNO} < ${INPUTSRC} 2>&1 | tee - a FCVS.OUT

        if [$? -eq 0 ]; then
            rm -f ${TESTNO}
        fi
done

#
# Check report results (pass, fail, or inspection
#
if [ -f FCVS.OUT ]
then
    nawk'
    BEGIN {
    teststart="FM[0-9]+BEGIN"
    testend="FM[0-9]+END"
    passed=0
    failed=0
    inspect=0
    deleted=0
    TestName="NO_TEST"
    }

    $1 ~ teststart {
    TestName=$5
    }

    $1 ~ testend {
    TestName="NO_TEST"
```

```
      passed=0
      failed=0
      inspect=0
      deleted=0
      }


        NF >= 3 && ($2 == "TESTS" || $4 == "TESTS"){
        if ($3 == "PASSED")
           passed=$1
        else if ($3=="FAILED")
           failed=$1
        else if ($3=="DELETED")
           deleted=$1
        else if ($3 == "INSPECTION")
           inspect=$1
        else if ($4 == "TESTS" && TestName != "NO_TEST"){
           printf("\n Test %s:", TestName)
           printf("%3d of %3d executed\n", $1, $3)
           printf("passed %3d", passed)
        }
        if (passed >1)
           print "tests"
        else
              print "test"
        if (failed >0)
           print "has ", failed, "failures"
        if (deleted >0)
           print "has ", deleted, "deleted"
        if (inspect >0)
           print "has ", inspect, "tests for inspection"
        }
        ' FCVS.OUT

# Save the output
cp FCVS.OUT 'date +%m.%d.%y'.FCVS
fi

${ECHO};${ECHO};${ECHO};${ECHO}
```

```
${ECHO}'-------------------------------------------'
${ECHO};${ECHO}
${ECHO} 'FCVS finished. Inspect the file FCVS.OUT'
${ECHO};${ECHO}
${ECHO}'-------------------------------------------'
#end of program
```

APPENDIX D

Alphabetical List of Companies

AccuWare, Inc.
Riverside Commons
700 River Avenue
Pittsburgh, PA 15212
Phone (412) 323-2650

Advanced Software Automation
2880 Lakeside Drive, Suite 226
Santa Clara, CA 95054
Phone (408) 492-1668
Fax (408) 492-1669

AIM Technology
4699 Old Ironsides Dr. Suite 150
Santa Clara, CA 95054
Phone (408) 748-8649

ApTest and 88Open Consortium Ltd.
c/o PowerOpen Assocation
10050 North Wolfe Road, Suite SW2-255
Cupertino, CA 95014
(408) 366-0460

ASTA, Inc.
1 Chestnut Street Suite 205/206
Nashua, NH 03060
Phone (603) 889-2230
Fax (603) 881-3740

Azor, Inc.
1032 Elwell Court Suite 111
Palo Alto, CA 94303
Phone: (415) 934-2869

Bender & Associates Inc.
P.O. Box 849 or 484 Magnolia Avenue
Larkspur, CA 94939
Phone (415) 924-9196
Fax (415) 924-3020

British Standards Institution (BSI) Quality Assurance
PO Box 375
Milton Keynes MK14 6LL
ENGLAND Attn: M.J. Horton
Phone 0908-220908
Fax 0908-220671

CAST Report
Cambridge Market Intelligence Ltd.
Letts of London House
Parkgate Road
London SW11 4NQ
Phone 071 924 7117l Fax 071 403 6729

Center for Software Development
111 West St. John, Suite 200
San Jose, CA 95113
(408) 494-8378

CenterLine Software
10 Fawcett Street
Cambridge, MA 02138
Phone (617) 498-3000
Fax (617) 868-6655

Cygnus Support
1937 Landings Drive
Mountain View, CA 94043
Phone (415) 903-1400
Hotline (415) 903-1401
email: 'info@cygnus.com'
Fax (415) 903-0122

Direct Technology
10 E. 21st St., Suite 1705
New York, NY 10010
212-475-2747
212-529-4941 (Fax)

Don Libes
National Institute of Standards and
Technology
Bldg 220, Rm A-127
Gaithersburg, MD 20899
Phone (301) 975-3535

DRA Maivem
St. Andrews Road
Great Maivern
Worcestershire
WR14 3PS, ENGLAND

Eastern Systems, Inc.
P.O. 1087
Westboro, Ma 01581-6087
Phone (508) 366-3220

Finite Computer Systems
6 Centre Court
Vine Lane, Halesowen
West Midlands B63 3EB
UK
44-215-856700

Free Software Foundation
675 Mass Ave.
Cambridge, MA 02139
Phone (617) 876-3296
gnu@prep.ai.mit.edu

Insignia Solutions
1300 Charleston Road
Mountain View, CA 94043
Phone (415) 694-7600
Fax (415) 694-3705

Interactive Development Environments
(IDE)
595 Market Street
San Francisco, CA 94105
Phone (415) 543-0900

Jan Newmarch (ReplayXt)
University of Canberra
Belconnen 2614
Canberra, Australia
+61 6 (06) 201 2422

Mercury Interactive Corporation
470 Potrero Avenue
Sunnyvale, CA 94086
Phone (408) 523-9900

Mindcraft
1410 Cambridge Avenue
Palo Alto, CA 94306
Phone (415) 323-9000

NCGA
2722 Merrilee Dr., Suite 200
Fairfax, VA 22301
Phone (703) 698-9600
Fax (703) 560-2752

Novell
190 River Rd.
Summit, NJ 07901
Phone (908) 522-6000

NTIS
5285 Port Royal Road
Springfield, VA 22161
(703) 487-4600

Open Software Foundation (OSF)
11 Cambridge Center
Cambridge, MA 02142
Phone (617) 621-8700

ParaSoft Corporation
2500 E.Foothit Blvd.
Pasadena, CA 91107
Phone (818) 792-9941

Perennial, Inc.
4699 Old Ironsides Dr. Suite 210
Santa Clara, CA 95054
Phone (408) 748-2900

Performance Awareness
8521 Six Forks Rd., Suite 200
Raleigh, NC 27615
Phone (919) 870-8800l Fax (919) 870-7416

Plum Hall
P.O. Box 44610
Kamuela, HI 96743
(808) 882-1255

Pure Software, Inc.
1309 South Mary Avenue
Sunnyvale, CA 94087
Phone (408) 720-1600

Quality Assurance Software Engineering
486 Leigh Avenue
San Jose, CA 95128
Phone (408) 298-3824

Quality Checked Software Ltd.
PO Box 6656
Beaverton, OR 97007-0656
Phone (503) 645-5610
Fax (503) 690-0201

Qualtrak Corporation
3160 De La Cruz Blvd., Suite 206
Santa Clara, CA 95054
Phone (408) 748-9500

Revision Labs, Inc.
10250 SW Greenburg Road, Suite 213
Portland, OR 97223

Reliable Software Technologies (RST)
1001 N. Highland Street, Suite PH
Arlington, VA 22201
Phone (703) 2276-1219

Remedy Corporation
1965 Landings Drive
Mountain View, CA 94043
Phone (415) 903-5200

RG Consulting
396 Ano Nuevo Avenue #216
Sunnyvale, CA 94086
Phone (408) 732-7839
Fax (408) 732-2609

Scopus Technology
1900 Powell St., Suite 900
Emeryville, CA 94608
Phone (510) 428-0500

Segue Software, Inc.
1320 Centre Street
Newton Centre, MA 02159
Phone (617) 969-3771

Software Emancipation Technology, Inc.
5201 Great America Parkway, Suite 320
Santa Clara, CA 95054
Phone (408) 562-6071

Software Management News
4546 El Camino Real, Suite 237
Los Altos, CA 94022
Phone (415) 969-5522
Fax (415) 969-5949

Software Quality Automation (SQA)
10 State Street
Woburn, MA 01801
Phone 800-228-9922
Phone 617-932-0110
Fax 617-932-3280

Software Quality Assurance Ltd.
Millfield, Ashwells Road
Brentwood, Essex CM15 9ST
Phone 44-277-374411
Fax 44-277-372151

Software Quality Engineering
3000-2 Hartley Road
Jacksonville, FL 32257
Phone 800-423-TEST (8378)
Fax 904-268-0733

Software Research, Inc.
625 Third Street
San Francisco, CA 94107
Phone (415) 957-1441
info@soft.com

Software Technology Support Center
(STSC)
00-ALC/TISE
Hill Air Force Base, UT 84056
Phone (801) 777-8045

Sparc International, Inc.
535 Middlefield Road, Suite 210
Menlo Park, CA 94025
Phone (415) 321-8692

Testing Tools Reference Guide - Order
R201
Software Quality Engineering
3000-2 Hartley Rd.
Jacksonville, FL 32257
Phone (800) 423-8378
Fax (904) 268-6733

Unisoft Ltd.
Spa House
Chapel Place
Rivington Street
London EC2A 3DQ
United Kingdom
Phone +44 717 293 773

VERITAS Software Corporation
1600 Plymouth Street
Mountain View, CA 94043
Phone (415) 335-8000

Workstation Labs
4324 N. Beltline Suite, C211
Irving, Tx 7503
Phone (214) 570-7100
Fax (214) 570-4201

X/Open Company Ltd.
Apex Plaza
Forbury Road
Reading, Berkshire
RG1 1AX ENGLAND
Phone +44 734 508311

APPENDIX E

Verification and Validation Plan Outline and Checklist

The following outline is provided as a sample plan that can be used for verification and validation of application or system software. This outline can also be used as a checklist during the product development life-cycle to determine items that have been successfully completed for project tracking and control. A sample checklist is also included after the outline. Project planning and estimation will also be improved by collecting data for each product release with specific V&V phase deliverables identified in the V&V plan.

A template can also be formed from this document that contains example or boiler-plate text. Using templates can provide both positive and negative rewards. One negative remark that is commonly made about templates is that the user often will focus so much on the format that the content of the V&V plan suffers and is not usable. Conversely, having a template can help new users to V&V methods to quickly get started in the creation of a V&V plan. This also forms a good foundation for agreement between members of the project team (i.e., marketing, engineering, quality, technical publications, support, etc.). Always have a plan in place before attempting to start a tool-based approach to testing and development.

E.1   Introduction and Purpose

A. Objectives
B. Background
C. Scope

E.2   Reference Documents and Test Items:

A. Requirements (Functional Specifications)
B. Design Specifications
C. User Guides
D. Operations Guides
E. Installation Guides
F. Application Notes
G. Known Problems and Solutions
H. Release Notes
I. Problem Change Requests
J. Others

E.3   Testing Activities and Approach (Tables Are Recommended):

A. Features to be tested and NOT to be tested (R&D and QA):
    A1. Unit Testing
    A2. Function Testing
    A3. Integration Testing
    A4. Flow Testing
    A5. Regression Testing
    A6. Reliability Testing
    A7. Performance Testing
    A8. Installation Testing
    A9. Security Testing
B. Item Pass/Fail Criteria (Expected Results)
C. Suspension and Resumption Criteria (Crashes, Hangs, etc.)
D. Test Deliverables (Test Plans, Reports, Tools, Tests, etc.)
E. Testing Tasks (Skills and Dependencies)
F. Environmental Needs (Hardware, Software, Network, etc.)

E.4   Customer Acceptance Tests

E.5   Standards, Practices, Conventions and Metrics

A. Approach (Techniques, Tools, Methods, Completion Criteria - Defect Density)
B. Pre-release and Post-release Quality Metrics
C. Others

E.6   Problem reporting and corrective action:

A. Technology (Problem Tracking System or Others)
B. Methodology for Problem Reporting and Resolution
C. Records Collection, Maintenance and Retention

E.7   Code Control (CM)

A. Technology (RCS, SCCS or Other)
B. Methodology for CM and Source Code Control
C. Tests vs. Source Code Changes
D. Configuration Items

E.8   Media Control

A. Technology For Control and Management
B. Methodology for Control and Management

E.9   Supplier Control

A. Acceptance Tests
B. Acceptance Test Procedure
C. Technology and Tools for Management of Product Development

E.10   Responsibilities

A. Management
B. Design
C. Preparation

D. Execution

E. Witness

F. Reviews and Audits

G. Resolution of Issues

E.11   Staffing and Training

A. Customer Flows and Use Model Validation

B. Customer Tools

C. Product/Tool Skills

E.12   Schedule

A. Test Milestones (Unit, Function, Integration, System and Flow Test Phases)

B. Testing Phase Complete and Accepted

C. Installation Phase Complete and Accepted

D. Release Phase Complete (to Manufacturing)

E. First Customer Shipment

E.13   Risks and Contingencies

A. High Risks

B. How to Compensate (Time, People, Resources, etc.)

E.14   Approvals

A. Engineering: _____ Date _____

B. Quality: _____ Date _____

C. Marketing: _____ Date _____

D. Customer Service: _____ Date _____

E. Publications: _____ Date _____

F. Training: _____ Date _____

E.15   Verification & Validation Checklist

A. Introduction

B. Goals and Objectives

C. Reference Documents

E.16 Testing Activities and Approach (Tables Recommended)

A. Unit & Function Testing

__ Each functional requirement has an associated test

__ Test Matrix (functions vs. Dirty Tests)

__ Boundary Values (Min, Max, -1 Min, +1 Max)

__ Equivalence Classes (valid and invalid data sets)

__ Syntax tests (missing arguments, flags, etc.)

__ Cause/Effect Mapping (Requirements inputs to outputs)

__ Performance to functions

B. Integration and Interface Testing

__ Bottom up method (driver used):_____

__ Top down (simulation libs used):_____

__ Each functional interface has an associated test

__ Execution of acceptance tests (function input validation)

__ Execution of data validators (function output validation)

__ Simulation libraries packaged (test stubs used)

__ Flow testing (customer use models validated)

C. System Testing

__ Product examples and tutorials

__ Documentation examples

D. Regression Testing and CM Control

__ All critical customer problems have a test written and checked into the CM system

__ All unit tests under CM control

__ All integration tests under CM control

__ All system tests under CM control

__ All system acceptance tests under CM control

E. Reliability Testing (Regression Test Build and Execution Cycle is Recorded)

__ MTBE (Mean Time Between Error)

__ MTBC (Mean Time Between Crash)

__ MTBH (Mean Time Between Hang)

__ MTBD (Mean Time Between core Dump)

__ Other:_____

__ Testability analysis (weak/strong mutation test analysis)

F. Performance Testing

The time required for completion of the full regression test suite will be recorded and compared with the previous baseline.

System Time:_____ User Time:_____

G. Installation Testing

The product must be installed on a freshly installed system. (Identify under environmental needs section below).

__ System disconnected from network and uses only local libraries and licenses.

__ Installation tests (product/package level)

__ Configuration tests (platform/system level)

E.17 Item Pass/Fail Criteria (Expected Results)

__ Each test must successfully complete build and execution operations without any loss of data or functionality within the required time limits

E.18 Suspension and Resumption Criteria (Crashes, Hangs, etc.)

__ Core dumps

__ Crashes

__ Hangs

__ Loss of data

__ Other critical failures (list)_____

__ Resolution of any of these activities must be provided to resume or restart testing activities

E.19 Test Deliverables (Test Plans, Reports, Tools, Tests, etc.)

__ Unit/Function tests under the CM system with test results

__ Capture/playback test scripts

__ Test plan

E.20 Testing Tasks (Skills and Dependencies)

__ Training with test harness and management system

__ Training with bug management/tracking system

__ Training with CM system

__ Training with regression test system

__ Training with structural testing and analysis tools

__ Training with reliability and testability tools

__ Training in coding and testability standards/guidelines

__ Training in requirements, design and code reviews

__ Training with capture/playback tools

E.21 Environmental Needs (Hardware, Software, Tools, Network, etc.)

__ Hardware systems (include peripherals)

_____
_____
_____

__ Software (Operating System, Compilers, etc...)

_____
_____
_____

__ Network Configurations

_____
_____
_____

E.22 Customer Acceptance Tests

__ All critical problems must be under CM control and included in the regression test system

__ All expert testing (e.g., customer support engineers) and beta tests should be collected for integration with the system regression test suite

E.23 Standards, Practices and Metrics (Values are for Example Only)

__ Each unit test must be associated with a functional requirement from the marketing requirements, functional specification or design specification

__ Each unit test will be measured for branch or decision coverage

__ 75% or greater decision coverage required during unit testing prior to integration test phase

__ No core dumps or memory leaks are accepted during unit testing

__ 85% call entry/exit coverage required during integration test prior to system test phase

__ 70% function call coverage required during system test phase prior to customer acceptance or beta test phase

E.24 Approach (Techniques, Tools, Methods, Completion Criteria—Defect Density)

__ Each functional test includes negative tests as well as positive test
__ Value equal to the minimum accepted value (from functional and design specifications)
__ Value equal to the maximum accepted value (from functional and design specifications)
__ One less than the minimum accepted value (from functional and design specifications)
__ One greater than the maximum accepted value (from functional and design specifications)
__ Data values equal to the accepted data type (from functional and design specifications)
__ Data values not equal to the accepted data type (from functional and design specifications)

E.25 Pre-release Quality Metrics

__ List each pre-release quality metric for:
__ Memory analysis
__ **lint** or static checker (coding guidelines, etc.)
__ Stress tools used (list)
__ Test coverage (**tcov**, MetaC, PureCov, ViSTA, etc.)
__ Call coverage
__ Block (statement) coverage
__ Branch (decision) coverage
__ Static structural complexity analysis)

E.26 System Testing

__ Test coverage (call coverage w/ **tcov**)
__ Schedule containment metrics
__ Content containment metrics

E.27 Acceptance Test Procedure

__ Each functional test will be under the control of a central test environment that can be used by members of other groups
__ Capture/playback tools used to execute acceptance tests

Beta Test and Customer Acceptance Test Checklist

F.1   Introduction

This document is organized according to objectives, ownership and process. Three phases are associated with successful beta testing. This is followed by a detailed checklist of steps required for successful customer acceptance and beta test. Each step is identified as either must, should or could. A must step is highly recommended. A should step should be considered very carefully. Finally, a could step is suggested, but may not be critical to success. I would like to thank the following individuals for creating the following checklist: Dick Albright, John Murphy, John Perry, Michael Griesbach, and Linda Prowse.

F.2   Objectives

- Beta testing should be a positive and desirable experience for customers and employees
- Customers must always have a feeling that their investment in beta testing is worthwhile

- New products must always be introduced using a rigorous process that includes testing in real customer environments
- Products or features must operate successfully in a customer environment
- A stable and repeatable process must always be used for conducting Beta tests
- Feedback from testing will be used to obtain input for future product releases

F.3   Ownership

The product team must own the process used for beta test. This is key to product release success. Individual dedicated resources on the team, such as marketing and QA, must own particular parts of the beta test process. Especially where their expertise and focus will add significant value.

F.4   Three Phases of Beta

1 Planning and customer engagement phase.
   This phase can start when product specification is first created and ends when the software has been successfully delivered to the customer for testing.
2 Execution Phase
   This is an intense period of time that starts when the software is first delivered to the customer for testing. This phase ends when the software reaches an acceptable level of stability according to the beta test objectives or customer acceptance test criteria.
3 Wrap-up phase.
   This phase is dedicated to collection of summary and evaluation information. This includes feedback and closure on all open issues.

F.5   Beta Test Best Practice Checklist

Beta Team Responsibilities

Resource Allocation

__ Identify an overall beta test coordinator from project team (Must).
This role may be taken on by any member of the product team depending
on resources and available skill sets. A dedicated marketing resource may
own the customer identification and qualification. A dedicated QA
resource may own the resolution of issues between the customer and the
R&D team. One person from the product team must be identified as the
technical support contact for questions received from each beta test customer.

__ R&D support budgeted, identified and available prior to beta test (Must).

__ A champion (contact) for each site is identified (Must).

__ Responsible parties (point of contact) are identified for both the customer
and company prior to the start of beta testing (Must).

__ All product and solution features to be tested must be identified in
advance (Must).

__ All primary features and functions are identified (Should).

__ A matrix of features to tests is created (Should).

__ All primary customer uses are identified (Should).

Site Selection

__ Strategic customers are involved in the requirements and design review
processes prior to the beta test phase. In general, these customers are
excellent candidates for beta test sites (Should).

__ Establish a qualification checklist to define good customer candidates
(Should).

__ Select beta test candidates (Must).

__ Sign and complete beta test agreement (Must).

__ Functional specification reviewed with customer (Must).

__ Non-disclosure documents complete by customer (Could).

__ Customer questionnaires completed (Could).

Project Plan

__ Customer feedback and metrics under a control system for weekly
review (Must).

__ Weekly conference calls are arranged prior to the start of the beta test
process (Must).

__ The project schedule includes sufficient time for feedback to customer during beta test period (Must).

__ The beta test customer provides sufficient breadth of testing. This includes installation, documentation, interoperability, stress, load, performance, and other system test methods. (Should)

__ The project schedule includes time to resolve and distribute corrections to problems discovered during the beta test period. (Should)

__ The test data and product use is documented (Should).

__ Buy-in across groups such as sales, sales management, field support, marketing, engineering, tech marketing is provided. Beta test can't be unilateral. (Should)

__ An email alias is created for feedback and sharing experience by marketing, management, field support and sales (Could).

__ Executive management provides visible support for beta test, especially for new product introduction (e.g., newsletters, etc.) (Could)

Execution Phase

Company Beta Team Responsibilities

__ A release mechanism is in place from the start of the beta test to provide timely updates to customer (Must).

__ Weekly telephone conference calls are scheduled (Must).

__ Feedback and metrics are reviewed weekly (Must).

__ Beta site field support personnel are trained with new technology prior to the start of beta testing (Should).

__ Customer data and usage (processes) are preserved for regression testing (Should).

Wrap-up Phase

Company Beta Team Responsibilities

__ A post review process (postmortem) is conducted after the beta test process (Should).

__ An improvement plan is constructed for the next Beta program (Should).

__ A "What worked and what didn't work" list is created (Should).

__ A beta customer day is scheduled (customer and project team meet). This includes final comments on product and beta process (Could).

Company Beta Test Champion Responsibilities

It is recommended that only one person is assigned for each beta test or customer acceptance test site. The beta test champion is usually a field support engineer. This individual must be very familiar with the company products used by the customer, as well as the customer's environment.

__ Assist with all beta test problems (Must).

__ Document and provide feedback and report problems using problem management system (Must).

__ Forward both new and unresolved feedback and problem reports to the beta project team (Must).

__ Beta site support engineers are trained with new product technology prior to the start of beta testing (Should).

__ The support engineer assists with loading the software (Should).

__ They will file, submit and record feedback and metrics (Should).

__ The field support and sales employees will collect and report (via email alias) how the competition is responding to the new product introduction. (Could)

__ Support engineer extends an invitation to the company beta customer appreciation day (Could).

Customer Responsibilities

For beta testing to be an advantage to both parties (win/win), strict criteria must be used to determine what customer are really interested in participating in serious beta testing.

__ A customer letter and agreement is received to test the features that the company needs tested. This is in the context of the customer's environment (Must). Note: This agreement is provided to ensure the success of the beta test process.

__ The schedule and resources available for beta testing are committed (Must).

__ Customer management support is in place for beta testing (Must).

__ The beta test process is presented and viewed as a collaboration with the company (a partnership) (Should).

__ The customer agrees to act as a reference account at end of the beta test period (Could).

__ The customer will test in a real-life situation or environment, not as a simple evaluation or demonstration (Could).

It is important that beta testing not be performed in a mission-critical or with a product that is already in the critical-path for production release. The risk are too great and the customer will not be able to give adequate attention to the process associated with beta testing.

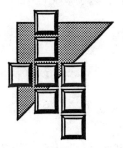# References

[ATT90] UNIX Software Operation. *System V Application Binary Interface.* Prentice Hall, Inc.

[BAC86] Bach, Maurice, J. (1986) *The Design of the Unix Operation System.* Prentice Hall, Inc.

[BAR74] Bard, Y. (1974) *Nonlinear Parameter Estimation.* New York: Academic Press.

[BEC77] J. V. & Arnold, K.J. (1977) *Parameter Estimation in Engineering and Science.* New York: John Wiley & Sons.

[BEI84] Beizer, Boris(1984) *Software System Testing and Quality Assurance.* Van Nostrand Reinhold Company, Inc.

[BEI90] Beizer, Boris. (1990) *Software Testing Techniques.* Van Nostrand Reinhold Company, Inc.

[BEI94] Beizer, Boris. (1994) *The Software QA Quarterly.* Vol. 1 No. 2

[BEN93] Bender, Dick. (1993) *Writing Testable Requirements*, Software Testing Analysis and Review Conference.

[BER91] Berry, Thomas H. (1991) *Managing the Total Quality Transformation.* McGraw-Hill, Inc.

[BOE81] Boehm, B. (1981). *Software Engineering Economics*, Prentice-Hall, Inc.

[BRO82] Brooks, Frederick P., Jr. (1982) *The Mythical Man-Month,* Addison-Wesley Publishing Company, Inc.

[BUR91] Burkett, Larry. (1991) *"The Coming Economic Earthquake".* Moody Press, Chicago.

[CHA77] Chambers, J.M. (1977) *Computational Methods for Data Analysis.* New York: John Wiley & Sons.

[CON82] Conner, Daryl R., et al.(1982) *Building Commitment to Organization Change, Training and Development Journal* Vol. 36 No. 4.

[COV89] Covey, Stephen R. (1989) *The 7 Habits of Highly Effective People.* Simon & Schuster, Inc. New York, New York 10020.

[CRO79] Crosby, Philip B. (1979) *Quality Is Free, The Art of Making Quality Certain.* Penguin Books USA, Inc.

[DEM82] DeMarco, Tom. (1982) *Controlling Software Projects.* Prentice-Hall, Inc. A Division of Simon & Schuster.

[DEM87] DeMarco, Tom and Lister, Timothy. (1987) *Peopleware.* Dorset House Publishing Co., Inc.

[DOW93] Dowd, Kevin. (1993) *High Performance Computing.* O'Reilly & Associates, Inc.

[FEN92] Fenton, Norman E. *Software Metrics A Rigorous Approach.* (1992) Chapman & Hall.

[GIL93] Gilb, Tom and Graham, Dorothy. (1993) *Software Inspection: An Effective Method for Software Project Management.* Addison-Wesley, Inc.

[GRA87] Grady, Robert B. and Caswell, Deborah L. (1987) *Software Metrics: Establishing a Company-wide Program.* Prentice-Hall, Inc.

[GRA91] Gray, Jim. (1991) *The Benchmark Handbook for Database and Transaction Processing Systems.* Morgan Kaufmann Publishers, Inc.

[GRA92] Grady, Robert B. (1992) *Practical Software Metrics for Project Management and Process Improvement.* Prentice-Hall, Inc.

[GRA93] Graham, Dorothy. (1993) *CAST REPORT Computer Aided Software Testing.* Cambridge Market Intelligence Limited.

[HAM93] Hamlet, Richard and Voas, Jeffery M. (1993) *Software Reliability and Testability.* "Software Quality Week Conference Proceedings", Paper 5-T-1&2.

[HET88] Hetzel, Bill. (1988) *The Complete Guide to Software Testing,* Second Edition. QED Information Sciences, Inc.

[HOL90] Hollingsworth, Jeff, Irvin, Bruce, and Miller, Barton P. (1990) *IPS User's Guide,* Version 3.0. University of Wisconsin-Madison.

[IEE94] IEEE. (1994) *IEEE Software Engineering Standards Collection,* The Institute of Electrical and Electronics Engineers, Inc.

[ISO91] ISO 9000. (1991) International Standards for Quality Management. ISBN 92-67-10165-x.

[KAN87] Kane, Gerry. (1987) *MIPS R2000 RISC Architecture.* Prentice Hall, Inc.

[KAN93] Kaner, Cem Falk, Jack and Nguyen, Hung Quoc. (1993) *Testing Computer Software,* Van Nostrand Reinhold.

[KER88] Kernighan, Brian W. and Ritchie, Dennis M. *The C Programming Language,* Bell Telephone Laboratories, Inc. Prentice Hall, Inc. Second Edition.

[LEW92] Lewis, R.O. (1992) *Independent Verification & Validation,* New York: Wiley.

[MAU90] Maurer, Peeter M. (1990) *IEEE Software.* Maurer Computer Science and Engineering Dept. ENG 119, University of South Florida, Tampa, FL 33620.

[MIL90] Miller, Barton P., Fredriksen, Lars and So, Bryan. (1990) *An Emphrical Study of the Reliability of UNIX Utilities.* "Communications of the ACM". Vol 33, No.12.

[MYE76] Myers, Glenford J. (1976) *Software Reliablity, Principles and Practices,* New York: Wiley.

[MYE79] Myers, Glenford J. (1979) *The Art of Testing Computer Software.* John Wiley & Sons, Inc.

[PHA89] Phadke, Madhav S. (1989) *Quality Engineering Using Robust Design.* Prentice-Hall, Inc.

[PRE92] Pressman, Roger S. (1992) *Software Engineering a Practitioner's Approach,* Third Edition. McGraw Hill.

[PUT78] Putnam, L. (1978) *A General Empirical Solution to the Macro Software Sizing and Estimating Problem.* "IEEE Trans. Software Engineering", Vol. 4, No. 4.

[RUM91] Rumbaugh, James., Blaha, Michael., Premerlani, William., Eddy, Frederick and Lorensen, William. (1991) *Object-Oriented Modeling and Design.* Prentice-Hall, Inc.

[SANKAR & HAYES] Sankar, Sriram and Hayes, Roger. *Specifying and Testing Software Components Using ADL.* Sun Microsystems Labs, Inc.

[SCH90] Schulmeyer, Gordon G. (1990) *Zero Defect Software.* McGraw Hill, Inc.

[SCH92] Schulmeyer, Gordon G. and McManus, James I. (1992) *Handbook Of Software Quality Assurance,* Second Edition. Van Nostrand Reinhold.

[STE91] Stern, Hal. (1991) *Managing NFS and NIS.* O'Reilly & Associates, Inc.

[VOA92] Voas, Jeff. (1992) *Improving the Software Development Process Using Testability Research,* "Proceedings of the 3rd Internation Symposium on Software Reliability Engineering".

[VOA93] Voas, Jeff. (1993) Software Testability Techniques Seminar. Reliable Software Technologies Corporation.

[WEB84] Webster, Howard. (1984) *Webster's II New Riverside Dictionary.* Houghton Mifflin Company.

[UTZ92] Utz, Walter J., Jr. (1992) *Software Technology Transitions, Making the Transition to Software Engineering.* Prentice-Hall, Inc.

Glossary

Acceptance Test Formal tests (often performed by a customer) to determine whether or not a system has satisfied predetermined acceptance criteria. These tests are often used to enable the customer (either internal or external) to determine whether or not to accept a system.

Baseline A process where control is placed on all configuration items including sources, libraries, compilers, include files, test suites, test plans and any other items required to build a product.

Baseline File A file that contains data used as a baseline for regression test comparisons (also known as back-to-back testing). This file is also commonly called a golden file.

Bashers Term often used for hardware-level diagnostics. The execution of many functional tests over the course of several hours or days.

Benchmarks Programs that provide performance comparisons for software, hardware and systems.

Black Book A supplement to the psABI and gABI for extensions to a specific processor family. For example, libraries and commands that are required for application support that are not included in either the psABI or gABI.

Black Box Testing A testing method where the application under test is viewed as a black box and the internal behavior of the program is completely ignored. Testing occurs based upon the external specifications. Also known as behavioral testing since only the external behaviors of the program are evaluated and analyzed.

Bottom-up Testing Test drivers are used to help perform unit testing with lower-level modules, even though the system, subsystem or entire function may be incomplete.

Boundary Value Analysis (BVA) Is different from equivalence partitioning in that it focuses on "corner cases" or values that are usually out of range as defined by the specification. This means that if a function expects all values in the range of -100 to 1000 test inputs would include -101 and +1001. BVA attempts to derive the value just above or below the maximum and minimum expected value. BVA is often used as a technique for stress, load or volume testing. This type of validation is usually performed after positive functional validation has completed (successfully) using requirements specifications and user documentation.

C0 coverage The number of statements in a module that have been executed during testing, divided by the total number of statements contained in the program under test.

C1 coverage The number of segments (branches or decisions) in a program that have been executed during testing, divided by the total number of segments in the program under test.

Call Graph A graphical representation of program caller-callee relationships. It is used to determine which function calls need further testing. Most useful during the system test phase.

Call Pair The connection between a caller and callee. Usually included in a call tree. See call graph.

Cause-and-effect graphing A functional testing method that uses combinations of inputs that are compared with specifications for matching error conditions (effects).

Complexity A metric of the degree of internal complexity of a program usually expressed in terms of some algorithmic measure. For example, the number operators, operands, decisions, tokens, etc.

Connected Digraph A directed graph (a set of nodes interconnected with entry and exit nodes) where there is at least one entry node to every exit node.

Cyclomatic Complexity A metric of the degree of internal complexity of a program's flow of control based on the number and arrangement of decisions.

Data Flow Graph A graphical presentation of a variable as used within a module or system. It can be expressed in either legal or illegal uses (transitions).

Defect Difference between the functional specification (including user documentation) and actual program text (source code and data). Often reported as a problem and stored in a defect tracking and problem management system.

Defect Containment The technologies and processes associated with discovering failures, defects or spoilage before product shipment.

Defect Detection The technologies and processes associated with preventing defects during requirements, design or implementation phases of the product life-cycle.

Directed Graph (digraph) A set of nodes interconnected with potentially many entry and exit nodes. A program must always have one entry and exit node. Also known as a digraph.

Driver A software program to control either the construction and/or execution of tests, like that of a test harness. Alternatively, a device driver controls the use of a specific hardware device.

Dynamic Metrics To focus on the collection of metrics information for the source code while under test execution management or control.

Equivalence Partitioning An approach where classes of inputs are categorized for product or function validation. This usually does not include combinations of input, rather a single state value based by class. For example, with a given function there may be several classes of input that may be used for positive or negative testing. If the function expects an integer and receives an integer as input, this would be considered a positive test assertion. On the other hand, if a character or any other input class other than an integer is provided, this would be considered a negative test assertion or condition.

Error Guessing   Another common approach to black box validation. Black box testing is when everything else other than the source code may be used for testing. This is the most common approach to testing. Error Guessing is when random inputs or conditions are used for testing. Random in this case includes a value either produced by a computerized random number generator, or an *ad-hoc* value or test condition provided by the engineer.

Errors   The amount by which a result is incorrect. Mistakes are usually a result of a human action. Human mistakes (errors) often result in faults contained in the source code, specification, documentation or other product deliverable. Once a fault is encountered, the end result will be a program failure. The failure usually has some margin of error, either high, medium or low.

Essential Segment   One method of performing selective path coverage analysis. A structural testing method where the segment of a program (entry and exit branches) exist on only one path.

Essential Paths   Another selective path method of performing structural testing analysis. Paths that include an edge that is not included in any other path (i.e., includes one essential edge) are identified.

Extended Differencing   EXDIFF is a component of the STW/Regression product from Software Research, Inc. This method of comparison ignores differences that are resident within a user-defined masked area. The mask area includes data to be ignored during golden file comparison.

Extended Finite State Machines (EFSM)   A Finite State Machine (FSM) with additional history based context. The context often represents various aspects of the history of a session. Using variables and predicates as an example, subsequent events can be determined based upon their dependence to previous events (i.e., history). EFSMs often reduce the number of total states or transitions provided by a regular FSMs.

Exercisers   Test programs oriented toward the basic use of a hardware device, software function or system feature. One example could be a tape exerciser that provides basic read, write and compare operations using various blocking factors.

Failures The result or manifestation of a fault. When a specific segment of source code is executed under certain conditions, a fault may be encountered. This fault will result in a program or system failure.

Faults The result of a mistake caused by an incorrect step, process or data definition. For example, a missing or extra code segment.

firm mutation Testing is determined by some internal state that detects the mutant later on during execution (i.e., longer association or coupling).

gABI generic Application Binary Interface. A top-level UNIX standard that defines a method for sharing and executing binary programs on systems that follow conformance guidelines of the same processor architecture.

gid Group Identification. A unique number that is used in the UNIX operating system for each unique group contained in the **/etc/group** file. Each member is assigned a default group by the **passwd** file for access and security purposes.

Harness A tool or program to control and manage the execution of both micro   and macro-level tests.

Inspection/Review A process commonly used to study requirements, design or source code documents with the intent to identify various types of errors by human rather than mechanical means. Reviews are often used for team-building, where inspections are oriented toward quality control goals (defects).

Instrumentation A process where source code is compiled or translated to an executable file that contains additional code for monitoring program execution.

Integration Testing Testing conducted after unit and feature testing. The intent is to f expose faults in the interactions between software modules and functions. Either top-down or bottom-up approaches can be used. A bottom-up method is preferred since it leads to earlier unit testing (step-level integration). This methods is contrary to the big-bang approach where all source modules are combined and tested in one step. The big-bang approach to integration should be discouraged.

Interface The boundary between two software systems, products, components or functions. An interface is usually defined on an information or data boundary. For example, communications to the hard disk device are usually provided through a set of interfaces defined in the standard C library (i.e., **open**, **close**, etc.).

Interface Tests   Programs that provide test facilities for external interfaces and function calls. Simulation is often used to test external interfaces that currently may not be available for testing or are difficult to control. For example, hardware resources such as hard disks and memory may be difficult to control; however, exception handlers must be tested for proper interface testing. Therefore, simulation can provide the characteristics or behaviors for a specific function.

Kiviat Chart   A graph that provides a method of viewing the impact of multiple metrics on a source code module or set of files. This presentation allows easy determination of values (test metrics) that fall either under or over the expected minimum or maximum limits.

Makefile   A file containing a set of rules for the construction and execution of a program or test. Often times is used as the front end or back end of a test harness.

Methods   Different from processes because they are closely associated with the technical or detail aspects associated with accomplishing a task. Methods are usually performed by an engineer, rather than manager.

mutant   When the existence of a data state error is discernible at a time later than when the mutant first occurred. A mutant can include either a valid or invalid equivalence class for program data or text.

POSIX   Portable Operating System Interface for UNIX.

Predicate   An expression contained in the source code that contains multiple groupings of program variables and/or constants. The following source code statement has two predicates. The first checks the value of the variable "a". The second the value of the variable "b". if ((a == 1) && (b == 2)) {;}

psABI   processor supplement Application Binary Interface. A processor-specific supplement to the gABI for system-dependent features. For example, **/usr/include** file structure definitions for a particular processor.

Quality Assurance (QA)   Consists of planning, coordinating and other strategic activities associated with measuring product quality against external requirements and specifications (process related activies).

Quality Control (QC)   Consists of monitoring, controlling and other tactical activities associated with the measurement of product quality goals.

Regression Testing   Testing conducted for the purpose of evaluating whether or not a change to the system (all CM items) has introduced a new failure. Regression testing is often accomplished through the construction, execution and analysis of product and system tests.

RISC   Reduced Instruction Set Computer, as opposed to Complex Instruction Set Computer (CISC). A CPU instruction set that is reduced to commonly used instructions for performance improvements.

S0 coverage   The number of modules executed at least once during the system test phase.

S1 coverage   The number of call pairs executed during system testing. For example, if a function requires no other functions (no call pairs), the S1 coverage will be 100% as soon as the function is called.

Scaffold   A component of software that provides services to another component. Any software used during development to simulate the other component is called a scaffold. See [IEE91] for further definition of test driver.

Segment   A branch that includes a decision-to-decision path within a program that is executed as a result of a conditional (predicate) expression.

Soak Tests   Also known as reliability, or life tests. Often a set of unit tests that are conducted over the course of several days or weeks.

St Coverage   Execution of all possible call pair subtrees at least once.

Static Analysis   Looks at the complexity of source code. It has been demonstrated that highly complicated modules or functions are more error prone and should be isolated for more rigorous inspection, verification and validation.

Static Structural Analysis   Can be provided without program execution and only requires a *map* of the source code structure. Includes McCabe's Cyclomatic and Essential Complexity, as well as Halstead's Software Science.

Stress/Load/Volume Tests   Tests that provide a high degree of activity, either using boundary conditions as inputs or multiple copies of a program executing in parallel as examples.

strong mutation testing   A comparison of program outputs which decide if a test case was able to distinguish between a mutant and the original program state.

Stub   A component that uses the services of another component. Any software used to simulate the other component during development is called a stub. See [IEE91] for further definition.

superuser or root   The system administrator. The user that can access any file or directory regardless of permission settings.

Syntax testing   A common form of testing where a command or function is often used (tested) without providing the required or necessary options or arguments.

Tally File   The file created by the ViSTA **audrep** command to consolidate all hits data from dynamic metrics-based testing.

test   Any activity in which a program is executed under specified conditions, the results are observed or recorded, and an evaluation is made (test success or failure). A [unit] test is commonly used for testing a single module. Ideally, a unit test isolates test inputs and outputs to the smallest degree possible (only one input and one output if possible). A unit test may or may not include the effect of other modules which are invoked during testing.

test assertion   A logical expression specifying a program state that must exist during testing.

test case   A set of test inputs, execution conditions, and expected results developed for a particular objective.

Test Harness   A test harness may also be called a test driver. It is commonly used to clean, build and execute test cases, test assertions or entire test suites. A test harness may include the use of a test scaffold. A test harness may also be considered part of the function of a test manager. A test harness is the same as a test driver.

Testability   Analysis to determine the probability of faults hiding in the source code under test. Low testability often means that testing will be difficult, if not impossible. See the section on PiSCES from Reliability Software Technologies.

Test Assertions and Cases   Test cases are similar to test assertions, however, a test assertion will test one specific behavior of a function. For example, does the UNIX **malloc** library call return ENOMEM when there is no more memory available for allocation? A test case, on the other hand, may use several behaviors (test assertions) in an integrated fashion for a specific purpose. For example, what happens when the **malloc** function fails while we are reading from a file?

Testing   The execution of tests with the intent of proving that the system and application under test does or does not perform according to the requirements specification.

Test Stub   A module that simulates the operations of a module during testing. The testing stub can replace the real module for testing purposes and is commonly used to test error conditions and exception handlers contained in the application under test.

Test Suites   A test suite consists of multiple test cases (procedures and data) that are combined and often managed by a test harness.

Top-Down Testing   Testing that starts with the main program. All subordinate units (features) are added to the testing process as they are completed; however, stub files can be created and used for units not yet complete.

uid or UID   Each user is assigned a unique **uid** after log in to the UNIX operating system. This integer value is contained in the **passwd** file and forms the basis for file and directory access security for the operating system.

Unit Testing   Testing performed to isolate and expose faults and failures as soon as the source code is available, regardless of the external interfaces that may be required. Often times the detailed design and requirements documents are used as a basis to compare how and what the unit is able to perform. White and black box testing methods are combined during unit testing.

Validation   The process of evaluating the software under test against the functional requirements (preferable defined and reviewed by the customer).

Verification   The process of determining if the products (outputs) of a previous development phase are acceptable as inputs. For example, product requirements must be complete (to an extent) prior to detail design and implementation (code development).

weak mutation   When the internal program state immediately after the mutant is different from the state immediately after the original state (short association).

White, Clear or Glass-box Testing   Analysis of the source code structure (implementation) to determine the integrity, reliability, testability and other related factors of the software under test. Test data is derived from the analysis of missing program control (e.g., executable statements) or data flow (e.g. missing variables). Approximately only 15% of all companies are believed to use any form static or dynamic structural testing or analysis.

XPG3, XPG4   X/Open Portability Guide 3. An international standard created by X/Open for Open Systems.

Index